# AMENDED

# CHARTER

AND

# ORDINANCES

OF THE

# CITY OF SAGINAW.

*Printed and Published by Authority of the Common Council of the City of Saginaw.*

CITY OF SAGINAW:
PRINTED AT THE SAGINAWIAN OFFICE.
1875.

*RESOLVED, That the City Attorney be and he is hereby directed to make and cause to be printed and published, a new compilation of the Charter of the City of Saginaw, and of all By-Laws and Ordinances of the City now in force. And such compilation, when published, shall be deemed to have been "printed and published by authority of the Common Council."*

CITY OF SAGINAW,
RECORDER'S OFFICE.

*I hereby Certify*, That a Resolution, of which the foregoing is a true copy, was duly passed by the Common Council of the City of Saginaw, on the 6th day of May, 1875, and that I have carefully compared said copy with the original thereof, now of record in my office, and that it is a true copy of said Resolution and of the whole thereof, that this book has been compiled, printed and published by D. P. Foote, City Attorney, in compliance with said Resolution.

IN WITNESS WHEREOF, I have hereunto set my hand, and affixed the seal of said City, this 20th day of October 1875.

F. F. Ormstead[?]
Recorder

# CHARTER OF THE CITY OF SAGINAW.

---

Act 496, Laws of 1867—Approved March 27, 1867.

---

**An Act to amend an Act entitled "An act to revise and amend the Charter of the City of Saginaw," approved February 5th, 1859.**

SECTION 1. *The People of the State of Michigan enact: That an Act entitled "An Act to revise and amend the Charter of the City of Saginaw," approved February 5th, 1859, be, and the same is hereby amended so as to read as follows:*

Corporate name.

SEC. 1. *The People of the State of Michigan enact:* That the corporation heretofore created and now known as the Mayor, Recorder and Aldermen of the City of Saginaw, shall be and continue to be, a corporation by the name of the City of Saginaw, and by that name may sue and be sued, implead and be impleaded, complain and defend in any court of record and place whatsoever, and shall be known at law; may have a common seal, and alter it at pleasure, and may take, purchase and hold, lease, convey and dispose of any real, personal, or mixed estate for the use of said corporation.

Power to purchase, hold and convey real and personal property.

Corporate boundaries. SEC. 2. The district of country in the County of Saginaw, and State of Michigan, hereinafter particularly described, is hereby constituted and declared to be a city by the name of Saginaw, and subject to the municipal government of said corporation; said district of country being bounded as follows, to-wit: Beginning at the center of Saginaw river, on the quarter line of Section Twenty-Four, in Township 12 north, of Range 4 east, thence west along the quarter line to the center of said section, thence north and northeasterly along the west line of the plat of the village of Florence to the quarter line of Section Thirteen, in said township; thence west along the quarter line of Sections Thirteen, Fourteen and Fifteen, to the west line of Section Fifteen in said township; thence south along the section line to the center of the Tittabawassee river, thence down and along the center of the Tittabawassee river to the center of the Saginaw river, and thence down and along the center of the Saginaw river to the place of beginning.

Division of City. SEC. 3. The said city shall be divided into six wards. First ward. The first ward shall comprise all that part of said city within boundaries, to-wit: Commencing at the west line of the village of Florence, where said west line intersects the east and west quarter line of section thirteen, town twelve (12) north, of range four east; thence west on said line to the section line between sections thirteen (13) and fourteen (14) in said town; thence south on said line to its intersection with Harrison street; thence south along the center of Harrison street to the center of Madison street; thence along the center of Madison street to the center of the Saginaw river; thence north along the center of the Saginaw river to the east and west quarter line of section twenty-four (24) town twelve (12) north, of range four (4) east; thence west on said quarter line to the west line of the village of Florence; thence north along the west line of the village of Florence to the place of beginning. The second ward shall embrace all that portion of said city within the following limits, to-wit: Commencing at the center of the Saginaw river at the foot of Court street; thence along the center of Court street to the north and south quarter line of section twenty-two (22), town twelve (12) north, of range four (4) east; thence north along said line to the east and west quarter line of section fifteen (15) of said town; thence west on said line to the center of Mackinaw street; thence along the center of Mackinaw street to the center of the Saginaw river; thence along the center of the Saginaw river to the place of beginning. The third ward shall embrace all that portion of said city within the following boundaries, to-wit: Commencing at the center of the Saginaw river at the foot of Mackinaw street; thence along the center of Mackinaw street to the east and west quarter line of section fifteen (15), town twelve (12) north, of range four (4) east; thence west along said line to the section line between sections fifteen (15) and sixteen (16) of said town; thence south on said section line to the center of the Gratiot State road, (so called); thence east along the center of said road to the center of First street; thence south along the center of said First street to the center of Waller street; thence south along the center of said Waller street to the center of the Saginaw river; thence north along the center of the Saginaw river to the place of beginning. The fourth ward shall embrace all that portion of said city lying south and west of the third ward. The fifth ward shall embrace all that portion of said city within the following boundaries, to-wit: Commencing at the center of Saginaw river, at the foot of Madison street; thence along the

Second ward.

Third ward

Fourth ward.

Fifth ward.

center of Madison street to the north and south subdivision line of the south-west quarter of section twenty-three (23), town twelve (12) north, of range four (4) east; thence north on said subdivision line to the east and west quarter line of section twenty-three (23) of said town; thence west on said quarter line to the center of the Bay City State road, (so called); thence north along the center of said road to the city limits on the north; thence west along said city limits to the north and south quarter line of section fifteen (15) of said town; thence south on said quarter line to the center of Court street; thence along the center of Court street to the center of

Sixth ward. the Saginaw river; thence along the center of the Saginaw river to the place of beginning. The sixth ward shall comprise all that part of said city embraced within the following boundaries, to-wit: Commencing at the center of Madison street, at its intersection with Harrison street; thence north along the center of Harrison street to the section line between sections twenty-three (23) and twenty-four (24), town twelve (12) north, of range four (4) east; thence north on said section line to the east and west quarter line of section fourteen (14) in said town; thence west on said quarter line to the center of the Bay City State road, (so called); thence south along the center of said road to the east and west quarter line of section twenty-three (23) in said town; thence east on said quarter line to the north and south subdivision line of the southwest quarter of section twenty-three (23) in said town; thence south on said subdivision line to the center of Madison street; thence east along the center of Madison street to the place of beginning. [*Act No. 305, Laws of 1869, Page 518.*]

City officers SEC. 4. The following officers of the corporation shall be elected at the annual city election, on a general ticket, by the qualified electors of the whole city, viz: A Mayor, one Recorder, a Treasurer, (who shall be *ex-officio* collector,) and four Justices of the Peace, as follows: The Mayor and Treasurer shall be elected annually, and hold their offices for one year and until their successors shall be elected and qualified; the Recorder on each alternate year, and shall hold his office for two years and until his successor shall be elected and qualified; and one Justice annually, who shall hold his office for the term of four years, and until his successor shall be elected and qualified, and whose term of office shall commence at the same time, and whose powers, duties and liabilities shall be the same as Justices of the Peace of the Townships of said County of Saginaw.

Term of

Justice of the Peace.

Terms of office.

Powers and duties.

SEC. 5. There shall also be elected at the same time, in and for each of the several wards of said city, one Constable, who shall hold his office for the term of one year; and one Alderman, who shall hold his office for the term of two years, and until their successors shall be elected and qualified; and every third year there shall be elected one Supervisor, who shall hold his office for the term of three years, and until his successor shall be elected and qualified. *Provided*, That at the election held in the year eighteen hundred and sixty-nine, there shall be elected, in the fifth ward, one Alderman for the term of one year and one Alderman for the term of two years, and until their successors shall be elected and qualified; also one Supervisor for the term of three years, and until his successor shall be elected and qualified. In the sixth ward there shall be elected one Alderman for the term of one year, and one Alderman for the term of two years, and until their successors shall be elected and qualified; also, one Supervisor for the term of two years,

Constable, election of.

Aldermen, election of.

Supervisor, election of.

Proviso.

1869.

Fifth ward.

Sixth ward

First ward. and until his successor shall be elected and qualified. In the first ward there shall be elected one Supervisor for the term of three years, and until his successor shall be Third ward. elected and qualified. In the third ward there shall be elected one Supervisor for the term of two years, and until his successor shall be elected and qualified. Each Supervisor, power of. of the said Supervisors shall be the Supervisor of the ward for which he is elected, with all the power of Supervisors of Townships of this State, and subject, in all respects, to the provisions of law regulating the duties of Township Supervisors, except as in this act otherwise provided. [*Act No. 305, Laws of 1869, Page 520.*]

Annual Charter Election. SEC. 6. The annual election, under this act, shall be held on the first Monday of April in each year, at such Time and place of holding. place in each of the several wards as the Common Council may designate. Notice of. Notice thereof shall be given by the Recorder at least eight days before the election, by publishing the same in some newspaper published in Inspectors of election. said city. The Aldermen of each ward shall be Inspectors of such election, and they shall also be Inspectors of Clerks of election. the State and County elections, and shall choose the clerks thereof; and in case of the absence of one or more Oath to be administered to Clerks of. of such Inspectors, the electors may choose *viva voce* from their number one or more to fill such vacancy or vacancies, to whom shall be administered the constitutional oath by either of said Inspectors, or by any Justice of Manner of conducting elections. the Peace. The manner of conducting all elections, and canvassing the votes and the qualifications of electors in the several wards shall be the same as that of townships, the word "ward" instead of "township" being used in the oath to be administered to an elector in case his vote shall be challenged. *Provided*, That at such charter elections the said ward Inspectors shall make one certificate of the number of votes given for each person for the several offices to be filled in and for said city; and also one certificate of the officers elected in and for each ward, which certificate shall be immediately filed in the office of the Recorder of said city; and upon the Thursday next following the day of such election the Common Council shall meet at the office of said Recorder, and thereupon determine who, by the greatest number of votes given in the several wards at such election, are duly elected to fill the respective city offices; and it shall be the duty of said Recorder, immediately after such determination, to cause notice to be given to each of the persons elected, of their election, and each of said officers so elected and notified shall, within ten days thereafter, take and subscribe the constitutional oath of office before any person authorized to administer oaths, and shall deliver the same to the said Recorder, who shall file the same in his office. *Provided*, That in case of the election of one or more Justices of the Peace, the said Recorder shall make a certificate thereof, and cause it to be delivered to the County Clerk in the same manner as is required of Township Clerks; and in case two or more shall receive for the same office an equal number, and not a plurality, of votes given at such election, the Common Council shall immediately proceed to determine by lot between the persons receiving the highest number of votes, which shall be considered elected to such office. *In case any of the officers so elected shall neglect, for the term of ten days, to qualify as aforesaid, the office shall thereby become vacant.*

Certificates for City and Ward Officers to be filed in the Recorder's office.

Meeting of Common Council to determine who elected.

Notice to persons elected.

Time and manner in which persons elected shall qualify.

Proviso.

Certificate to be filed with County Clerk of election of Justices.

Tie.

Proceedings in case of.

Failure of Officers to qualify.

SEC. 7. The Mayor, Recorder and Aldermen, when assembled together and organized, shall constitute the Common Council of the City of Saginaw; and a majority

Who Constitutes the Council.

Quorum. Mayor may call a meeting. Recorder may call a meeting when Mayor is absent. Council may compel attendance of members. Mayor to preside at all meetings. Mayor may vote. Recorder to keep record of the proceedings. President or Recorder pro tem. Members not to vote when they have interest. When Recorder shall vote. Less than a quorum may adjourn. No proceedings to lapse by an adjournment. Mayor may suspend the operation of certain proceedings.

of the Aldermen elect, with the Mayor or Recorder, shall be necessary to constitute a quorum for the transaction of business, and the Common Council may be summoned to hold its meetings at such time and place as the Mayor, or in case of his absence or inability from any cause to act, the Recorder may appoint. The Common Council shall have power to send for and compel the attendance of any of its members, and to impose, levy and collect such fines as it may deem proper, not exceeding five dollars, for the non-attendance at any meeting of any officer of the corporation who has been duly notified to attend the same. The Mayor shall preside at all meetings of the Common Council, and shall have the right to vote upon all questions. The Recorder shall keep a record of the proceedings of the Common Council. In the absence of the Mayor or Recorder from any meeting, the members present may appoint a President or Recorder *pro tem.* from among its members. No member of the Common Council shall be allowed to vote upon any question in which he has a direct personal interest, but upon all other questions he shall vote. *Provided,* That the Recorder shall vote only in the absence of the Mayor. A less number than a quorum may adjourn a meeting of the Common Council, and no business or proceedings, set down or noticed for any special, regular or adjourned meeting shall lapse, fail or become invalid by reason of a failure to hold such meeting, but the same shall go over to the next regular or adjourned meeting. No ordinance imposing a fine or penalty, and no ordinance, resolution or vote of the Common Council, appropriating or creating the liability to pay money, or conferring upon any person, corporation or company, any special franchise or privileges, or providing for any improvements, shall have any force or effect if on the day of its passage, or the next day thereafter, the Mayor, or other officer legally discharging the duties of Mayor, shall lodge in the office of the Recorder, a notice, in writing, suspending the immediate operation of such ordinance, resolution or vote. If the Mayor, or other officer legally exercising the office of Mayor, shall, before the next regular meeting of the Common Council after the passage of such ordinance, resolution or vote, lodge in the office of the Recorder his reasons, in writing, why the same shall not go into effect, the same shall not go into effect nor have any legal operation, unless it shall, at a subsequent meeting of the Common Council, be passed by a vote of two-thirds of all the members elect of the Common Council, exclusive of the Mayor or other officer legally discharging the duties of Mayor, and if so re-passed, shall go into effect according to the terms thereof. If such reasons, in writing, shall not be lodged with the Recorder, as above provided, such ordinance, resolution or vote, shall have the same operation and effect as if no notice suspending the same had been lodged with the Recorder; and no such ordinance, resolution, or vote of the Common Council shall go into effect or operation until after the expiration of one day after the day of its passage, unless the Mayor, or other officer legally acting in the place of the Mayor, shall vote in favor of the adoption of the same. It shall be the duty of the Recorder to communicate to the Common Council, at the next meeting thereof, any paper that may be lodged with him as in this section provided. [*Act No. 302, Laws of 1875.*]

Mayor may veto, when.

Council may pass question over the veto, when.

Suspended proceedings when to have effect.

Mayor must vote for a measure to give it immediate effect.

Recorder must lay before Council any notice suspending measures.

SEC. 8. The Common Council shall have power to appoint an Attorney, a Street Commissioner, and one or more Assistant Street Commissioners, a Director of the Poor, a Marshal, a Chief and one or more Assistant

Common Council may appoint certain officers.

Engineers for the Fire Departmeut, and a Controller, who shall be *ex-officio* Assesor of said city, and such other officers whose election is not herein specially provided for, as they may deem necessary to carry into effect the powers granted by this act and to remove the same at pleasure. They shall also have power to remove from office any of their own members, or any other officer holding office by election, (except the Mayor and Recorder) for corrupt or willful malfeasance or misfeasance in office, or for willful neglect of the duties of his office, or for any violation of any of the ordinances of the Common Council, by a vote of two-thirds of all the Aldermen elect; and in each case the reason for removal shall be entered on the records of the Common Council, with the names and votes of the members voting on the question. No officer holding office by election shall be removed by said Council, unless first furnished with a copy of the charges against him in writing, and allowed to be heard in his defence, with aid of counsel; and the Common Council shall have power to issue subpœnas to compel the attendance of witnesses and the production of papers when necessary, and they shall proceed, within twenty days after service of a copy of the charges, to hear and determine the case. If such officer shall neglect to appear and answer to such charges, his default may be deemed good cause for removal. [*Act No. 305, Laws of 1869, Page 521.*]

How may remove officers.

Reasons for removal to be recorded.

Elected officers; proceedings in case of removal of.

Power to issue subpœna.

Default cause of removal.

Resignations; how made.

SEC. 9. Resignations of office shall be made in writing to the Common Council, and subject to their approval and acceptance. In case of the death, resignation, removal from office, neglect to qualify, removal from the city or ward for which he has been elected, or permanent disability to perform the duties of his office, of any officer holding by election, the Common Council shall appoint some person eligible under this act to serve in such office *pro tempore*, until such vacancy shall be filled by a special election for that purpose; and on the occurrence of such vacancy, the Common Council shall, at the first meeting held after such vacancy, order a special election to fill such vacancy; said election shall be conducted in the same manner, as near as may be, as the annual charter election provided for in this act; such vacancy shall be so filled for the residue of the official term. They may also fill, by appointment, any vacancies in office held by appointment under this act. [*Act No. 305, Laws of 1869.*] Vacan cies; how filled.

SEC. 10. The Common Council, in addition to the powers and duties specially conferred on them by this act, shall have the management and control of the finances, rights, and interests, buildings and all property, real and personal, belonging to the city, and make such order and by-laws relating to the same as they shall deem necessary and proper. They shall also have power within the limits and jurisdiction of said corporation— General powers of Council.

*First*, To provide for and preserve the purity and salubrity of the waters of the Saginaw River; to prohibit and prevent the depositing therein of all filthy and other matter tending to render said waters impure, unwholesome or offensive; to preserve and regulate the navigation of said river within the limits of said city; to prohibit and prevent the depositing or keeping therein any structure, earth or substance tending to obstruct or impair the navigation thereof, and remove all obstructions that may, at any time, occur therein, and to direct and regulate the stationing, anchoring and mooring of vessels, and laying out of cargoes and ballast from the same. To provide for purity of Saginaw river. To regulate navigation.

To license ferries.

*Second,* To license, continue and regulate so many ferries from within said city to the opposite shore of Saginaw river, for carrying and transporting persons and property across said river, in such manner as shall seem most conducive to the public good.

*Third,* To erect, repair, and regulate public wharves and docks at the ends of streets, and on the property of the corporation; to regulate the erection and repair of private wharves and docks, so that they shall not extend into the Saginaw river beyond a certain line to be established by the Common Council, and to prohibit the incumbering of all public wharves and docks with boxes, carriages, carts, sleighs. sleds, or other vehicle, dray or thing whatsoever.

Wharfing privileges.

*Fourth,* To lease the wharves and wharfing privileges at the ends of streets on the Saginaw river, in said city, upon such terms and conditions, and under such covenants, and with such remedies, in case of non-performance, as the Common Council may direct; but no building shall be erected thereon: no lease thereof shall be executed for a longer period than twenty years, and a free passage shall at all times be secured for all persons, with their baggage, over said public wharves.

Free passage of passengers.

Draining of swamps.

*Fifth,* To provide for the draining of any swamp, marsh, wet or low lands in said city, or within the distance of three miles therefrom, by the opening of ditches; but a jury of not less than six disinterested freeholders of the County of Saginaw, before any proposed ditch can be opened, shall ascertain that the opening thereof is necessary or proper; also, whether the benefits which will accrue to the owner or owners of any land, from the opening of the ditch, will or will not be equal to any damages he or they will sustain thereby; if such benefits

Opening ditches.

are exceeded by the damages, they shall ascertain and certify the damages to which the owner or owners will be entitled, after deducting therefrom the amount of benefits their lands will receive from the opening of the proposed ditch. On payment or tender of the damages thus ascertained and certified, the Common Council shall have the power to enter upon any land through which the proposed ditch will run, with the necessary agents, teams and implements, to cut and open said ditch; to protect, clean and scour it, from time to time, so as to preserve its original dimensions, and to prohibit and prevent all obstructions thereof or injury thereto.

Settling with owners of land.

May enter on any land.

*Sixth.* To prohibit and prevent the location or construction of any wooden or frame house, store, shop, or other building, on such streets, alleys, and places, or within such limits, in said city, as the Common Council may, from time to time, prescribe; to prohibit and prevent the removal of wooden or frame buildings from any part of said city to any lot on such streets, alleys, and places, or within said limits, and the rebuilding and repairing of the same; to prevent the rebuilding or repairing of wooden buildings on said streets, alleys, and places, or within said limits, when damaged by fire or otherwise.

Wooden houses.

Removal of buildings.

*Seventh,* To appoint one or more inspectors, measurers, weighers, and gaugers of articles to be measured, inspected, weighed and gauged; to prescribe and regulate their powers and duties, fees and compensation.

Inspectors.

*Eighth,* To provide for the protection and care of paupers, and to prohibit and prevent all persons from bringing, in vessels, or in other mode, to said city, from any other port or place, any pauper or other person

Paupers.

likely to become a charge upon said city, and to punish therefor.

City Hall. *Ninth,* To erect, and provide for the erection of a City Hall, and all needful buildings and offices for the use of the corporation or of its officers, and to control and regulate the same, and to purchase the necessary real estate on which to erect the same.

Purchasing land.

Vice. *Tenth,* To prevent vice and immorality; to preserve public peace and good order; to appoint, organize, regulate and maintain a police of the city, and to prevent and quell riots, disturbances, and disorderly assemblages and conduct.

Police.

Gaming. *Eleventh,* To restrain and prevent disorderly and gaming houses, and houses of ill-fame; the holding, keping, or using of all instruments and devices used for gaming, and to prohibit all gaming and fraudulent devices, and regulate or restrain billard tables and bowling alleys.

Billiard tables.

Liquors. *Twelfth,* To prevent the vending or giving away of spirituous or fermented liquors, and to license and regulate the sale thereof whenever such sale shall hereafter be authorized by the laws of this State.

Drunkards. *Thirteenth,* To apprehend, restrain, and punish all drunkards, vagrants, mendicants, street beggars, prostitutes, and persons soliciting alms or subscription for any purpose, and to punish and prevent all intoxication and disorderly conduct.

Public exhibitions. *Fourteenth,* To prohibit and prevent, or license and regulate, the public exhibition, by itinerant persons or companies, of natural or artificial curiosities, caravans, circuses, menageries, theatrical representations, concerts, musical entertainments, exhibitions of common showmen, and shows of any kind.

*Fifteenth*, To prohibit, prevent, abate, and remove all nuisances within said city, and to compel the owner or occupant of any grocery, tallow chandler shop, butcher shop or stall, soap factory, glue factory, tannery, slaughter house, stable, privy, hog-pen, sewer, or other offensive house or place; to cleanse, remove, or abate the same as often as they may deem necessary for the health, comfort and convenience of the inhabitants of the city. Nuisances.

*Sixteenth*, To direct and regulate the location and maintainace of all slaughter-houses, markets, and buildings for storing gunpowder or other combustiable substances, and to prohibit or regulate the buying, selling, keeping for sale, storing and transporting gunpowder, naptha, saltpeter, benzine, benzole, petroleum, kerosene oil, fire-crackers, fire-works, and all other conbustible substances, and the using thereof; the use of lights in barns, stables, and other buildings, and the making of bonfires. Slaughter houses. Markets. Gunpowder Lights.

*Seventeenth*, To prevent the encumbering or obstruction of streets, side or cross-walks, lanes, alleys, bridges, wharves or slips, in any manner whatsoever, and to compel persons owning or occupying adjoining premises to keep the streets and sidewalks in front of such premises free from dirt and obstructions. Encumbering streets.

*Eighteenth*, To prevent immoderate riding or driving in any street; to compel persons to fasten or secure their horses, oxen, or other animals, while standing in any of the streets, lanes, or alleys of the city, and to prevent persons from riding or driving upon, or across any sidewalk. Immoderate driving.

Muzzling dogs.

*Nineteenth*, To prevent or regulate the running at large of dogs; to impose taxes for the keeping of dogs; to require them to be muzzled, and to authorize their destruction when running at large in violation of any ordinance.

Locomotives.

Lighting of railroads.

*Twentieth*, To restrain and regulate the use of locomotives, engines and cars upon the railroads within the city; to provide, by ordinance, for the lighting of any railroad or portion thereof which may be located within the corporate limits of the city, in such mode and manner as the Common Council shall prescribe; and when it shall be deemed necessary and proper by said Common Council to provide for the lighting of any such railroad, or portion thereof, within the city, said Common Council shall pass and adopt an ordinance requiring such railroad company or companies, within a specified time, (which shall not be less than thirty days,) so to light their track or tracks, or such portion thereof as may be designated by such ordinance; and such ordinance shall prescribe the mode and manner in which the same shall be done; the number, style, and size of lamp posts, burners, lamps, and all other fixtures and apparatus necessary for such lighting; the points of location for such lamp posts, and the time or times for lighting and keeping such lamps or burners lighted; and in case the said lighting shall not be done in conformity with the provisions, directions, and specifications of such ordinance, or in case any railroad company fail, neglect, or refuse to light its track, or such portion thereof as may be designated, and within the time limited by such ordinance, the Common Council may proceed immediately to cause such lighting to be done in conformity to the provisions of such ordinance, the expenses of which shall be a proper charge against such company or

Action in case railroad company refuse to put up lights.

companies; and the Common Council may provide in such ordinance the mode and manner in which the charge on any railroad company or companies shall be assessed and determined. Such charge, when so assessed and determined, shall be payable by such railroad company or companies at the time of the assessment, and shall also be a lien upon the lots, land, and any and all property, real or personal, in the possession of and belonging to such company or companies, from the time of making such assessment; such charge may be collected as provided for in such ordinance, and lien enforced by action or procedure at law or in equity, in the corporate name of said city; in any such proceedings at law, when pleadings are required, it shall be sufficient to declare generally for work and labor done, and materials furnished on the particular railroad, part or parts thereof; and in case any company or companies shall neglect or refuse to pay such assessment in the manner and at the time provided for in such ordinance, said city shall be entitled to demand, receive and recover, in addition to the amount assessed, with interest from the time of such assessment, the additional sum of five per cent. on such amount assessed, to defray the expense of collection, and which shall be included in any judgment or decree rendered under the provisions of such ordinance.

Collection of charges against company.

*Twenty-first,* To prohibit and prevent any indecent exposure of the person; the show, sale, or exhibition of any indecent or obscene books, pictures, or pamphlets, and all indecent or obscene exhibitions or shows of every kind, and all indecent, immoral, profane, or disorderly conduct or language; and to prohibit or regulate the bathing in any public waters within or adjoining said city.

Indecent books and shows.

Bathing.

Pounds. *Twenty-second,* To establish, regulate, and maintain one or more pounds; and to restrain and prevent, or regulate the running at large of horses, cattle, swine, and other animals, geese and poultry, and to authorize the impounding and sale of the same for the penalty incurred and the cost of keeping and impounding.

Cattle.

Gaming. *Twenty-third,* To prevent every species of gaming; and to prevent the violation of the Sabbath, and the disturbance of any religious congregation, or any other public meeting assembled for any lawful purpose.

Violation of the Sabbath

Cemeteries. *Twenty-fourth,* To protect and regulate all cemeteries or grave-yards within the city, and all such without the limits of said city, as such corporation may acquire, and to regulate the burial of the dead, and the keeping of bills of mortality.

Offensive substances. *Twenty-fifth,* To prohibit the bringing or depositing, within the limits of said city, any dead carcass, or other unwholesome or offensive substance, and to provide for the removal or destruction thereof, wheresoever found.

Market places. *Twenty-sixth,* To lay out, establish, make, alter and regulate market places and public parks and grounds, and regulate the measuring and selling of fire-wood, and the weighing and selling of hay, and the selling of meats, vegetables, fish, fruits, and provisions of all kinds.

Hay.

Awning and sign posts. *Twenty-seventh,* To regulate the setting of awning and other posts, and to direct and regulate the planting of shade or ornamental trees in the streets and other public grounds, and to provide for the preservation of the same.

Trees.

Meetings of electors. *Twenty-eighth,* To provide for calling of meetings of the electors of the city, and to determine and regulate the compensation of all officers elected or appointed under this act, except as is herein otherwise provided; but the compensation of no officer fixed by an annual or periodical salary shall be increased or diminished during the term for which he was elected or appointed, unless by a two-thirds vote of the Common Council; to authorize and regulate the demand and receipt, by officers, of such fees and costs, and in such cases as the Common Council shall deem reasonable, and to prescribe, fix, determine and regulate the powers and duties of all officers of the city, subject to the provisions of this act.

Compensation of officers.

Powers and duties of officers.

*Twenty-ninth*, To survey, ascertain, and establish the boundaries of the city, and of all highways, streets, avenues, lanes, alleys, parks, squares and spaces in said city; to prohibit and remove all encroachments upon the same in any manner, and to number the buildings.

Boundaries of city.

Encroachment on streets.

*Thirtieth*, To license and regulate the keeping of hotels, taverns, and other public houses, grocers and other keepers of ordinary saloons, and victualing and other houses or places for furnishing meals, food or drink, and the keepers of billiard tables and pin alleys; also, to license and regulate or prohibit auctioneers, hawkers, peddlers and pawn-brokers, and regulate auctions, hawking and pawn-brokerage.

Hotels.

Saloons.

Auctions.

*Thirty-first*, To license and regulate butchers, and the keepers of shops, stalls and stands for the sale of meats, vegetables, and provisions of all kinds, and all draymen, common teamsters, hackmen, and all persons who carry or transport persons or property for hire; to designate stands for all carriages, carts or drays used in carrying persons or property for hire, and prescribe their fares and compensation.

Butchers.

Draymen.

Stands for carriages.

Weights and measures.

*Thirty-second,* To regulate the weights and measures used in the city, to appoint one or more sealers of weights and measures, and prescribe the powers and duties thereof, and the penalties for using false weights and measures, not conforming to the standard as established by the laws of this State.

Taxes on property for corporation purposes.

*Thirty-third,* To assess, levy and collect taxes, for the purposes of the corporation, upon all property made taxable by law for State purposes, which taxes shall be liens upon the property taxed until paid; to appropriate money, provide for the payment of the debt and expenses of the city, and make regulations concerning the same.

Punishing all offenders

Imprisonment of convicted persons.

*Thirty-fourth,* To punish all offenders for violation of or offenses against this act, or any by-law or ordinance of the Common Council, adopted or passed under this or any other act of the Legislature, by holding to bail for good behavior, by (imprisoning) imposing fines, penalties, forfeitures and costs, and by imprisonment in the jail of Saginaw County, or any jail, prison or work-house of said city, or by either, in the discretion of the court or magistrate before whom such (criminal) conviction may be had. If only a fine, penalty or forfeiture be imposed, with or without costs, the offender may be sentenced to imprisonment until the payment thereof, for a term not exceeding three months. All punishment for offenses against the ordinances of the Common Council shall be prescribed in the ordinance creating or specifying the offence to be punished, and no penalty or forfeiture shall exceed five hundred dollars. No fine shall exceed three hundred dollars, and no imprisonment shall exceed one year.

Limit of fines.

*Thirty-fifth*, To employ all persons confined for the non-payment of any fine, penalty, forfeiture or costs, or for any offense under this act, or any ordinance of the Common Council, in any jail, work-house or prison, at work or labor, either within or without the same, or upon any street or public work under the control of the Common Council; to allow any person thus confined for the non-payment of any fine, penalty, forfeiture or costs, to pay and discharge the same by such work and labor, and to fix the value and price of such work and labor. The said Common Council shall have power to make all such other by-laws, ordinances or regulations as they may deem necessary for the safety and good government of the city, and to preserve the health, and to protect the persons and property of the inhabitants thereof. They shall also have power to purchase, for the use of the city, so much land without the limits of the city as may be required for the purpose of a cemetery, the same to be located not exceeding four miles beyond the boundary of the city; and in case said Council is unable to agree with the owner or owners for the purchase of such land, they shall have the right to acquire the title to the same for the city, in the manner and by the proceedings, as near as may be, as is prescribed in this act relative to laying out or altering streets, lanes or alleys. [*Act No. 302, Laws of 1869, Page 522-531.*]

**Employing any convicted person in work-house.**

**Necessary regulations.**

**Purchasing lands for cemetery.**

**Eminent domain.**

**Same as in case of streets.**

SEC. 11. The Common Council shall have power to make all such by-laws and ordinances as they shall deem necessary and proper to secure said city and the inhabitants thereof against injuries by fire; to compel the owners or occupiers of buildings to procure and keep in readiness such number of fire-buckets as they may direct, to establish, maintain and regulate all such fire engines, hook and ladder, and hose and bucket companies,

**Power of Common Council to make by-laws and ordinances to secure against injury by fire.**

as they may deem expedient, to construct reservoirs and provide such companies with necessary and proper buildings, engines and other implements to prevent and extinguish fires; to appoint from among the inhabitants of said city such number of persons, not exceeding eighty to one company, as are willing to accept or may be deemed proper to be employed as firemen; and every such company shall have power to appoint its own officers, and to pass by-laws for its organization and government—subject to the approval of the Common Council—and to impose and collect such fines for the non-attendance or neglect of duty of its members, as may be deemed necessary and proper; and every person belonging to such company shall annually obtain from the Recorder a certificate, which shall be *prima facia* evidence of his membership for one year from the date thereof. Every member of such company, during his membership, shall be exempt from service on juries, from military duty in time of peace, and from payment of a poll-tax.

To appoint firemen.

Duties of fire companies.

SEC. 12. It shall be the duty of each company to keep in good order and repair its fire engine, hose, ladders and other implements; to assemble at least once in each month for the purpose of working its engine, and upon any alarm or breaking out of fire within said city, each company shall forthwith assemble at the place of such fire, with its fire engine and implements, and be subject to the orders of the chief engineer of the fire department.

Duty of Marshal on breaking out of fire.

SEC. 13. Upon the breaking out of any fire in said city, the Marshal shall immediately repair to the place of such fire, and aid and assist, as well in extinguishing the fire, as in preventing any goods or property from being stolen or injured, and in protecting, removing and securing the same, for which purpose, and as Chief of Police, he may require the assistance of all bystanders; and in the performance of his said duties, the Marshal shall, in all respects, be subject to the orders of the Mayor, or such of the Aldermen as may be present.

SEC. 14. The Common Council shall have power, and it shall be their duty to adopt measures for the preservation of the public health of said city; to restrain or prohibit the exercise of any unwholesome or dangerous avocation within the limits of said city; to regulate and prescribe, by ordinance, the location of all barns, stables, and privies, within said city; to establish a Board of Health, and to invest it with such powers, and to impose upon it such duties as shall be necessary to secure the inhabitants of said city from contagious, malignant, and infectious diseases; to provide for its proper organization, and for the appointment of proper officers; they shall have authority to make all such by-laws, ordinances, and regulations for the government of such Board of Health, and for the preservation of the health of the inhabitants of said city, as shall secure a prompt and efficient discharge of the duties imposed upon the Common Council by this act. [*Act No. 224, Laws of 1871, Page 493-494.*]

Power of Council as to public health.

To prohibit unwholesome and dangerous avocations.

To regulate the location of barns, &c

Board of Health.

SEC. 15. The Common Council shall have power to regulate the time and manner of working upon the streets, lanes and alleys in said city; to provide grading, planking or paving, and railing the sidewarlks, and to prescribe the width thereof: to prevent the obstruction or encumbering of any of the streets, lanes, alleys, sidewalks, or public grounds in said city; to lay out, open, make, grade and repair streets, lanes and alleys, and the same to alter or vacate, and to alter or vacate those

Common Council to regulate time of working on streets.

To open streets, lanes, etc.

Proviso.

already laid out: *Provided*, That before any street, lane, or alley shall be vacated or altered, the person or persons applying therefor shall give public notice, specifying the time and place at which such application will be made, by causing the same to be published in a newspaper published in said city, for three successive weeks, and by personally serving upon each owner residing in said city, or occupant of any lot, or part of lot, contiguous to such street or alley proposed to be altered or vacated, a copy of such notice.

When street shall be vacated.

Upon the hearing of such application, all parties in interest shall be entitled to be heard in person or by counsel; and no street or alley shall be vacated except upon sufficient cause shown, and with the concurrence of three-fourths of all the Aldermen elect.

Proceedings when private property is taken for streets.

If, in laying out or altering any street, lane, or highway, the Common Council shall require for such purpose the grounds of any person, they shall give notice thereof to the owner or person interested, or his or their agent or representative, by personal service, or by written or printed notices posted in three of the most public places of said city, at least three weeks next preceding the meeting of said Common Council, for the purposes aforesaid; and the Common Council are authorized to treat with such person or persons for such grounds or premises; and if such person or persons shall refuse to treat for the same, or the parties cannot agree therefor, it shall and may be lawful for the Mayor or Recorder of said city to issue

Summoning of jury.

*venire facias*, to command the Marshal of said city to summon and return a jury of twelve disinterested freeholders, residing within said city, to appear before said Mayor or Recorder, at any place therein to be stated, to inquire into and determine the necessity for using such grounds, and the just compensation to be paid therefor to the owner or owners of, or parties interested in said grounds and premises, which jury, being first duly sworn by said Mayor or Recorder, faithfully and impartially to inquire into the necessity for taking or using such grounds, and to ascertain and determine the just compensation to be paid therefor, and having viewed the premises, if necessary, shall inquire into and assess such damages and recompense as they shall judge fit to be awarded to the owner or owners of, or the parties interested in such ground or premises, for their respective injuries, according to their several interests or estates therein; and the said Mayor or Recorder shall, upon the return of such assessment or verdict, enter judgment therefor, confirming the same; and such sum or sums so assessed, together with all costs, shall be paid, or legally tendered, before such street, lane, or alley shall be made, laid out, altered or opened, to the claimant or claimants thereof, it shall thereupon be lawful for said Common Council to cause such grounds to be occupied for the purpose aforesaid: *Provided*, That any party claiming damages, as aforesaid, may have the right to remove such proceedings, by appeal to the Circuit Court, or any court of competent jurisdiction, upon giving notice of his, or her, or their intention so to do to said Mayor or Recorder, in writing, within ten days, or in case of the absence of said party from said city, at the time of the rendition of said judgment, then within thirty days after the verdict of said jury, and the judgment of said Mayor or Recorder, as aforesaid: *And provided further*, That the said Common Council may have the right to remove such proceedings by appeal to the Circuit Court, or any court of competent jurisdiction, within thirty days after the rendition of such judgment, as aforesaid; such determination on the part of said

Jury to assess damages.

Compensation tendered to owners.

Proviso.

Council may appeal.

Council to remove said proceedings by appeal, as aforesaid, shall be, by resolution of said Common Council, adopted by a vote of at least two-thirds of all the Aldermen elect. A notice of such determination to appeal, as aforesaid, together with a certified copy of such resolution, signed by the Mayor or Recorder, shall, within ten days after the passage of such resolution, be personally served on each and every person or party interested in such verdict and judgment, residing within said city; and in case any person or persons, interested as aforesaid, reside without said city, then said notice and copy of resolution shall be published in a newspaper published in the County of Saginaw for three successive weeks next after the passage of such resolution as aforesaid; and upon filing a transcript of the proceedings aforesaid, duly certified by said Mayor or Recorder, within forty days after the rendition of the judgment aforesaid, in the Circuit Court, or any other court of record having appellate jurisdiction, and to which such appeal is made, the same proceedings shall be had as is prescribed in other cases of appeal: *Provided*, That the appellant or appellants shall not recover costs in such case, unless the judgment in the appellate court shall be ten dollars more favorable to him or them than the assessment before the Mayor or Recorder. [*Act No. 305, Laws of 1869, Page 531-533.*]

Council judge of the election of its members

SEC. 16. The Common Council shall be the judge of the election and qualification of its own members, and shall have the power to determine contested elections, to compel the attendance of absent members, to determine the rules of its proceedings, and pass all by-laws and rules necessary and convenient for the transaction of business, and not inconsistent with the provisions of this act.

SEC. 17. All appointments to office shall be made and all assessments be ordered by a majority vote of all Aldermen elected; and removals from office shall be made by the like vote, except in cases where, by this act, a different vote may be required. Requisite vote for making appointments, removals from office, and ordering assessments.

SEC. 18. The Common Council may, at any time, require an officer, whether elected or appointed, to execute and file with the Recorder of the city, new official bonds in the same, or in such further sums, and with new and such further securities as said Council may deem requisite for the interest of the corporation. New official bonds may be required.

SEC. 19. All meetings of the Common Council shall be public, and it shall cause to be kept a record of its proceedings, which, with all other records of said city, shall be open to public inspection at reasonable times. The concurrence of a majority of all the aldermen shall be necessary to pass any ordinance, and no ordinance granting rights, privileges, or franchises to any person or corporation shall be adopted, amended, or repealed without the concurrence of two-thirds of all the Aldermen. Meeting of Common Council to be public, and record of the same kept. Requisite vote to pass ordinance.

SEC. 20. The Common Council shall have the power to grant the right of way through any of the streets of said city, to railway companies, by a two-thirds vote of said Council; to cause the streets, lanes, and alleys to be paved, planked, graveled and lighted, and to cause the expense of making, grading, paving, planking, graveling, lighting, and opening streets, lanes, and alleys, and of making, grading, paving, and planking sidewalks, and of making drains and sewers, and other local improvements, to be assessed against the owners or occupants of the lots or premises which are in front of, or adjoining such Right of way may be granted. To pave, plank, &c., streets. To light and open streets. To build sidewalks and make local improvements

To cause the expense to be assessed to owners or occupants.

To make ordinances relative to mode of assessing taxes for local improvements.

Fees for collecting such assessments to be added.

Council may provide for sale of personal property.

Sale of real estate.

Lien upon real estate for local improvement tax, real estate may be sold.

improvements, and against the owners or occupants of any other lots or premises, which, in the opinion of the Common Council, are benefited thereby, or by general tax, as it may deem just and proper, and the Common Council shall have power to make all by-laws and ordinances relative to the mode of asssessing, levying, and collecting such tax, with such fees for collecting the same as shall be provided in such ordinances, which collection fees shall be added in making such assessments and be a part thereof; and the Common Council may, by such by-laws and ordinances, provide for the sale of the personal property of the person or persons so assessed, to pay such assessment, and that the real estate, lots, or premises in front of, or adjoining such improvements, and the lots or premises which, in the opinion of the Common Council, are benefited thereby, shall be and remain subject to a lien thereon for the amount of such assessment, and may be sold to pay the same, and the

Interest on local assessments returned unpaid.

Interest and charges to be a lien on real estate.

Council may provide for the sale and redemption of real estate.

Deed prima facia evidence of regularity and of title.

Common Council may, by such by-laws or ordinances, provide for the payment of interest on such assessment or tax as shall be returned unpaid, at a rate not exceeding twenty-five per cent. per annum, and such charges of advertising and selling the same as to the Common Council shall seem just, which interest and charges shall be a lien on said lots and premises, to the same extent as said original assessment, and may provide for the sale, redemption, and conveyance of all lands, lots, and premises, upon which such tax or assessments, interest, and charges shall not be paid, in the manner, and within the time fixed by such by-laws or ordinances, and such deed of conveyance, executed and delivered pursuant to such by-laws, or ordinances, shall be *prima facia* evidence of the regularity of all proceedings required prior to, and including its execution, and of title in fee in the grantee therein named. And whenever any special assessment made for any of the purposes mentioned in this section, or for any other public work or improvement, shall, in the opinion of the Common Council, be invalid, said Council may vacate and set the same aside; and when any special assessment, or any re-assessment, shall be so vacated, or shall be held invalid by the judgment or decree of any court of competent jurisdiction, said Council may cause a new special assessment to be made for the purpose for which the original assessment was made. Such new assessment shall be made in the manner provided for making original assessments of like nature, in force at the time when such assessment should be made, and when the tax, or any part thereof, assessed as aforesaid by the original assessment set aside, or so held invalid as aforesaid, has been paid, and has not been refunded, it shall be the duty of the receiver of taxes, to apply said payment upon the re-assessment, and to make a minute thereof upon the new assessment roll, and such re-assessment shall, to the extent of such payment, be deemed paid and satisfied. All the provisions of the charter, by-laws, and ordinances of said city making special assessments a lien upon the lots, parcels, and premises embraced therein, and also those relative to the levying and collecting of special assessments, and sale of property therefor, shall apply to re-assessments made under this section. The provisions of this section shall apply to assessments heretofore made, as well as to those which shall be hereafter made. [*Act No. 302, Laws of 1875.*]

Invalid special assessments may be vacated.

Invalid special assessments vacated may be re-assessed.

Re-assessments, how made.

Payments on invalid assessments to be credited on the re-assessment

Law of original assessment to govern all re-assessments.

SEC. 21. The Common Council shall have power to assess and collect from every male inhabitant of said city over the age of twenty-one and under fifty pears (except paupers, diots and lunatics, and all others by law exempt) an

Assessment of poll tax.

annual capitation or poll tax, not exceeding one dollar, and they may provide by their by-laws for the collection of the same; and the money raised by such poll tax shall be expended under the direction of the Common Council.

Powers and duties of Common Council as township boards.

SEC. 22. The Common Council of said city is hereby authorized and required to perform the same duties in and for said city as are by law imposed upon the township boards of the several townships in this State, in reference to school taxes, county and State taxes, the support of the poor, and State, district and county elections, and the Supervisors, Justices of the Peace, Recorder, Director of the Poor, and all other officers of said city who are required to perform the duties of township officers of this State, shall take the oath, give the bond, perform like duties, and receive the same pay, and in the same manner, and be subject to the same liabilities as is provided for the corresponding township officers, except as is otherwise provided in this act, or as may be provided by the ordinances of the Common Council.

Style of all ordinances.

Prosecutions under ordinances and Charter in the name of the City of Saginaw.

SEC. 23. The style of all ordinances of the Common Council shall be: "It is hereby ordained by the Common Council of the City of Saginaw;" and all prosecutions for offenses arising under this act, or any ordinance or regulation of the Common Council, shall be in the name of the City of Saginaw.

Tax for expense other than bonded debt; when and amount Council may raise.

SEC. 24. For the purpose of defraying the expense, and all other liabilities of the city, except the bonded debt thereof, and the interest thereon, and paying the same, the Common Council may raise annually, by tax levied upon the real and personal property within said city, such sums as they may deem necessary, not exceeding two per cent. on the valuation of such real and personal estate within the limits of said city, according to the valuation thereof, taken from the assessment roll of the year preceeding the levying of such tax; and the Common Council may, in addition thereto, levy such sum, not exceeding three per cent. of the valuation of the preceeding year, as they may deem necessary for highway purposes, which shall be raised, assessed, and collected on the same roll, and in the same manner as the other taxes.

Amount to be raised limited.

Tax, highway, in addition to other taxes, Council may raise.

Amount limited.

Highway tax, how raised, &c.

If the said Common Council shall deem it expedient, for the purposes of the city, to levy a larger tax than is allowed by this section, they may, by giving *ten days notice*, by publishing the same in a newspaper published in said city, and posting a notice thereof in three public places in said city, call a meeting of the inhabitants of said city, at some place therein, who may, then and there, vote to levy, assess and collect a further money tax upon all the real and personal property in said city, in such sum as the meeting shall direct, and such tax shall be levied, assessed and collected in the same manner as is provided for the levying or collection of other taxes mentioned in this act: *Provided*, That no person shall vote at such meeting who is not a taxpayer in said city. The Mayor of said city shall preside, or in his absence, the then acting Mayor shall preside at such meeting. [*Act No. 305, Laws of 1869, Page 533-534*.

When extra tax may be raised.

Notice of meeting of inhabitants.

Notice to be published and posted.

Inhabitants may vote to raise extra tax.

How extra tax shall be collected.

Voters at meeting of inhabitants must be tax-payers.

Mayor to preside.

SEC. 25. All State, county and school taxes in said city, and all city taxes, which shall be raised by general tax, shall be levied and collected, as near as may be, in the same manner as is provided by law for the assessment

General taxes; how levied and collected.

and collection of taxes by township officers, and all the proceedings for the return, sale and redemption of real estate for the non-payment of taxes shall be in conformity with the proceedings for the return, sale, and redemption of real estate by township officers.

Proceedings same as in case of townships.

Taxes for specific purposes; how apportioned and how placed on tax roll.

SEC. 26. Whenever the Common Council shall be authorized by a vote of the property holders of said city to raise a tax for any specific purpose, it shall be lawful for the Common Council to apportion such tax upon the property according to the valuation as contained in the the last city assessment roll, and shall place the tax in a column opposite the valuation of the property; and when such roll is completed the Recorder shall make and deliver a copy thereof to the City Treasurer, together with a warrant signed by the Mayor and Recorder, commanding the Treasurer to collect the same and make return of his proceedings by virtue of said warrant within a time in said warrant to be specified—not less than thirty nor more than ninety days from the date thereof; and it shall be the duty of the Treasurer to collect said taxes within the time specified in said warrant, or within such further time as the Common Council may by resolution direct.

Recorder's duty when special tax is assessed.

Council may make ordinances relative to levy of taxes.

Sale of personal property for taxes and assessments.

Sale of real estate for taxes and assessments

SEC. 27. The Common Council may by ordinance provide for the collection of all taxes and assessments necessary to be raised, other than such as may be raised as provided in section twenty-five, and for the sale of the personal property of the person assessed therefor, and for the sale of any real estate for the non payment of such taxes or assessments, and for the redemption thereof. *Provided*, That all proceedings relative to the sale of personal property, and to the notice of sale, and the time to redeem real estate sold for such taxes or assessment shall be in conformity, as near as may be, to the provisions of law regulating the notice of sale and redemption of lands delinquent for township taxes. [*Act No. 224, Laws of 1871, Page 494-495.*]

Proceedings to conform to like proceedings in townships.

SEC. 28. No bond or note, or other obligation or evidence of indebtedness of said corporation, shall be given or issued by said corporation, except as provided in section eighty-four (84) of this act, or by any officer thereof in his official capacity, whereby the said city shall become obligated to pay any sum of money; but the Common Council may endorse on all accounts which may be presenteda gainst said city the amount allowed by them thereon.

No bond, note or obligation to be given except as authorized by sec. 84.

SEC. 29. The Common Council shall, in the month of March in each year, make out a detailed statement of all receipts and expenditures of the corporation for the past year, which statement shall state particularly upon what account all moneys were received; and it shall also specify all appropriations made by the Common Council during the year, and the particular purpose for which each appropriation was made; such statement shall be signed by the Mayor and Recorder, and be recorded and filed in the Recorder's office; a copy thereof shall be published in a newspaper printed in said city for at least two weeks.

Common Council to make, file, and publish detailed statements of all rec'pts and expenditures.

Time and manner.

SEC. 30. The Mayor shall be chief executive officer of the City of Saginaw and conservator of its peace. It shall be his duty to see that all officers of said city faithfully comply with, and discharge their official duties; to see that all laws pertaining to the municipal government of said city, and all ordinances and resolutions of the Common Council be faithfully observed and executed,

Mayor chief executive.

His duties.

and he shall have power, in his discretion, to report to the Common Council any violations thereof. He shall from time to time, give to the Common Council such information and recommend such measures, as he shall deem necessary or expedient.

Powers of Mayor ex-officio.

SEC. 31. The Mayor shall, by virtue of his office, be authorized to take the acknowledgement of deeds and other instruments in writing; to administer oaths and affirmations, perform marriage ceremonies, and to do all other like acts which Justices of the Peace are by law authorized to do, and may affix to any official certificate the seal af the city.

Powers of Recorder ex-officio.

Title of Recorder's court and where to be held.

Records and files of Recorder's court to be delivered to successor.

SEC. 32. The Recorder shall, by virtue of his office, be a Justice of the Peace, with all the like powers and duties as other Justices of the Peace in said city, and shall give bond and take oath of office as Justice before entering upon the discharge of the duties thereof; but his title as such Justice shall be *Recorder*, and his court shall be denominated the *Recorder's Court of the City of Saginaw*, and shall be held in the Recorder's office or Common Council room. The records of such court, and all papers filed therein shall be delivered by the Recorder to his successor in office, who shall proceed in all cases undetermined without notice to (the) parties.

Recorder to be clerk of Common Council and give bond as such.

SEC. 33. The Recorder shall be the clerk of the Common Council, and shall give bond for the faithful performance of his duties in such sum as the Common Council shall by ordinance direct, and shall keep a record of their proceedings in proper books provided therefor, and shall open and keep the books of account, and such other books of receipts and expenditures, as the Common Council may direct, and in such form and manner as they may order. He shall also perform for the city all such duties as township clerks are required by law to perform for the several townships, and for such services he shall receive the same fees and compensations as they are entitled to receive under the laws of this State. [* He shall keep a record of any (every) ordinance enacted, and of the time of its publication, which record shall be signed by the Mayor and Recorder. No ordinance subjecting any person to fine or imprisonment shall take effect until it shall have been published for at least one week in a newspaper published in said city.]

To perform duties required of township clerks.

To keep record of ordinances and time of publication.

Time when certain ordinances to take effect.

SEC. 34. All official bonds of said city, except as herein otherwise provided, shall be deposited with the Recorder of the city for safe keeping, and it shall be his duty to deliver the same to his successor in office.

Official bonds.

Where deposited.

SEC. 35. The Recorder shall possess the some powers and perform and discharge the municipal duties of Mayor during the absence, inability, death, resignation or removal of the Mayor.

Duties and powers of Recorder n absence of Mayor.

SEC. 36. The Recorder shall be subject to impeachment and removal from office for corrupt conduct in office, or for crimes and misdemeanors, in the same manner as judicial officers, pursuant to the provisions of the Constitution of this State.

When Recorder subject to impeachment.

SEC. 37. It shall be the duty of every Alderman of said city to attend the regular and special meetings of the Common Council, to act upon committees when thereunto appointed by the Mayor or Common Council, to

Duties of Aldermen.

* This section, to the bracket, is the same as Section 42 of the Charter of 1859 [Laws of 1859, page 183.] That part of the section included in the brackets was added by the revision of 1867. [Laws of 1867, vol. 2, page 1,006-1,007.] The word "any" is probably to be read "every." Before March 27th, 1867, it was not necessary for the Mayor to sign ordinances on the record. Under the Charter of 1857 and that of 1859 they properly appear on the record of the Council proceedings.

order the arrest of all persons violating the laws of this State, or the ordinances, by-laws or police regulations of the city; to report to the Mayor all subordinate officers who are guilty of any official misconduct, or neglect of duty, to maintain peace and good order, and to perform all other duties required of them by this act.

Powers of Supervisors

SEC. 38. The Supervisor of each ward shall have and exercise within his ward all the powers, authority and functions of Supervisors of townships as now provided, or as may hereafter be provided by law, except as herein otherwise provided; and each of them, with the Comptroller of said city, shall be members of the Board of Supervisors of Saginaw County, and as such shall be entitled to the same compensation and paid in the same manner as other members of said Board. [*Act No. 305, Laws of 1869, Page 534. See same section, Act No. 596, Laws of 1867.*]

Annual assessment of taxable property; when and how and by whom to be made.

SEC. 39. The annual assessment of taxable property in the city shall be made by the Comptroller at the same time and in the same manner as assessments are taken and made in the townships in this State, except as herein otherwise provided; and

Proviso.

*Provided*, That the Common Council may, by ordinance, regulate and determine the time and manner of taking such assessment..

Accounts against the city; how presented

SEC 40. The accounts and demands of all persons against the city shall be verified by affidavit, and shall set forth the items thereof in detail, which affidavit may be taken and certified by any member of the Council.

Comptroller and his duties.

SEC. 41. The Comptroller shall perform such duties in relation to the finances, accounts, and other matters of the city as shall be prescribed by ordinance, and shall, in addition to his other duties, be the assessor of said city, and as such, shall have and exercise within the city all the powers and duties and authority of Supervisors of townships, as provided by the laws of this State, except as herein otherwise provided. He shall be a member of the Board of Supervisors of Saginaw County, and shall have a seat in and attend the sessions of the Common Council, and may discuss all questions and matters which come before the Council, but shall have no vote therein.

Member of Board of Supervisors of Saginaw County and have a seat in the Common Council.

SEC. 42. The Comptroller of said city shall complete his assessment of all taxable property in said city on or before the fourth Monday in June, and upon the completion thereof, shall file a notice of said completion with the Recorder, who shall report the same to the Common Council at its next meeting. [*Act No. 302, Laws of 1875.*]

Comptroller when to complete assessment and to file notice with Recorder, who lays it before Council.

SEC. 43. The Comptroller, City Attorney, City Treasurer, and two tax-paying citizens, appointed by the Mayor and approved by the Common Council, shall constitute a Board of Review, four of whom shall constitute a qurom. They shall have the power, and it shall be their duty, to examine said assessment and correct any errors found therein, and on cause shown, to reduce, equalize, or increase the valuation of any property found in said roll, and to add thereto any taxable property in said city that may have been omitted, and to value the same. The assessment roll of said city shall be open for the inspection of any tax-payer of said city, from the time of its completion until the meeting of said Board of Review; and whenever said Board shall decide to increase the valuation of any property on said roll, as fixed by the Comptroller, and the owner thereof, or person to whom the same shall be assessed, shall not

Board of Review how constituted.

Quorum.

Powers and duties of Board of Review.

Board may add property to tax roll.

Assessment roll to be open to inspection.

Notice required in certain cases before valuation can be raised.

appear before said Board during its session, said Board shall cause a notice to be published in some newspaper published in said city, at least two weeks, directed to the several persons to whom such property is assessed, stating that it is the intention of said Board, at a time and place to be named in such notice, to increase the valuation of the property assessed to the persons whose names appear in said notice, to which time and place said Board may adjourn, and at said adjourned meeting may make such increase in the valuation of such property as it may deem just. They shall meet at such time and place as shall be appointed by the Common Council, of which time and place notice shall be given by the Common Council, at least two weeks prior to the meeting, by publishing a notice thereof in some newspaper published in said city, and also by posting the same in three public places in each ward of said city, and shall continue in session at least three days successively, and as much longer as may be necessary, at least six hours in each day during said three days; and any person desiring so to do, may examine his or her assessment on said rolls, and may show cause, if any, (there may be) why the valuation thereof should be changed, and the said Board shall decide the same, and their decision shall be final; and the said Board shall keep a record of their proceedings, and of all changes made by them in said rolls, and their record shall be deposited with the Recorder. [*Act No. 302, Laws of 1875.*]

Notice served by publication. Notice, contents of. Board may adjourn to time fixed in notice. First meeting of Board fixed by the Council. Council to give notice of first meeting of Board. Notice to be published and posted. Session of Board not less than three days. All persons may examine assessment roll. May show cause for a reduction. Decision of Board final. Board to keep record. Records where deposited.

Comptroller to deliver assessment roll to Board of Review.

SEC. 44. The Comptroller shall deliver the assessment rolls to said Board of Review at their first meeting, and after the same shall be confirmed by resolution of said Board, to be entered on their record, he shall again take such roll into his possession and retain the same in his office, and present the same for equalizstion to the Board of Snpervisors of Saginaw County.

SEC. 45. It shall be the duty of the Common Council, on or before the third Monday in October in each year, to determine, by resolution, the amount necessary to be raised by tax for city purposes for such year, and also the amount to be raised for highway purposes; and the Recorder shall thereupon certify such amount, together with the amount of school taxes for the year, to the Comptroller.

Common Council to determine the amount of tax necessary to be raised for current year on or before third Monday in October.

SEC. 46. The Comptroller shall levy the sums so ordered to be raised, with all other taxes required by law, upon the taxable property of said city, in the same manner that taxes are required by law to be levied in townships; he shall extend the several taxes upon the said roli, and complete the same and deliver a copy thereof, with his warrant thereto attached in the form required by the general laws of the State, to the City Treasurer within the the time prescribed by law for the completion and delivery of the tax rolls of townships in this State: *Povided*, Security has been given by such City Treasurer as required by law or in this act provided; but if such security shall not have been given by such City Treasurer, in the manner and within the time required, the Common Council shall immediately appoint some suitable person who will give the requisite security, to col ect such tax roll, and the person so appointed shall thereupon be entitled to receive said tax roll, and shall collect and pay over such taxes and make return of his doings thereon in the same manner and shall have all the powers and shall perform all the duties and be

Comptroller to levy taxes.

Proviso.

Common Council to appoint suitable person to collect tax in case of failure of Treasurer to give requisite security.

Powers and duties of such appointee.

subject to the same liabilities in this act conferred upon the City Treasurer of said city for the purpose of the collection and return, and paying over such taxes.

Taxes to be a lien.

SEC. 47. The taxes so levied shall be and remain a lien upon the property on which the same was levied, in the same cases, to the same extent, and in like manner, as taxes required by law to be levied on property in the several townships in this State are liens upon such property; and all provisions of law relating to the collection of taxes, and to the return and sale of property for the non-payment of taxes for State, county and township purposes, shall apply to the collection of such taxes, and to the return and sale of property for the non-payment of such taxes of said city, except as herein otherwise provided. [*Act No. 302, Laws of 1875.*]

Collection to be according to the general law of the State.

Exception.

Fees of Treasurer for collecting taxes.

SEC. 48. For the collection of all such taxes, the City Treasurer, or other person appointed to collect the same, shall be entitled to receive such percentage as shall be prescribed by the Common Council, *by ordinance*, not exceeding three *per centum* upon the sum to be collected, which sum shall be added in the computation of taxes on said tax roll of said city: *Provided*, That on all taxes paid during the first thirty days after said tax roll shall be delivered to said Treasurer or collector, there shall be deducted all collection fees beyond *one per cent.*, which shall be in full compensation for collecting all taxes so paid, and the said Treasurer, or other person appointed to collect taxes, shall remain in his office during ordinary business hours, for the said thirty days, and receive such taxes as may be offered; and immediately upon receiving such tax roll, he shall give *public notice* of the time and place at which he will receive such taxes, by publishing the same in some newspaper published in

Fees fixed by ordinance.

Fees to be added to tax on the roll.

One per cent first thirty days.

Deduction of fees.

Treasurer to remain in his office first thirty days.

Treasurer to give notice of tax roll.

said city, at least two weeks, and by posting said notices in at least five public places in each ward of said city; and all such taxes shall be payable at the place so designated. [*Act No. 302, Laws of 1875.*]

How notice shall be given.

SEC. 49. The Treasurer of the city shall be, by virtue of his office, the collector of all the taxes and assessments, both general and special, levied and made therein; and for that purpose, within ten days after his election, he shall give bonds to the city in such sum and with such surety, or sureties, as the Common Council shall require and approve; he shall also give to the Treasurer of the County of Saginaw such further security as is or may hereafter be required by law of the several Township Treasurers of this State; and for the purpose of the collection and return of all such taxes, and the return of property delinquent for the non-payment of taxes, the said Treasurer, on giving the bonds or surety so required, shall possess all the powers, and perform all the duties of the several Township Treasurers of this State, as prescribed by law, and shall also perform such other duties respecting the collection and return of taxes as the Common Council shall require. He shall have power to appoint a deputy, to be approved by the Common Council, and may revoke such appointment at his pleasure, which appointment and revocation shall be in writing and filed in the office of the Recorder; and the deputy may perform the duties of such Treasurer. The Treasurer and his sureties shall be responsible for the acts of his deputy.

Treasurer's duties ex-officio.

Treasurer to file bonds within ten days after election, to be approved by Common Council.

Powers and duties.

Power to appoint deputy.

Duties of deputy.

Treas. and surety responsible for acts of deputy.

SEC. 50. All moneys drawn from the treasury shall be drawn in pursuance of an order of the Common Council by warrant signed by the Recorder, and countersigned by the Comptroller; such warrant shall specify for what

Moneys how drawn from treasury.

Treasurer to keep account of warrants paid by him

Treasurer's books to be open for inspection.

To exhibit to Common Council at last meeting in March an account of all receipts and expenditures, and the state of the treasury.

purpose the amount named therein is to be paid, and the Treasurer shall keep an accurate account, under appropriate heads, of all the warrants paid by him, and his books shall be open to the inspection of any elector of the city at all reasonable hours. The Treasurer shall exhibit to the Common Council, at their last regular meeting in the month of March, and at such other times as the Council may require, a full and fair account of the receipts and expenditures from and after the date of the last annual report, and also the state of the treasury, which account shall be referred to a committee for examination, and if found to be correct shall be filed.

Marshal to give security.

Chief of Police and have the powers of a Constable.

Marshal to give security required of Constables.

Duties of Marshal.

Obey orders of Mayor.

May command aid.

Marshal may appoint deputies.

SEC. 51. The Marshal of said city shall, before entering upon the discharge of the duties of his office, give such security for the faithful performance of his duties as the Common Council shall direct and require. He shall be Chief of Police, and by virture of his office shall have all the powers conferred upon, and perform the duties required of, Constables elected under the general laws of this State, and shall take and subscribe the same official oath, and give the like security, required of such Constables; and it shall be his duty to serve all process that may be lawfully delivered to him for service; to see that all the by-laws and ordinances of the Common Council are promptly and efficiently enforced, and especially those which may be passed to carry into effect the powers granted by section ten of this act. He shall obey all lawful orders of the Mayor, and may command the aid and assistance of all Constables, and (of) all other persons, in the discharge of the duties imposed upon him by law. He may appoint such number of deputies as the Common Council shall direct and approve, who shall have the same powers and perform the same duties as the Marshal, *except the power to serve civil process*, and for whose official acts he shall be in all respects responsible; and the Marshal and his deputies shall have the same powers to serve and execute all process in behalf of the corporation of said city, or of the people of this State, for offences committed *within* said city, as Sheriffs and Constables have by law, to execute similar process. [*Act No. 224, Laws of 1871.*]

Deputy Marshals, powers of.

Powers of Marshal and his deputies.

SEC. 52. The Directors of the Poor, and City Constables shall have the powers and perform the duties of township officers elected under the general laws of this State, subject to the provisions of this act; and the Police Constables shall have like power and authority with the Marshal.

Duties and powers of Director of the Poor and Constables.

SEC. 53. The Street Commissioner shall, under the direction of the Common Council, superintend the making, grading, paving or planking, repairing and opening of all streets, lanes, alleys, bridges, sidewalks, drains and sewers within the limits of the city, in such manner as he may from time to time be required; and before entering upon the discharge of his duties, and within ten days from the notice of his appointment, shall take the oath of office and give such security for the faithful discharge of his duties as the Common Council shall direct and require; and he may appoint one or more assistants, who shall be approved by the Council.

Street Commissioner's powers and duties.

Oath of office and bond to be filed.

May appoint assistants.

SEC. 54. The City Attorney shall appear in, and conduct all suits, prosecutions and proceedings, in any court, to which the City of Saginaw is a party, to the end thereof, subject to the rules and practice of such court; and if the same be removed to any other tribunal, by writ of error, *habeas corpus*, or otherwise, he shall

City Attorney; powers and duties.

To conduct all suits of the city.

conduct the same before such tribunal, and shall perform such duties, as attorney, as the Common Council may require. He shall have a seat in, and attend the sessions of, the Common Council, and may discuss all questions and matters which may come before said Council, but shall have no vote therein. [*Act No. 302, Laws of 1875.*]

To have seat in sessions of Common Council.

SEC. 55. Whenever any officer shall resign or be removed from office, or the term for which he shall be elected or appointed shall expire, he shall, on demand, deliver over to his successor in office all the books, papers, money and effects in his custody as such officer, or in any way appertaining to his office, and every person violating this provision shall be deemed guilty of a misdemeanor, and may be proceeded against in the same manner as public officers generally for like offense under the general laws of this State, now or hereafter in force and applicable thereto; and every officer appointed or elected under this act shall be deemed an officer within the meaning and provisions of such general laws of the State.

Officers to deliver all books, papers, etc, to successor on demand.

Persons violating this section to be guilty of a misdemeanor, and punished under the general laws of this State.

SEC. 56. In addition to the rights, powers, duties and liabilities of officers prescribed in this act, all officers, whether elected or appointed, shall have such other rights, powers, duties and liabilities subject to and consistent with the provisions of this act, and shall give such security as the Common Council may deem expedient and shall prescribe by ordinance or resolution.

Powers, duties, &c, of officers not otherwise provided for regulated by Common Council.

SEC. 57. The Common Council shall prescribe, by ordinance or resolution, the term of office of all officers appointed under this act, and shall determine the salary or compensation to be paid to the several officers of said

Common Council to determine by ordinance or resolution the term of office and city, which sum, when so fixed, shall not be changed during the term, except as provided in Section 10 of this act. Salary of all officers appointed.

SEC. 58. All fines imposed by any by-law or ordinance of the Common Council may be sued for by the City Attorney, in the name of the corporation, before the Recorder, or any Justice (of the Peace) of said city. Fines to be collected by City Attorney.

SEC. 59. In all suits in which the corporation of the City of Saginaw shall be a party, or shall be interested, no inhabitant of said city shall be deemed incompetent as a witness or juror on account of his interest in the event of such suit or action: *Provided*, Such interest be such only as he has in common with the inhabitants of said city. No inhabitant incompetent as a witness in suits in which the City of Saginaw is interested. Proviso.

SEC. 60. In all trials before the Recorder, or any Justice of the Peace, of any person charged with a violation of any by-law or ordinance of the Common Council, either party shall be entitled to a jury of six persons; and all the proceedings for the summoning of such jury and in the trial of the cause, shall be in conformity, as near as may be, with the mode of proceeding in similar cases before Justices of the Peace; and in all cases, civil and criminal, he shall have the right of appeal from the Justice's Court to the Circuit Court, and shall abide the order of the court therein on the same terms as is or may be required by law in appeals from Justices' Courts in similar cases. Parties entitled to jury in trials for violating city ordinances, &c. Practice in Recorder's and Justices Court. Right of appeal.

SEC. 61. In all prosecutions for the violation of any of the by-laws or ordinances passed by the Common Council, upon complaint being made in writing by the City Attorney, or the oral or written complaint of any other person upon oath, before the Recorder or any Justice of Proceedings upon complaint and warrant.

the Peace of said city, setting forth the substance of the offense complained of, the Recorder or Justice shall issue a warrant in the name of the People of the State of Michigan, for the apprehension of the offender, directed to the Marshal of the City of Saginaw, or any Constable of the County of Saginaw, (except in the case mentioned in section 65,) and such process may be executed by any one of said officers, anywhere within the County of Saginaw, and shall be returnable the same as other similar process issued by Justices of the Peace in townships.

*What officer to execute warrant.*

*Return of warrants.*

*Wher person brought before Recorder or Justices; proceedings.*

SEC. 62. Upon bringing the person so charged before the Recorder or Justice, he shall plead to said complaint, and in case of his refusing to plead, or standing mute, the Recorder or Justice shall enter the plea of not guilty for the person so charged, that upon the said complaint and plea a trial shall be had; and upon the conviction of said offender, and the imposition of a fine, it shall be the duty of the Justice to issue an execution, directed to the Marshal of said city, or any Constable of said county, commanding him to collect of the goods and chattels of the person so offending the amount of fine, with interest and costs; and for the want of such goods and chattels wherewith to satisfy the same, that he take the body of the defendant and commit him to the common jail of said county, and the Sheriff shall safely keep the body of the person so committed until he be discharged by due course of law; and in case where imprisonment alone shall be imposed upon the person so convicted, the said Justice shall issue a commitment, directed as aforesaid, commanding his commitment until the expiration of the time for which he shall be sentenced to imprisonment, or until he be discharged by due course of law; and in cases where both fine and im-

*Conviction and fine.*

*Execution to issue.*

*Manner of collecting.*

*For want of goods, &c., to take the body of def't and commit to county jail.*

*When commitment to issue.*

prisonment are imposed upon the person so convicted by the judgment of such Justice of the Peace, he shall issue the necessary process to carry such judgment into effect: *Provided*, That the Common Council may remit such fine, in whole or in part, if it shall be made to appear that the person so committed is unable to pay the same. [*Compare this section with clause 34, of section 10.*]

Proviso.

Common Council may remit fine.

SEC. 63. Any Justice of the Peace residing in said City of Saginaw, and the Recorder of said city, shall have full power and authority, and it is hereby made the duty of such Justice or Recorder, upon complaint to him in writing by the City Attorney, or upon oath of any other person, to inquire into and try and determine all offenses which shall be committed within said city against any of the by-laws or ordinances which shall be made by the Common Council in pursuance of the powers granted by this act, and to punish the offenders as by the said by-laws or ordinances shall be prescribed or directed; to award all process and take recognizance for the keeping of the peace, for the appearance of the persons charged, and upon appeal, and to commit to prison as occasion shall lawfully require, and to commit to the Detroit House of Correction in all cases where, by the general laws of this State, such imprisonment is lawful.

Recorder and Justices of the Peace duties of upon complaint by City Attorney or other person for violation of by-laws or ordinances.

When may commit to the Detroit House of Correction.

SEC. 64. The corporation of the City of Saginaw shall be allowed the use of the common jail of the County of Saginaw for the imprisonment of all persons liable to imprisonment under the by-laws and ordinances of the Common Council; and all persons committed to jail by any Justice of the Peace for any violation of a by-law or ordinance of said Common Council, shall be in the

Use of county jail to be allowed to City of Saginaw.

custody of the Sheriff of the county, who shall safely keep the person so committed until lawfully discharged, as in other cases.

Powers of Recorder or Justices to issue warrant to any Sheriff of any county in certain cases.

SEC. 65. Whenever any person charged with having violated any ordinances of the Common Council, by which the offender is liable to imprisonment, shall have escaped from said city, or shall reside or be without the limits thereof, the Recorder or any Justice of the Peace, residing in said city, to whom complaint shall be made, shall issue a warrant to any Sheriff of any county in the State, commanding him forthwith to bring the body of such person before him, to be dealt with according to law; and every Sheriff, or other officer, to whom such warrant shall be delivered for service, is hereby required to execute the same under the penalties which are by law incurred by Sheriffs and other officers for neglecting or refusing to execute other criminal process; and in case the person charged as aforesaid, shall be within the county of Saginaw, the said warrant may be served by the Marshal of the city, or by the Sheriff, or any Constable of the county.

Marshal to serve warrant in the county in certain cases.

SEC. 66. All process issued by the Recorder or any Justice of the Peace to enforce or carry into effect any of the by-laws or ordinances of the Common Council (except in the cases mentioned in Section 65 of this act) shall be directed "To the Marshal of the City of Saginaw," or "To any Constable of the County of Saginaw;" and such process may be executed by any of said officers anywhere within the County of Saginaw, and shall be returnable the same as other similar process issued by Justices of the Peace.

Process—to whom to direct.

Fines must be paid into City Treasury.

SEC. 67. All fines, penalties, or forfeitures, recovered before any of the said Justices, or the Recorder, shall, when collected, be paid into the city treasury; and each of said Justices, and the Recorder, shall report on oath to the Common Council, at the first regular meeting thereof in each month, during the term for which he shall perform the duties of such Justice or Recorder, the number and names of all persons against whom judgment shall have been rendered, for such fine, penalty, or forfeiture, and all moneys by him received for, or on account thereof; which moneys so received, or which may be in his hands, collected on such fines, penalty, or forfeiture, shall be paid into the city treasury, on the first Monday of each and every month during the time such Justice or Recorder shall exercise the duties of said office; and for any neglect in this particular, he may be suspended or removed, as hereinafter provided. [*Act No. 305, Laws of 1869.*]

Recorder and Justices must report fines to Council, and the number and names of persons fined.

Fines, when paid over by Recorder and Justices

Fines; penalty for not paying over.

SEC. 68. Any Justice of the Peace, and the Recorder of said city, may be suspended or removed from his said office, by the Circuit Court for the County of Saginaw, for neglect or refusal to pay over as required by law, any moneys by him collected for, or on account of any fine, penalty, or forfeiture, or the unfaithful or insufficient performance of his duties in relation to the internal police of the State, or for any official misconduct, on charges specially preferred by said Common Council of said city, or any member or any officer thereof, or by three electors of said city, founded on affidavit filed in said Circuit Court, specially stating the charges complained of, a copy whereof shall be served upon him, in such manner as said Circuit Court shall direct, and opportunity shall be given him to be heard in his defence. [*Act No. 305, Laws of 1869.*]

Recorder and Justices may be removed.

Neglect to pay over money.

Charges may be preferred by Council.

Electors may prefer charges.

Charges; copy must be served.

SEC. 69. In addition to the security now required by law to be given by Justices of the Peace, each of the

Bond to be given by Justices. Justices of the Peace shall, before entering upon the duties of his office, execute a bond to the City of Saginaw, with one or more sufficient surities, to be approved by the Mayor and Recorder of said city, which approval shall be endorsed on said bond, in the penalty of one thousand dollars, conditioned for the faithful performance of his duties as a Police Justice of said city, and to pay over the moneys so collected, and make his report as in this act required, which bond shall be filed in the office of the Treasurer of said City.

Dockets and office books of Justices to be at all times subject to inspection by the Common Council.

SEC. 70. All dockets and office books kept by the Justices of the Peace shall at all times be subject to inspection and examination by the Common Council, or or any member or officer thereof, and it shall be the duty of said Justices of the Peace to produce such dockets and books at all times, whenever and wherever the said Common Council shall require or direct, and if they shall neglect or refuse to produce such docket or office books as directed and required, the Circuit Judge of the Circuit Court for the County of Saginaw may, on a proper application to him for the purpose, make an order requiring the same to be produced and enforce obedience thereto in the same manner in which other orders made by him are enforced.

Further duties of Justices of the Peace in certain cases.

SEC. 71. It shall be the duty of each Justice of the Peace, at the first regular meeting of the Common Council in each of the months of August, November, February and May, in every year, to account on oath before the Common Council for all such moneys, goods, wares and merchandise seized as stolen property, as shall then remain unclaimed in the officef of either said Justices of the Peace, and immediately thereafter to give notice for four weeks in one of the public newspapers printed in the said City of Saginaw, to all persons interested or claiming such property: *Provided, always*, That if any goods, wares, merchandise or chattels of a perishable nature, or which shall be expensive to keep, shall at any time remain unclaimed in the offices of either of said Justices, it shall be lawful for such Justice to sell the same at public auction, at such time, and after such notice, as to him and the said Common Council shall seem proper. Proviso.

SEC. 72. It shall be the duty of each of the Justices of the Peace aforesaid, who may recover or obtain possession of any stolen property, on his receiving satisfactory proof of property from the owner, to deliver such property to the owner thereof, on his paying all necessary and reasonable expenses which may have been incurred in the recovering, preservation or sustenance of such property, and the expenses of advertising the same. Duties of Justices on taking possession of stolen goods

SEC. 73. It shall be the duty of each of the Justices of the Peace aforesaid, to cause all property unclaimed after the expiration of the notice specified in the last preceeding section but one of this act, money excepted, to be sold at public auction to the highest bidder, unless the Prosecuting Attorney of the County of Saginaw shall direct that it shall remain unsold for a longer period, to be used in evidence in the administration of justice—and the proceeds thereof forthwith to pay to the Treasurer of the said City of Saginaw, together with all money, if any, which shall remain in his hands after such notice as aforesaid, first deducting the charges of said notice of sale. Duties of Justices in case of stolen property unclaimed.

SEC. 74. The Recorder shall report to the Common Council the names of such officers as shall have neglected to give the bond and security required by the provisions of this act. Recorder to report to the Common Council the names of officers neglecting to qualify.

*Fees of Justices and Constables. Fees of the Marshal.*

SEC. 75. The Justices of the Peace and the Constables shall receive the same fees as are by law allowed to Justices and Constables in townships. The Marshal and Police Constables shall receive the same fees for making arrests and serving process in behalf of the corporation as Constables are allowed by law for similar services.

*Qualifications of electors at city elections. Proviso. Residence of elector in the ward where he boards or takes regular meals.*

SEC. 76. At all city elections every eleetor shall vote in the ward where he shall have resided ten days preceding the day of election, otherwise he may vote in the ward from which he removed: *Provided*, He shall have resided in such ward ten days prior to such removal. The residence of an elector, under this act, shall be the ward where he boards or takes his regular meals.

*Perjury.*

SEC. 77. Any person who may be required to take any oath or affirmation under or by virtue of any provision of this act, who shall, under such oath or affirmation, in any statement or affidavit, or otherwise, wilfully swear falsely as to any material fact or matter, shall be guilty of perjury.

*Double costs when recovered.*

SEC. 78. If any suit shall be commenced against any person elected or appointed under this act to any office, for any act done or omitted to be done under such election or appointment, or against any person having done any thing or act by the command of any such officer, and if final judgment be rendered in such suit whereby any such defendant shall be entitled to costs, he shall recover double costs in the manner defined by law. Every such suit shall be commenced before theRecorder or some Justiceof said city, or in the Circuit Court for the County of Saginaw, whether such action be civil or criminal in form.

SEC. 79. The record of any ordinance enacted, and of the time of its first publication, made by the clerk as required in this act, or a copy thereof, certified by such clerk, under the seal of the corporation, shall be presumptive evidence in all courts, places and proceedings, of the due passage of such ordinance—of its having been duly published, and of the time of its first publication. Copies of all other records and papers duly filed in and pertaining to the office of the clerk, certified by him under the seal of the corporation, shall be evidence in all courts and places to the same effect as the originals would be if produced.

Record of ordinances or certified copy presumptive of due passage of such ordinance.

SEC. 80. Proof of the requisite publication of any ordinance, resolution or other proceedings required to be published in any newspaper, by the affidavit of a printer or publisher thereof, taken before any officer authorized to administer oaths and take affidavits, and duly filed with the Clerk of the city, or any other competent proof, shall, in all courts and places, be conclusive evidence of the legal publication of such ordinance, resolution or other proceeding. All ordinances and by-laws of the Common Council, printed and published by their authority, shall, in all courts, places and proceedings, be received without further proof as *prima facia* evidence thereof, and of their legal enactment and publication. [*See sec. 5,953, Page 1,711, C. L.*]

Legal publication of ordinances; when conclusively proved.

SEC. 81. No person shall be an incompetent Judge, Justice of the Peace, or other officer, witness or juror, by reason of his being an inhabitant or freeholder in the City of Saginaw, in any prosecution or proceedings in the Recorder's Court, in any action or proceedings in which the corporation shall be a party in interest, or in any judicial or other proceedings.

Inhabitant or freeholder not disqualified to act as Judge Justice, juror ro witness in any prosecution or proceeding in Recorder's Court in which this city is a party.

Legal acts by Mayor or other officer not to be invalidated by this act.

SEC. 82. This act shall not invalidate any legal act done by the Mayor or Recorder, Aldermen and Freemen of the City of Saginaw City, or by the Common Council or any officer of said city now or hereafter in office.

Defaulters to the city not to be elected or appointed to any office

Who are defaulters.

Office to become vacant by default.

SEC. 83. No person shall be elected or appointed to any office created by this act who is now, or may hereafter be, a defaulter to said city, or to any board of officers thereof, or to the State of Michigan or any county or township thereof; and any person shall be considered a defaulter who has refused or neglected, or may hereafter refuse or neglect, for thirty days after demand made, to account for and pay over to the party authorized to receive the same, any public money or papers pertaining to his office, which may have come into his possession; if any person holding any such office shall become a defaulter while in office, the same shall thereby be vacated.

Bonds; when and how to issue.

Mayor, or in his absence, Recorder to preside at certain meetings.

SEC. 84. Whenever the Common Council shall deem it necessary to issue the bonds of the city for any purpose, they shall call a meeting of the property-holding taxpayers of the city, being electors thereof, by posting notices in five of the most conspicuous places of said city, at least eight days previous to the time of said meeting, giving notice of the time and place of such meeting, also specifying the amount of, not exceeding twenty-five thousand dollars, and the object for which it is proposed to issue said bonds. The Mayor, or in his absence, the Recorder, shall preside at such meeting, and the electors present shall choose, *viva voce*, from among their number the inspectors and clerks of said election, who shall, before proceeding to the discharge of their duties, make an oath or affimation faithfully to discharge the duties of their respective offices at such election, which oath or affirmation may be administered by any person authorized to administer oaths. Said election shall be conducted in the same manner, and the canvass of votes, as nearly as may be, as other elections under this act. At the close of such election the inspectors shall make two certificates of the number of votes given for and against such issue of bonds, one of which shall be forthwith deposited with the Recorder of said city, and the other filed in the office of the County Clerk of the County of Saginaw: *Provided*, That not more than two such meetings shall be called in any one year. **Proviso.**

Sec. 85. Whenever the Common Council shall be authorized by a vote of the tax-payers as aforesaid, they may issue the bonds of said city for the amount as aforesaid, and provide for the payment of the interest thereon, and for this purpose shall annually levy, assess and collect on the assessed value of all the real and personal estate in said city, made taxable by the laws of this State—taxes for this purpose not to exceed in amount a sufficient sum to pay the interest accrued or to accrue on said bonds for the year for which said taxes are levied. **Common Council may issue bonds when authorized by vote of tax-payers.**

Sec. 86. All ordinances, by-laws, regulations, resolutions and rules of the Common Council of the City of Saginaw City, now in force and not inconsistent with this act, shall remain in force until altered, amended or repealed by the Common Council under this act, and after the same shall take effect. **Ordinances to remain in force.**

Sec. 87. So much of the "Act to incorporate the City of Saginaw City," and only so much of said act as may be inconsistent with the provisions of this act, is hereby repealed. **What by this act repealed.**

Certain officers to remain in office until expiration of the term for which they were elected

SEC. 88. All the officers of said city who may be in office at the passage of this act shall continue to exercise the duties of their respective offices until the term for which they were elected shall have expired.

Public act.

SEC. 89. This act shall be deemed a public act, and shall be favorably construed in all courts.

SEC. 90. The Legislature may at any time alter, amend, or repeal this act.

SEC. 91. This act shall take immediate effect.

Council may build road to cemetery beyond city limits.

SEC. 92. The Common Council may construct, grade, gravel, plank, or repair, any street, road, or highway within, or without the corporate limits of the city, leading to the burying ground or cemetery owned by it, and may join with the township of Saginaw in the construction, grading, graveling, planking, or repairing, from time to time, of any such road or highway without the limits of said city, leading to such burying ground or cemetery, on such terms and conditions as may be agreed upon with the Township Board of said township, and may contract with the Saginaw & Gratiot Plank Road Company to keep in repair that part of its road lying between the city and said cemetery. [*Laws of 1875.*]

May join with township of Saginaw to build road to cemetery.

City may bid in lands on the five year list.

SEC. 93. The Common Council may, in its discretion, authorize the Comptroller to attend the annual tax sales held in the County of Saginaw, and bid in, in the name of the City of Saginaw, all descriptions of property lying within the corporate limits of said city, known as State tax lands, which have remained unsold for five years or more, from the time such lands were bid off to the State, under the general tax law of this State, which lands, so bid in for the city, shall be liable to taxation the same as if they were not the property of the city, and such tax

Liable to taxation.

shall be a lien on the land, and the city shall have the same right to take any proceedings in law or equity, given to individuals, to quiet title in cases provided for in the general laws of this State, and provide for the sale and conveyance thereof, and all deeds of conveyance made of such lands, pursuant to the order, or direction of the Common Council, or ordinances of said city, shall be *prima facia* evidence of the regularity of all proceedings prior to, and including such deed, and of title in fee in the lands therein described. [*Laws of 1875.*]

City may take proceedings to quiet title.

May re-sell such lands.

Deeds made by Council.

Evidence of title.

SEC. 94. No plat of lands within the limits of the city, executed as a sub-division thereof, or addition to said city, for the purpose of being recorded in the office of the Register of Deeds, shall be entitled to record without the approval of the Common Council, and a copy of the resolution containing such approval, certified by the Recorder, under the seal of said city endorsed thereon; a copy of such plat shall also be filed with the Comptroller of said city. [*Laws of 1875.*]

Plats must be approved by Council.

Copy of all plats to be filed with the Comptroller.

SEC. 95. The Common Council shall have power, by ordinance, adopted by a vote of two-thirds of all the Aldermen elect, and approved by the Mayor, to create and provide for a Board of Sewer Commissioners, and from time to time to fix and prescribe the powers and duties of such Board. [*Laws of 1875.*]

Sewer Commissioners.

SEC. 96. The Common Council shall have power, by a two-thirds vote of all the Aldermen elect, to enter into a contract with any bank, banker or bankers, doing business in the City of Saginaw, to receive on deposit, and pay interest on, any money in the city treasury belonging to the city, and to receive from any such bank, banker or bankers, such security, by way of bond, or otherwise, for the safe keeping, and prompt paying over

Interest on city money.

Security to be given for deposits.

of such money, and the interest thereon, on the order of City Treasurer, as the Common Council may, by resolution, adopted by a two-thirds vote of all the Aldermen elect, demand and approve; and such contract, being made and filed with the Recorder, and the security for the faithful performance thereof being approved, and filed with the Recorder, and such contract and security entered and recorded at length upon the journal of the Common Council in the proceeding of the meeting at which the security was approved, the Common Council shall have power, by resolution, to direct the City Treasurerto deposit with such bank, banker, or bankers, all moneyof the city in, and thereafter coming into, his hands, during the time fixed in such contract, and the City Treasurer and his bondsmen shall not be liable for any loss the city may sustain from, or by reason of any defalcation of such bank, banker, or bankers. In any contract for the deposit of the city funds, made in pursuance of the authority herein given, the Common Council shall reserve the right to terminate the same, and to withdraw such deposits, and remit the same to the custody of the City Treasurer at its pleasure, by a two-thirds vote of all the Aldermen elect. Money so deposited shall be drawn only on the order of the City Treasurer, and he shall draw the same only when he is authorized to pay the same according to the provisions of section fifty of this charter, or directed by the Common Council to withdraw such deposits in the manner above provided. [*Laws of 1875.*]

Interest contract to be recorded on the journal.

Treasurer not liable for money deposited by Council.

Council may terminate interest contracts.

Money deposited on interest contracts; how drawn.

# SCHOOL LAW OF THE CITY OF SAGINAW.

[Act No. 260, Laws of 1865.]

## An Act to Organize Union School District of the City of Saginaw.

SEC. 1. *The People of the State of Michigan enact:* That the City of Saginaw shall constitute One School District, which shall be a body corporate, by the name and style of Union School District of the City of Saginaw, and by that name may sue and be sued, and shall be subject to all the general laws of this State relative to corporations, so far as the same may be applicable, and such district shall have all the powers and privileges conferred upon school districts by the general laws of this State, all the general provisions of which, relating to common or primary schools, shall apply and be in force in said district, except such as shall be inconsistent with this act, or with the by-laws and ordinances of the Board of Education hereinafter mentioned, made in pursuance of this act.

Body corporate.

Powers of Board.

SEC. 2. All schools organized in said district under this act shall be open to all children, actual residents within the limits of said city, between the ages of five and twenty-one years, inclusive, and to such other persons as the said Board shall admit.

Who to be admitted to school.

Board of Education. Terms of

SEC. 3. The officers of said district shall cousist of Six Trustees, to be called the Board of Education ; and the term of office of said Trustees shall be three years, two of whom shall be elected annually, at the annual meeting of said district, which shall be held on the first Monday of June in each year ; and within ten days after each annual election the Trustees shall meet and elect from their own number, a President, Secretary and Treasurer, who shall severally hold their offices for one year, and until their successors shall be elected and qualified, and may at any time fill, by a new election, any vacancies that may occur in either of said offices ; and their powers and duties shall severally be the same as those of the moderator, assessor, and director, in school districts organized under the general laws of this State, except as the same are varied by the provisions of this act, and the ordinances and by-laws of said Board.

Officers.

Powers and duties of

Notice of elections.

SEC. 4. The Secretary of said Board shall give at least ten days previous notice of the annual and all special meetings of said district by posting notices thereof, specifying the hour, place, and object of holding the same, in at least three public places in said city ; and a copy of such notice shall be recorded in the book in which the records of the proceedings of such meeting shall be kept, and such record shall be *prima facia* evidence that due notice of such meeting has been given according to its terms.

Vacancies how filled.

SEC. 5. Said Board of Education shall have power to fill all vacancies that may occur in the office of Trustee until the next annual meeting of the district ; and each Trustee within ten days after notice of his election, whether elected by said district or by said Board, shall file with the Secretary an acceptance of office in writing.

SEC. 6. The treasurer of said district shall, before entering upon the duties of his office, give a bond to said district, in such sum and with such surety or sureties as the said Board shall approve, conditioned for the faithful performance of the duties of his office, which bond shall be filed with the Secretary. Treasurer to give bond.

SEC. 7. The Treasurer shall receive and hold, subject to the order of said Board, all moneys, belonging to said district, from whatever sources derived; and it shall be the duty of the County Treasurer and the Treasurer of said city to pay over to him, on his application therefor, all moneys that shall come into their hands respectively, belonging to said district. Treasurer to hold moneys belonging to district.

SEC. 8. No money of said district shall be paid by said Treasurer except on the order of said Board, signed by the Secretary and countersigned by the President; and it shall be the duty of such Treasurer to pay such orders to the extent of the funds in his hands on presentation thereof. Moneys how paid.

SEC. 9. A majority of the members of said Board shall constitute a quorum, and the said board shall meet from time to time, at such place in said city as they may designate. Said Board shall succeed to, and exercise all the powers and perform all the duties of school inspectors for said city, and the office of School Inspector of said city, except as vested in and to be executed by said Board, is hereby abolished; said Board, before hiring any teacher, shall examine into his or her qualifications, and all teachers employed by said Board shall be considered and deemed legally qualified; and said Board shall deliver to them respectively a certificate, stating the branches they have been found qualified to to teach, which shall continue in force so long as said Board shall continue to employ such teachers in the schools of said district, unless expressly annulled by the said Quorum. Powers of board. Examination of teachers.

Board; and on such certificate being annulled, any contract for the employment of the teacher named therein, shall cease and determine, as though the term of such employment had expired.

Board to determine amount of money necessary to be raised.

SEC. 10. The said Board shall also have power, and it shall be its duty, annually to determine by vote, which shall be entered in the records of its proceedings, the amount of money necessary to be raised by tax on the property of said district, to defray the expenses of the schools of said district for the current year, and the amount necessary to pay the interest and principal of any liquidated debt due within such year, from such district, and to file with the Recorder of said City on or before the first day of October in each year, a statement in writing, of the sum so voted; and it shall be the duty of the Common Council to apportion said sum to be raised among the wards of said city, according to the valuation of the taxable property in the same, and to cause the same to be assessed on such property in the first general tax thereafter made; and the assessment of such tax, for said district, shall be in a separate column in said roll; and the same shall be collected at the same time, and shall be and remain a lein on the property on which the same is levied; and the Treasurer of said city shall have the same authority, and may resort to the the same modes and proceedings, by virtue of the said roll and the warrant annexed thereto, to collect the the same, as the other taxes therein contained; and it shall be the duty of rhe City Treasurer to pay over to the Treasurer of said district all such moneys as may be collected belonging to said district, as indicated by said column, as follows, to wit: All such moneys as shall have been collected on the first Monday of January next succeeding the date of issuing such tax roll, and on the

Council to apportion sums among the wards.

Taxes to be a lein on property.

first day of February such sum as shall equal one-half the amount of the total school tax, the same to be paid out of any moneys collected by him on said roll, and the balance of the school moneys on the return of the roll. *Provided*, That in case the time for the collection of the roll shall be extended, then on or before the twentieth day of February he shall pay over one-half of the balance remaining unpaid after the payment of the first of February, and the remainder, on the return of the roll. [*Act No. 353, Laws of 1869, page 821.*] **Proviso.**

SEC. 11. Said Board shall also have power to order special meetings of said district whenever any such meeting shall be deemed necessary: and at any such special as well as at any annual meeting of said district, a majority of the tax payers, resident therein, in attendence, shall be entitled by vote to order any number of school houses to be erected, and sites for the same in said city to be purchased; and to vote for raising by tax on the taxable property of said city, or partly by tax and partly by loan, on the bonds of said district, all sums necessary to purchase said sites, and to improve and ornament the same, and to erect and furnish such school-houses. **Special meetings of district.**

SEC. 12. Said Board shall have power, and it shall be its duty, to select and purchase such number of sites for school-houses, as shall be directed by the vote of any district meeting or meetings; and in case a loan, for any purpose authorized by the last preceding section shall be voted by a district meeting, it shall be the duty of said Board, if possible, to borrow the money so directed to be procured, by loan, and on the time directed by said district meeting; and for this purpose a bond may be made in the name of said district, signed by the Secretary, and countersigned by the President, and delivered to the **School-house sites.** **Loans.**

lender, providing for the payment of the sum borrowed, and such rate of interest as shall be agreed on, not exceeding ten per centum per annum, and a statement of any sum directed by said district meeting to be raised by tax, shall be filed with the Recorder of said city within the same time as the statement of moneys voted by said Board is required to be filed, and on the filing of the same, the same proceedings shall be had and taken to collect the same as is by section ten of this act act authorized to collect the moneys voted by said Board, and said section, as to the collection and paying over the moneys, directed by said Board to be raised by tax, shall apply to the collecting and paying over of the moneys voted by said district meeting, to be raised by tax.

School-house sites, etc.

SEC. 13. It shall be the duty of said Board to improve and ornament the sites for such school-houses as it shall deem proper and expedient, and adopt plans of school-houses to be erected, and to erect the same and furnish them in such manner, as in the judgement of said Board will best subserve the purposes of their erection.

District library.

SEC. 14. Said Board shall establish a district library for the use of the schools in said district, and for the increase of the same, shall appropriate annually the sum of two hundred dollars of the moneys raised by tax for school purposes; and in addition thereto, all fines collected for breach of the State or municipal laws within said city, shall be applied for the support of such library.

Board authorized to make by-laws, ete.

SEC. 15. Said Board shall also have full power and authority to make by-laws and ordinances relative to taking the census of all children in said district between the ages of four and eighteen years; relative to making all necessary reports and transmitting the same to the proper officers, as designated by law, so that said city may be entitled to its proportion of the primary school fund ; relative to the levying and collecting of rate bills ; relative to supplying with books, the children who are destitute of the means to procure them ; relative to the grading, disciplining and visitation of schools ; relative to the course of study and the books to be used in the schools , relative to the appointment of necessary officers and servants in and about said schools, their powers, duties and compensation, including a Superintendent of the schools of said district.

High schools.

Scholarship.

SEC. 16. Said Board shall also have power to establish a high school, and prescribe the course of study for the same, and to grant such certificates of scholarship and in such form as such Board shall deem proper, to pupils completing satisfactorily the said course of study.

Entitled to moneys etc., belonging to present district.

SEC. 17. Said school district hereby organized, shall succeed to, and be entitled to demand and receive all moneys and other rights, of whatsoever name or nature, belonging to the present school district in said city, hitherto known as school district number one, of the City of Saginaw, to the same extent as said last named district could do, if this act had not been passed ; and all real and personal property, situate in said city, hitherto belonging to said district, or to school district number one, of the town of Saginaw, now embraced within said city, shall, by the force of this act, become the property of said union school district hereby organized ; and all moneys [raised] or being raised by tax, or accrued or accruing to said former district in said city, shall hereby become the money of said union school district, and no tax of said district, or other proceeding, shall be invalidated or affected by the change in the organization of said district by means of this act. [*Act No. 440, Laws of 1867, page 922.*]

Liable for its debts.

SEC. 18. All debts and liabilities of said school district number one, of the City of Saginaw, whether in the form of bonds or other express contracts, or in any other form, and whether liquidated or not, shall become the debts and liabilities of said union school district of the City of Saginaw, to the same extent as they existed and were valid against said former district; and said union school district hereby organized shall be subject to be sued in the same manner, and all other proper and suitable proceedings against it, may be taken as though it had been the original debtor; and in no such suit or proceeding shall the defense be urged or allowed that said school district number one was not a valid organization, but the said school district number one is hereby declared to have been duly organized, and its organization shall be deemed a valid school district, by the name aforesaid, from the date of the act incorporating the said city, to the time when this act shall take effect.

Offiicers of

SEC. 19. The trustees and officers of said school district number one, shall be and they are hereby constituted the trustees and officers of said Union School District of the City of Saginaw, and the moderator shall be the president, and the director the secretary of said board, and said trustees and officers shall continue to hold their offices respectively, for the same time as though this act had not been passed, except as modified by the time of holding the annual meetings of said district, it being the intention that the school year shall annually expire on

School year.

the first Monday of June, and that all terms of office which expire in any year, shall terminate with the school year, on the election and acceptance of office, of the officers then elected, or at the first meeting of the trustees thereafter.

SEC. 20. The Secretary of the Board of Education of the City of Saginaw is directed, and hereby required, at least ten and not more than fifteen days before the annual school meeting of said school district, to be held in the year eighteen hundred and sixty-nine, make out and publish in some newspaper published in the County of Saginaw, a detailed statement of all moneys received and from what sources, and all moneys expended and for what purpose, from the organization of said district, and also submit such statement to the electors of said district at the said school meeting; and in each and every year thereafter, the said Secretary shall, at least ten and not more than fifteen days before the annual school meeting of said district, make out and publish in some newspaper published in the County of Saginaw, a detailed statement of all moneys received, and from what sources, and all moneys expended, and for what purpose, for the expiring year. [*Act No. 353, Laws of 1869, page 822.*]

Secretary of Board to make statement.

# ORDINANCES OF THE CITY OF SAGINAW.

(From Laws of 1865, Page 487.)

(5953) SECTION 1. *The People of the State of Michigan enact:* That all laws by-laws, regulations, resolutions and *ordinances* of the Common Council, or of the Board of Trustees, of any incorporated city or village, in this State, may be read in evidence in all Courts of Justice, and in all proceedings before any officer, body or board, in which it shall be necessary to refer thereto, either from a record thereof kept by the Clerk or Recorder of such city or village, or from a printed copy thereof, purporting to have been published by authority of the Common Council or Board of Trustees in a newspaper published in such city or village, *or from any volume of ordinances purporting to have been printed by authority of the Cammon Council, or Board of Trustees of sueh city or village;* and such record, certified copy, or volume, shall be *prima facia* evidence of the existence and validity of such laws, regulations, resolutions, and ordinances, without proof of the enactment, publishing, or any other thing concerning the same. (*C. L. of 1871, page 1711.* See also Sec. 79 and 80 of the Charter, page 57.)

When the charter of a city provides that the printed volume of the city ordinances shall be evidence, in all Courts, they are placed on the same footing, as regards proof, as the statutes. (*Napman vs. People, 19 Mich., 352.*)

**The Ordinances contained in this Book, are printed and published by authority of the Common Council of the City of Saginaw.**

*An Ordinance relative to the apprehension and punishment of Drunkards and Disorderly Persons.*

*Be it ordained by the Mayor, Recorder and Aldermen of the City of Saginaw City, in Common Council convened:*

SECTION 1. Any person who shall be found intoxicated in any street or elsewhere, in the City of Saginaw, city shall on conviction thereof, before any Justice of the Peace, be punished by a fine not to exceed fifteen dollars, or by imprisonment in the common jail of the County of Saginaw, for a period not exceeding ten days, Intoxiacted persons. Punishment. Fine.

Imprisonment. or by both such fine and imprisonment, in the discretion of the Justice who shall try the offender, together with the costs of prosecution.

Powers and duties of Marshal, etc., to arrest without process in certain cases. SEC. 2. The Marshal, any Deputy Marshal, or Constable of said city may, and it shall be their duty to arrest without process any person found in a state of intoxication in said city, and bring him forthwith before a Justice of the Peace; or in case such arrest be made in the night time, or on Sunday, or in case no Justice of the Peace of said city be found in his office, the officer making the arrest shall convey the person arrested to said common jail, the keeper whereof shall safely keep such person therein until he shall be taken away by the same or some other officer possessing similar powers, or until such person shall have remained in jail twenty-four hours, or in case his imprisonment commenced on Sunday, until four o'clock in the afternoon of Monday following. And it shall be the duty of the officer conveying any person to jail under the provisions of this section, within twenty-four hours thereafter, or in case such person was taken to jail on Saturday afternoon, or on Sunday, previous to four o'clock in the afternoon of Monday following, to cause such person to be brought before a Justice of the Peace of said city.

Officers to give notice to City Attorney. SEC. 3. It shall be the duty of the officer bringing any person before a Justice of the Peace, in pursuance of the provisions of section two of this ordinance, forthwith to give notice thereof to the City Attorney. And upon complaint being made to said Justice in writing, charging such person with being found intoxicated in said city, the said Justice shall proceed to inquire into and try such charge, and if it shall appear, by the confession of the person so charged, or by competent evidence, that such offense has been committed, the said Justice shall render judgment in the name of the People of the State of Michigan against such person for such penalty, within the above prescribed limits, as he may judge proportionate to the offense, and shall forthwith issue the appropriate process to carry such judgment into effect.

SEC. 4. No person shall, within said city, sell or give away spirituous or fermented liquor to any drunkard, or to any person while in a state of intoxication; and any person who shall offend against any provision of this section shall, for each offense, forfeit and pay a fine not to exceed fifty dollars, in the discretion of the Justice who shall try the offender, with the costs of prosecution.

Furnishing intoxicating liquors to drunkards prohibited.

SEC. 5. Any person who shall, in the City of Saginaw City, make or aid, countenance or assist in making any riot, disturbance or improper diversion, or who shall be guilty of any indecent, immoral or disorderly conduct or language, or of any assault or battery, or other breach of the peace, and all persons who shall collect in crowds, in said city, for any unlawful purpose, shall for each offense forfeit and pay a fine, in the discretion of the Justice who shall try the offender, not to exceed one hundred dollars, with costs of prosecution.

Persons aiding in disturbance.

Disorderly conduct, etc.

Penalty.

SEC. 6. It shall be the duty of the Marshal, Deputy Marshals and Constables of the City of Saginaw City to arrest, without process, any person found offending against any provision of the fifth section of this ordinance, and bring him forthwith before a Justice of the Peace in said city, or in case such arrest be made in the night time, or on Sunday, or in case no Justice of the Peace in said city be found in his office, the officer making the arrest shall convey the person so arrested to said common jail, the keeper whereof shall safely keep such person therein until

Duty of Marshal, etc., to arrest offenders without process.

he shall be taken away by the same or some other officer possessing similar powers, or until such person shall have remained in jail twenty-four hours, or in case his imprisonment commenced on Saturday afternoon, or on Sunday, until four o'clock in the afternoon of Monday following. And it shall be the duty of the officer conveying any person to jail, under the provision of this section, within twenty-four hours thereafter, or in case such person was taken to jail on Saturday afternoon, or on Sunday, previous to four o'clock in the afternoon of Monday following, to cause such person to be brought before a Justice of the Peace of said city. And whenever any person shall be brought before a Justice of the Peace under the provisions of this section, such further proceedings shall be thereupon had as prescribed in section three of this ordinance in respect to persons arrested in a state of intoxication.

Adotped May 13, 1857.

GARDNER D. WILLIAMS, Mayor.

C. GARRETT, Recorder.

[*Journal of Common Council, May 13, 1857, page 14; Record Ordinance Book, page 12.*]

---

*An Ordinance relative to closing stores and shops, and the sale of intoxicating or spirituous liquors on the Sabbath.*

*Be it ordained by the Mayor, Recorder and Aldermen, of the City of Saginaw City, in Common Council convened :*

Buildings for sale of intoxicating liquors to be closed on Sunday.

SECTION 1. No person shall keep open any store, shop or building of any kind, in this city, on the first day of the week, for the sale of any spirituous or intoxicating liquors, or any mixed liquors, a part of which is spirituous or intoxicating, or any beer, wine or cider ; that no person shall, on the first day of the week, sell within said city, directly or indirectly, or give away or furnish to any person or persons any spirituous or intoxicating liquors, or any mixed liquors, a part of which is spirituous or intoxicating, or any beer, wine or cider.

SEC. 2. If any person, by himself, his clerk, agent or servant, shall directly or indirectly keep open any store, shop or building of any kind in this city, on the first day of the week, for the sale of any spirituous or intoxicating liquors, or any mixed liquors, a part of which is spirituous or intoxicating, or any beer, wine or cider, or shall within said city, on the first day of the week, sell directly or indirectly, or give away or furnish to any person or persons any spirituous or intoxicating liquors, or mixed liquors, any part of which is spirituous or intoxicating, or any wine, beer or cider, he shall forfeit and pay, on the first conviction, the sum of ten dollars and the cost of suit or prosecution, and shall be at once committed to the common jail of Saginaw County until the same shall be paid, provided that the term of imprisonment shall not exceed thirty days, and on the second and every subsequent conviction for the like offense, he shall forfeit and pay the sum of twenty dollars and the cost of prosecution, and shall be committed as aforesaid until the same is paid, provided the term of imprisonment shall not exceed the term of thirty days.

**Penalty for violation of preceeding section.**

Adopted August 17, 1857.

GARDNER D. WILLIAMS, Mayor.

COE GARRETT, Recorder.

[*Journal of 1857, page 49. Proof of publication, rec. Ord. Bk., p. 95.*]

*An Ordinance relative to Nuisances.*

*It is hereby ordained by the Common Council of the City of Saginaw as follows:*

Nuisances prohibited.

SECTION 1. No person or persons, within the limits of this city, shall permit or suffer on his or their premises, or on any premises of which he, she or they may be occupants, any nuisance; nor shall he, she or they exercise any calling or trade which is unwholesome or offensive, by which a nuisance shall be created by offensive and noisome stenches or otherwise, which shall or may become offensive or dangerous to the neighborhood or travelers, or which may endanger the neighboring buildings by any liability from fire or fires used on his, her or their premises.

Offensive substances not to be deposited in said city.

SEC. 2. No person shall deposit, or cause to be deposited, in any part of said city any dead animal, or any animal, vegetable, or other substance which is offensive, or which by process of decomposition may become offensive, unless the same shall be buried at least three feet below the surface of the ground.

Keeping of swine.

SEC. 3. No person shall erect or maintain a pen for the confinement or keeping of swine within fifty feet of the line of any street, within the limits of the city. [*See Journal No. 4, page 414, of April 1st, 1875.*]

Nuisances how abated.

SEC. 4. Whenever any nuisance shall be found to exist in any part of said city, the Common Council may, by resolution, cause the same to be abated or removed at the expense of the person creating the same, or permitting the same to remain.

Marshal's duties.

SEC. 5. It shall be the duty of the Marshal to cause any nuisance to be abated or removed when thereto directed by the Common Council.

SEC. 6. Whoever shall violate any of the preceding sections of this ordinance shall be liable to pay a fine not less than three dollars nor more than fifty dollars upon conviction thereof. Penalty for violation.

SEC. 7. All ordinances, or parts of ordinances, heretofore passed by the Common Council of this city, contravening the provisions of this ordinance, be and the same are hereby repealed. Ordinances repealed.

Adopted May 14, 1859.

G. W. BULLOCK, Mayor.

H. L. MILLER, Recorder.

[*Record Ordinance Book, page 15*]

---

*An Ordinance relative to obstructions in the streets, and nuisances.*

*It is hereby ordained by the Common Council of the City of Saginaw, as follows :*

SECTION 1. No person shall leave any wagon, cart, carriage, sleigh, or other vehicle, standing or remaining in any of the puclic streets of the city, the same not being in use at the time, under a penalty not exceeding ten dollars and the costs of prosecution for each offense. Prohibited. Penalty.

SEC. 2. No person shall leave any horse or horses in any of the public streets of said city, without being sufficiently tied, under a penalty not exceeding five dollars and costs for each offense. Penalty.

SEC. 3. No person shall place, or cause to be placed, any stone, brick, timber, lumber, planks, boards, or other materials, in or upon any of the public streets, lanes or alleys of said city, unless for the purpose of building, and for that purpose only for a period of time not exceeding thirty days, without leave obtained from the Obstructions in streets prohibited.

Exception. Section.

Mayor or Common Council, and any person offending against any provision of this section shall pay for each offense a penalty not exceeding fifty dollars and costs of prosecution.

Gutters, etc., not to be obstructed.

SEC. 4. No person building shall, without permission of the Common Council, obstruct, or cause to be obstructed, any gutter or sidewalk, or more than one-quarter of the carriage-way of said street opposite the lot owned by such person, or on which he is building, under a penalty not exceeding twenty-five dollars, and a further penalty of five dollars for every forty-eight hours that such gutter, sidewalk or street shall afterwards remain so obstructed.

Penalty.

Building materials to be removed.

SEC. 5. Immediately after the completion of any building, or within the period of thirty days aforesaid, if such building be not completed, (unless otherwise permitted by the Mayor or Common Council,) all building materials and rubbish arising therefrom shall be removed from the street, and every person offending in the premises shall be liable to pay a penalty not exceeding five dollars for every forty-eight hours such material or rubbish shall be or remain in such street after the time limited aforesaid, with costs.

Penalty.

Duty of owner or occupant of lots.

SEC. 6. It shall be the duty of every owner or occupant of any house, or other building or premises in the City of Saginaw, at all times to keep the drain or gutter in front of the same clear and free from any obstruction that may hinder the free passage of water, and every person who shall neglect such duty shall be liable to a penalty of not exceeding ten dollars and costs for each offense.

Penalty.

SEC. 7. No person shall cast or throw, or cause or permit to be thrown, into any drain, sewer or gutter in said city, any straw, shavings, wood, stones, rubbish, or any other filth or other substance, or cause any obstruction, nuisance or injury in or to the same by diverting or stopping the water-course thereof, or otherwise, under a penalty not exceeding ten dollars and costs for each offense. Obstructions in sewers. Penalty.

SEC. 8. No person shall throw, place or deposit, or suffer his or her servant, child or family to throw, place or deposit any dung, dead animal, carrion, putrid meat or fish, entrails or decayed vegetables, or nuisance of any kind, nor knowingly suffer the same to remain in any street, lane or alley of said city adjacent to his, her or their premises, and any person who shall violate any of the provisions of this section shall forfeit and pay a fine not exceeding ten dollars and costs of prosecution for each offense. Nuisances in streets, etc. Penalty.

SEC. 9. It shall not be lawful for any person to leave any wagon, cart, carriage or sleigh, wood, timber, or any other encumbrance or obstruction, in any of the streets, lanes or alleys of the said city during the night time, and every person offending herein shall forfeit and pay a fine not exceeding twenty dollars and costs of prosecution for each offense, and it shall be the duty of the Street Commissioner to remove all such obstructions at the expense of the person creating or causing the same. Obstructions in streets, etc. Penalty.

SEC. 10. No person or persons shall run or race any horse or horses, or drive any carriage or vehicle of any kind, within the limits of said city, at a faster rate than at the rate of six miles per hour, under a penalty not exceeding twenty dollars and costs for each offense. Racing horses prohibited. Penalty.

Removing soil, etc., from streets etc., prohibited.

SEC. 11. No person shall, unless authorized specially by the Common Council, dig, remove, or carry away any earth, loam, gravel, stone or sand from any street, lane or alley or public ground in the City of Saginaw, under a penalty for each offense not exceeding fifty dollars, with costs of prosecution.

Penalty.

Teams, etc., not to stand on cross-walks.

SEC. 12. No person shall leave, or keep for any longer time than is necessary to cross the same, any horse, team, cart, wagon, dray, sleigh or other vehicle, on any cross-walk in any street or alley in said city, under a penalty for each offense not exceeding twenty dollars and costs of prosecution.

Penalty.

Obstructions in streets, etc., not to be permitted.

SEC. 13. No person shall knowingly permit or suffer his property to be or remain in any street or alley of said city so as to become a nuisance, under a penalty for each offense not exceeding twenty-five dollars and costs of prosecution, together with the expense of removing such nuisance.

Penalty.

Boxes, etc., not to be placed on sidewalks.

SEC. 14. No person shall place, or cause to be placed, on any street or upon any sidewalk in this city any box, barrel, article of merchandise, or any other obstruction whatsoever, except so far as the same may be necessary in transporting such articles across the sidewalks, under a penalty for each offense not exceeding ten dollars and costs of prosecution.

Penalty.

Street Commissioner to enforce this ordinance.

SEC. 15. The Street Commissioner of this city is hereby directed and required to see that the provisions of this ordinance are carried into effect, and to give notice to the City Attorney of all violations thereof.

Street Commissioner's duties.

SEC. 16. It shall be the duty of the Street Commissioner, upon knowledge or information that any sidewalk in the city is obstructed or encumbered, to request the occupant or occupants of the lot or premises in front of which such obstruction or encumbrance exists to remove it, and every such occupant neglecting to comply with such requisition shall, for every twenty-four hours of such neglet, be subject to a penalty not exceeding five dollars and costs of prosecution. It shall be the duty of the Street Commissioner to remove all obstructions from the sidewalks in front of all unoccupied lots or premises. The above restrictions shall not extend to posts for awnings, shade trees, or the boxes to protect them, which are now standing, or may be hereafter set without a violation of any by-law or ordinance of said city, nor to ladders necessarily used in building or repairing buildings, nor be construed to affect the ingress or egress to and from the yards of houses and buildings across said sidewalks. Penalty.

SEC. 17. Except for the purpose of ingress or egress, no person shall drive, ride or lead any horse, cart or carriage on any sidewalk within the city, or remove, take up, or otherwise injure any such sidewalk, or any part thereof, or any crosswalk, under penalty not exceeding twenty dollars for each offense, and being liable to repair and make good all damages caused by him, and if the party offending in the premises shall neglect to have the same repaired within twenty-four hours after the damages done, it shall be the duty of the Street Commissioner of the city to repair such damages, and the expense attendant thereon shall be recovered of the party offending in the same manner as the said penalty. Trespass on sidewalks, etc. Penalty. Duty of Street Commissioner.

SEC. 18. All ordinances, or parts of ordinances, heretofore passed by the Common Council of this city, con- Ordinances repealed.

travening the provisions of this ordinance, be and the same are hereby repealed.

Adopted April 26, 1865.

STEWART B. WILLIAMS, Mayor.

A. F. R. BRALEY, Recorder.

[*Record Ordinance Book, page 35.*]

---

*An Ordinance relative to nuisances.*

*It is hereby ordained by the Common Council of the City of Saginaw:*

Nuisances prohibited.

SECTION 1. That no person shall deposit, or cause to be deposited, any dead animal, fish, or putrid meat, entrails, shells of oysters or clams, decayed fruit or vegetables, or any other offensive substance, in or upon any public street, square or alley, or on the surface of the ground in any lot, or in the Saginaw River, or on the banks or shores thereof, or upon or under any dock or wharf in the City of Saginaw, or suffer or permit any stagnant or filthy water, or putrid or unwholesome meat, decayed fruit or vegetable, or other filthy or offensive substance, to remain on his or her lot, or in his or her house, or other building, or cellar, or in or upon any boat or vessel in the Saginaw River within said city, under a penalty of not exceeding twenty-five dollars for each offense, and the expense and charges which shall be incurred by said city in removing or abating such nuisance.

Penalty.

Board of Health and other officers may enter any premises to abate nuisances.

SEC. 2. The Board of Health of said city, or any member thereof, or any person appointed by said Board, or the City Marshal, or Street Commissioner, or either of them, may at any time enter into or upon any house, building, cellar, boat, lot, or other place within said city, and remove or abate such nuisance as he or they may judge best ; and if at any time any lot, yard, building, cellar, alley, sink, drain, vault or privy, within said city, is found by such officers or persons, or either of them, to be foul, encumbered with rubbish, damp, sunken, or ill-conducted, or to contain any filth, or other offensive substance or nuisance, he or they shall have power, and it shall be the duty of such officers, officer or person, to direct the removal of all such matter, filth, rubbish, or offensive substance, or the cleaning or repairing of any cellar, drain, vault, privy, stable, pig-sty or yard upon such lot or premises, by the owner or occupant thereof, within twenty-four hours thereafter ; any person who shall refuse or neglect to comply with such direction, after such notice as aforesaid, shall, upon conviction thereof, be punished by fine not exceeding twenty-five dollars, or by imprisonment not exceeding twenty-five days, or by both such fine and imprisonment for each and every twenty-four hours the same shall be suffered to remain after such notice.

Powers and duties of certain officers to abate nuisances.

Penalty for refusing to abate nuisances.

SEC. 3. No person shall cast or throw, or suffer to run from his or her house, lot or premises, into any street, lane or alley, or upon any adjoining house, lot or premises, any stinking, noxious, impure, offensive or unwholesome water, substance or thing, and any person violating the provisions of this section shall be punished by a fine not exceeding twenty-five dollars, or by imprisonment not exceeding twenty-five days.

Offensive water,

SEC. 4. No brewer, salt manufacturer, dyer, soap manufacturer, tanner, or other person, shall cast or throw, or suffer the water or other substance, in a flowing state, from his, her or their manufacturing houses or establishments, to run into and upon the surface of any street, alley or public place, or upon any adjoining

Refuse from manufactories,

Penalty. lot or premises, and any person violating the provisions of this section shall be punished by a fine not exceeding twenty-five dollars, or by imprisonment not exceeding twenty-five days.

Meat markets and slaughter houses to be cleansed.

SEC. 5. Every butcher or other person occupying any slaughter-house in said city shall, on every day on which an animal shall be killed or dressed therein, between the first day of May and the first day of November in each year, cause the same to be thoroughly washed and cleansed, and shall, immediately after killing any animal, destroy the offal, garbage and other offensive and useless parts thereof, or cause the same to be removed to such place as may be designated by the Common Council, and there disposed of as such Common Council may direct. Any person violating the provisions of this section shall be punished by a fine not exceeding twenty-five dollars, or by imprisonment not exceeding twenty-five days.

Offal, how disposed of.

Penalty.

Slaughter houses prohibited within the city limits, except by permission of Common Council.

SEC. 6. No person shall build, make or use, or permit to be built, made or used, any slaughter-house or building for the slaughtering or dressing of animals within said city, without permission from the Common Council. Every butcher, or other person, whose business shall be wholly or in part the selling of fresh meat within said city, shall keep the inside of his locker, and the tables and the blocks and the floor of his shop or market clean and free from filth and dirt. No person shall slaughter any hog, beeve, calf, sheep or lamb, or render any lard or tallow, or boil any bones or parts of animals not used for food, between the first day of May and the first day of December in each year, within the city limits, without a license from the Common Council of said city. Any person violating the provisions of this section shall be punished by a fine not exceeding twenty-

Meat markets to be kept clean.

Slaughtering prohibited within certain periods, without license.

Penalty.

five dollars, or by imprisonment not exceeding twenty-five days, or both such fine or imprisonment.

SEC. 7. It shall be the duty of the several members of the Board of Health, and of the Marshal and Street Commissioner, to enforce the provisions of this ordinance, and to make complaint for any violation which shall come to their knowledge, before the Recorder or some Justice of the Peace of said city. Duties of members of Board of Health.

SEC. 8. All ordinances, or parts of ordinances, contravening the provisions of this ordinance, are hereby repealed. Ordinances repealed.

Adopted April 17th, 1866.

WM. M. MILLER, Mayor.

A. F. R. BRALEY, Recorder.

[*Record Ordinance Book, page 3.*]

---

*An Ordinance concerning pounds, animals impounded, and the duties of poundmasters.*

*It is hereby ordained by the Common Council of the City of Saginaw, as follows :*

SECTION 1. There shall be one or more public pounds in the said city, in such place or places as the Common Council shall designate and provide. Pounds.

SEC. 2. The Common Council of said city shall appoint one or more poundmasters in and for said city, who shall hold their office during the pleasure of said Common Council, who shall take and file the oath of office and shall give bonds to the city in the sum of one hundred dollars, with one or more sureties, to be approved by the Mayor or Recorder of said city, conditioned to pay to the City Treasurer all moneys that shall come into his Poundmasters appointed by Common Council. Bond.

hands as poundmaster, excepting his fees allowed him by this ordinance.

Animals prohibited from running at large.

SEC. 3. No cattle, horses, asses, mules, swine, sheep, goats, geese, or domestic fowls, shall run at large in the streets, or elsewhere, within the limits of the City of Saginaw.

Proviso.

*Provided*, That it shall be lawful for cows and calves to run at large therein between the first day of April and the first day of December in each year, except within the following described limits, viz: All that part of the city bounded as follows: on the easterly side by the Saginaw River, on the southerly side by Jackson street, on the westerly side by Bond street, and on the northerly side by Farley street.

Excepted limits within which cows are prohibited from running in the night time.

And it shall be lawful for cows to run at large within said excepted limits during the day time (between the hours of five o'clock in the forenoon, and nine o'clock in the afternoon), from the first day of April to the first day of December in each year.

As amended April 15th, 1875.

[*Record Ordinance Book, page 175.*]

Animals to be impounded.

SEC. 4. Any horses, cattle, asses, mules, swine, sheep, goats, geese, or domestic fowls, except as hereinbefore provided, running at large within said city limits, each and every of them may be inpounded in said public pounds.

Who may impound animals.

SEC. 5. All persons, except minors under the age of eighteen years, may take up and drive to the public pound, any of the animals mentioned in the preceding section found so running at large.

Pound-keepers' duties.

SEC. 6. It shall be the duty of the pound-keepers to receive and safely keep and sustain in the public pounds any of said animals so as aforesaid taken up and driven to said pounds.

SEC. 7. It shall be the duty of the pound-keepers to register in a book, to be kept for that purpose, the time when any animal was received into the public pound, the name and residence of the person by whom said animal was taken up, and the place where said animal was found running at large. He shall provide necessary sustenance for all animals impounded, and shall sell at public auction, on Wednesdays and Saturdays of each week, any animal which has been impounded in said pound seven days, and is unclaimed by any person, or whose owner refuses to pay the fees, costs, and charges of impounding and keeping said animal, first giving, five days previous, written or printed notice of the sale of said animals, which notice shall state, as near as may be, a description of said animal, the person by whom and the place where it was taken up, and the time when it was impounded, which notice shall be posted in four different public places in said city, and to be posted at the post office and on the front door of the Court House in said city, and such sale shall be held at the public pound.

Book of registry.

Sustenance to be provided to animals impounded.

Unclaimed animals to be sold.

Notices of sale.

SEC. 8. Any person owning any animal impounded in the public pounds may redeem said animal any time before it is sold, by paying to the pound-keeper the costs, charges and fees hereinafter provided, and by proving to the satisfaction of the pound-keeper the ownership of said animal.

Owner of animal may redeem.

SEC. 9. Pound-keepers shall exact and receive for his or their fees, in receiving and discharging, or selling every horse, ass, mule, and for each head of cattle, seventy-five cents ; for each swine, sheep, or goat, fifty cents ; and for each goose or domestic fowl, the sum of ten cents ; and for the sustenance of each head of cattle,

Fees of pound keepers.

each horse, ass or mule, seventy-five cents per day ; for the sustenance of each swine, sheep or goat, thirty-five cents per day ; and for the sustenance of each goose or domestic fowl, twenty cents per day ; and for taking up any of the said animals aforesaid, he shall receive the sum of twenty-five cents for each animal, except geese and domestic fowls, and for each of them the sum of five cents.

Proceeds of sale of animals to be paid to Treasurer.

SEC. 10. All the moneys received by the pound-keepers, by virtue of this ordinance, for animals sold by him, after deducting therefrom the fees and charges for sustenance, shall be promptly paid by him to the City Treasurer, but the city shall not in any case be liable to the pound-keeper for or on account of any fees or expenses due to him on account of any animal which may be impounded.

Violation of duty by pound keepers, how punished.

SEC. 11. If said pound-keeper shall refuse to receive into the public pound and keep therein any animal which may be legally impounded therein, or if he shall receive into and keep in the pound, or sell as pound-keeper, or receive any fees, costs or charges for any animal not legally liable to be impounded, he shall, on conviction thereof, be punished by a fine not exceeding twenty dollars, or fifteen days' imprisonment in the county jail.

Punishment for illegally impounding animals.

SEC. 12. If any person shall take up and drive to the public pounds any animal not legally liable to be impounded therein he or they shall, on conviction, be punished by a fine of five dollars for each and every offense.

Obstructing the impounding of animals, how punished.

SEC. 13. Each and every person who shall hinder, delay or obstruct any person or persons in driving to the pound any animal or animals, beast or beasts, liable to be impounded in the city pounds, shall, for each and every hindrance, delay or obstruction, and for each and every person delayed, upon conviction, pay a fine of not less than five nor more than twenty dollars.

Breaking open of pound, how punished.

SEC. 14. If any person or persons shall break open, or in any manner, directly or indirectly, aid or assist in breaking open any city pounds, said person or persons shall severally, on conviction thereof before the Recorder's Court, or before any Justice of the Peace of said city, be punished by a fine not exceeding fifty dollars and costs of prosecution, and imprisonment in the county jail for a period not exceeding sixty days, or either, in the discretion of the court trying the same.

Fees for impounding animals.

SEC. 15. Any person authorized by this ordinance, taking to said pound any animal or animals, herein prohibited from running at large, shall receive from said pound-keeper, after the said animals have been sold or redeemed as aforesaid, the sum of fifty cents for each of said animals, except geese and domestic fowls, and for each goose and domestic fowl the sum of ten cents.

Permitting animals to run at large, how punished.

SEC. 16. Every owner or possessor of any horse, neat cattle, or other animal liable to be impounded, who shall permit the same to run at large within the limits of said City of Saginaw, contrary to the provisions of this ordinance, shall, upon conviction thereof, pay a fine for each offense not exceeding the sum of twenty-five dollars and the costs of prosecution, and imprisonment in the county jail not exceeding twenty days, or both or either, in the discretion of the court trying the same.

Duties of Street Commissioner as fence viewer.

SEC. 17. The Street Commissioner of said city shall have and exercise the same powers, duties and privileges, and be subject to the same restrictions and penalties as the laws of this State prescribe relative to fence viewers.

Ordinances repealed.

SEC. 18. All ordinances, or parts of ordinances, heretofore passed by the Common Council, contravening the provisions of this ordinance, be and the same are hereby repealed.

Passed April 26th, 1865.

STEWART B. WILLIAMS, Mayor.

A. F. R. BRALEY, Recorder.

[*Record Ordinance Book, page 20.*]

---

*An ordinance relative to excavations in the streets and public grounds of the City of Saginaw.*

*It is hereby ordained by the Common Council of the City of Saginaw:*

Prohibitions.

SECTION 1. That no person or persons shall make or dig, or cause to be made or dug, any ditch, drain, sewer, or any excavation whatever, in any of the streets, lanes, alleys or public grounds, or remove any plank, pavement or other improvement in the streets, lanes, alleys, or public grounds of said city, without having first obtained permission therefor by ordinance or resolution of the said Common Council.

Prohibitions.

SEC. 2. No person or persons shall make or dig, or cause to be made or dug, any ditch, drain, sewer, or any excavation whatever, in any of the streets, lanes, alleys, or public grounds, or adjacent to any streets, lanes, alleys or public grounds of said city, without, immediately upon commencement of such excavation, placing and maintaining proper and sufficient safeguards about and around such ditch, drain, sewer or excavation.

Penalty.

SEC. 3. Any person or persons violating any of the provisions of this ordinance shall, upon conviction, pay a fine not exceeding fifty dollars, and the costs of prosecution, or be imprisoned in the county jail of Saginaw County not exceeding sixty days, in the discretion of the court or magistrate before whom such offender may be convicted, or such court may, in its discretion, impose both such fine and imprisonment.

SEC. 4. It shall be the duty of the Street Commissioner and the Marshal, and each of them, strictly to enforce the provisions of this ordinance. Duty of Street Commissioner and Marshal.

SEC. 5. Any ordinance, or ordinances, heretofore passed, contravening any portion of this ordinance, are hereby repealed. Ordinances repealed.

Adopted October 6, 1868.

A. F. R. BRALEY, Mayor.

JOHN B. SCHICK, Recorder.

[*Record Ordinance Book, page 92.*]

---

*An Ordinance relative to licensiug draymen and others.*

*It is hereby ordained by the Common Council of the City of Saginaw :*

SECTION 1. That no person shall ply any cart, dray, wagon, truck, or other vehicle, within the limits of said city, for hire, without a license. License required.

SEC. 2. No person who has not resided in said city at least three months shall be licensed as a cartman, drayman, truckman or wagoner, without the special consent of the Common Council, but any person who has resided in said city three months or more, and who shall be deemed by the Mayor, Recorder, or Common Council a proper person, may obtain such license from the Recorder by first paying the City Treasurer the following Qualifications for license. Fees for licenses.

fees, viz : For each one-horse vehicle $3, and for each two-horse vehicle $5, and presenting his receipt therefor.

License not assignable.

SEC. 3. No person licensed under this ordinance shall assign his license, or permit any other person to drive his wagon, cart, dray, truck, or other vehicle, without permission of the Mayor, Recorder or Common Council, and every such person shall cause the number of his license to be conspicuously and distinctly painted upon each side of said cart, dray, wagon, or other vehicle.

Vehicle to be numbered.

Draying, price per load.

SEC. 4. The price to be demanded and received by persons licensed as aforesaid shall not exceed twenty-five cents for each load, unless drawn more than one mile, when ten cents per mile may be added : *Provided*, That the price for removing each load of household furniture from one dwelling house to another shall not exceed forty cents, and no greater sum per load shall be asked, demanded or received, unless by previous agreement.

Proviso.

License may be revoked.

SEC. 5. The Mayor, Recorder or Common Council may at any time revoke any such license for such cause as he or they may deem sufficient, and no person whose license is so revoked shall be entitled to hold a license within twelve months from the date of such revocation, without the special permission of the Common Council.

Stand for unoccupied drays, etc.

SEC. 6. All carts, wagons, drays, trucks, and other vehicles, used for the transportation of goods and property, plying for hire within the limits of the city, shall, while waiting for employment, occupy the following stand, and no other, viz : At the foot of Court street, on the easterly side of Water street, and wholly on the river side of the sidewalk on that side of Water street. The driver of any such vehicle shall, while waiting for employment, remain upon or by his said vehicle, and such vehicle shall stand in a line parallel with the course of said Court street.

[*Journal No. 3, page 334, Oct. 6th, 1870.*]

SEC. 7. Any violation of the provisions of this ordinance shall be punished by a fine not exceeding fifty dollars, or an imprisonment not exceeding three months, or both such fine and imprisonment, in the discretion of the court. Penalty.

SEC. 8. All licenses granted under this ordinance shall expire on the first Monday in July next ensuing the date thereof. Time license expires.

Adopted July 5, 1865.

STEWART B. WILLIAMS, Mayor.

A. F. R. BRALEY, Recorder.

[*Record Ordinance Book, page 49.*]

---

*An Ordinance to provide for licensing hawkers, peddlers and auctioneers.*

*It is hereby ordained by the Common Council of the City of Saginaw:*

SECTION 1. That no person shall travel from place to place, in the city of Saginaw, for the purpose of carrying to sell, or exposing for sale, any goods, wares, or merchandise, unless he shall have obtained a license as a hawker and peddler in the manner hereinafter described. Peddlers to obtain license.

SEC. 2. No person shall sell any goods, wares or merchandise at auction, within said city, except he be a Circuit Court Commissioner, Sheriff, Treasurer, Marshal, Constable, or other person, acting under an order, decree, judgment or execution of a court, or an assignee of an Sale of goods at auction prohibited without license.

insolvent residing in said city, without first having taken out a license, as hereinafter provided, as an auctioneer.

Resident license.

SEC. 3. No resident of said city shall be entitled to a license as a hawker and peddler, or as a hawker or peddler, until he shall have paid into the city treasury the sum of *one hundred dollars*, nor as auctioneer until he shall have paid into the city treasury the sum of *fifteen dollars*. And no person who is not a resident of said city shall be entitled to a license as a hawker and peddler, or as a hawker, peddler, or auctioneer, until he shall have paid into the city treasury the sum of *two hundred dollars*, and the term of a license of a non-resident of said city, under this ordinance, shall not exceed three months: *Provided, however*, That the provisiens of this ordinance shall not apply to any person who only peddles farm produce, nor to any resident of said city who peddles only articles wholly or principally of his own manufacture or production, nor to any person employed by a resident of said city to peddle articles wholly or principally manufactured or produced by such resident employer.

Amount of.

Non-resident license

Farm produce and articles made in the city. No license required.

[*Record Ordinance Book, page 170, March 19th, 1874.*]

Recorder to issue license

SEC. 4. Upon the presentation to the Recorder, by any person desiring a license as a hawker and peddler, or auctioneer, of an application in writing for such license, signed by the applicant, and the receipt of the City Treasurer, showing the payment of the sum required therefor, and upon payment of a fee of one dollar to the Recorder, he shall issue a license to such person in accordance with his application, under his hand and the seal of said city, which license, except as hereinbefore provided, shall continue in force and authorize such person to carry on the business therein mentioned for the term of one year next ensuing the date thereof, unless sooner revoked.

SEC. 5. This ordinance shall not be construed to prevent the sale of farm produce or fish within the limits of said city. **Farm produce excepted.**

SEC. 6. Any person who shall be convicted of the violation of any provision of this ordinance, shall be punished by a fine of not less than *one hundred dollars* and not more than *three hundred dollars,* and costs of prosecution; and the court before whom any person shall be convicted under this ordinance shall make a further sentence that the person so convicted be confined in the Saginaw County jail until such fine and costs shall be paid, but such confinement shall not exceed ninety (90) days. And it shall be the duty of the Marshal, Deputy Marshal, and each policeman and constable of said city, to arrest without process any person who shall be found by them or either of them, within the limits of said city, carrying on the business of a hawker, peddler or auctioneer, without a license, and to convey the person so arrested forthwith before the Recorder or some Justice of the Peace of said city, and then to make a complaint against such person. **Penalty.** **Duty of Marshal, etc.**

[*Record Ordinance Book, page 170, March 19th, 1874.*]

Adopted April 22d, 1867.

A. F. R. BRALEY, Mayor.

ROBERT MCQUEEN, Recorder.

[*Record Ordinance Book, page 61.*]

*An Ordinance in relation to the burying ground.*

*Be it ordained by the Mayor, Recorder and Aldermen, of the City of Saginaw City, in Common Council convened:*

Sexton, duties of.

SECTION 1. It shall be the duty of the Sexton of said Saginaw City at all times when called upon, to dig all graves in the burial ground of said city, and shall take the entire supervision of said ground, and shall see that the fences are kept in repair, and that all gates, through which teams may pass, are at all times kept securely locked, when not opened by himself, or by his permission, for the purpose of ingress or egress of burial processions.

Digging of graves prohibited except by permission.

SEC. 2. No person shall dig any grave in the burial ground of this city, unless permitted to do so by the Sexton of said city. No person or persons shall at any time, or under any pretense whatsoever, (except the Sexton,) unlock, or break the fastenings of any gate or gates, or in any manner injure the same, or move, deface or break the fence of said ground or any trees belonging thereto.

Unfastening cemetery gate.

Penalty for violation of preceding section.

SEC. 3. Any person or persons that shall violate any of the provisions of section two of this ordinance, shall forfeit and pay a sum not less than three dollars and not more than twenty dollars.

On complaint of City Attorney, duty of Justice, etc.

SEC. 4. Upon the City Attorney making complaint in writing, charging any person or persons with violating any of the provisions of section second of this ordinance, it shall be the duty of any Justice of the Peace of said city, to whom such complaint shall be delivered, to forthwith issue his warrant for the arrest, immediately, of all persons named in such complaint, and upon said persons being brought before such Justice, he shall, without delay, proceed to examine into and try the charge made in said complaint, and if he shall find that the person or persons so arrested and brought before him have violated any of the provisions of said second section of this ordinance, he shall impose such fine as in his judgment the nature of the case may require within the aforesaid limits, together with the costs of prosecution. Penalty.

Adopted July 31, 1858.

GARDNER D. WILLIAMS, Mayor.

NEWTON D. LEE, Recorder.

[*Journal of 1858, page 124. Record Ordinance Book, page 18.*]

---

*An Ordinance relative to Cemeteries.*

*It is hereby ordained by the Common Council of the City of Saginaw:*

SECTION 1. The east half of the so-called Battell farm, in the town of Saginaw, county of Saginaw, bounded on one side by the Gratiot State Road, on the other side by the River Road, is hereby declared the city cemetery and public burial ground, under the name of "Oakwood Cemetery," and no person or persons, society or congregation, shall establish or locate any burying ground within the limits of the City of Saginaw. Location of cemetery. No cemetery to be located in the city.

SEC. 2. No interments shall be made in any place within the limits of the City of Saginaw. No interments to be made in any other place.

SEC. 3. The government of said cemetery is intrusted to a Board of six trustees, designated by the name of Cemetery Commissioners, said trustees to be appointed out of the freeholders, electors of said city by the Com- Board of Trustees, or Commissioners, how appointed.

mon Council at their first regular meeting in May each year, to serve for the term of three years, and till their successors are appointed and qualified, at the passage of this ordnance six to be appointed, two to serve one year, two two years, and two three years, afterwards two, and such more as would be necessary to fill vacancies to be appointed each year. Said trustees not to receive any salaries, emoluments or fees for their services.

Term of office.

Officers to be elected.

SEC. 4. Said Cemetery Commission shall elect annually a President, Secretary and Treasurer out of their number. The Treasurer shall give such bonds, and with such sureties, as shall be determined and approved by said Commission: said bond to be deposited with the Controller of the City of Saginaw.

Treasurer to give bond.

Powers and duties of Cemetery Commissioners.

SEC. 5. The Cemetery Commission shall have power, and it is their duty to lay out, embellish, protect and keep in order said cemetery, establish all necessary rules and regulations, make and repair all fences, roads, walks, alleys, bridges, buildings and plantings, fix and graduate the price of the lots for sale, appoint and remove sextons and other officers, define their duties and regulate their salaries and fees, receive and disburse all moneys granted to them by the Common Council, or received from sale of lots, audit and allow all the accounts against said cemetery, keep correct records of all their proceedings, as well as accounts, and keep a register of all lots, the sale of them, and of all interments.

Report of Cemetery Commission.

SEC. 6. The Cemetery Commission shall make out a full report of their doings during the preceding year, and present it, with their balance sheet and a statement of what is to be done for the next year, to the Common Council at the first regular meeting in March in every

year, and all moneys shown to be in the hands of the Treasurer by such report shall be subject to the order of the Common Council, to be applied for improvement of the grounds, or the extinguishment of the debt incurred in the purchase of said cemetery grounds.

SEC. 7. The Cemetery Commission shall designate suitable lots in the city cemetery for the interment of deceased strangers and poor persons. Potter's Field.

SEC. 8. On application to the Director of the Poor, with satisfactory proof that the deceased left no means with which to pay funeral expenses, the corpse shall be buried at the expense of the city, and the Director of the Poor shall give an order in writing commanding the city sexton to dig a grave, furnish a suitable coffin, place the body in the coffin when directed, convey the body to the cemetery and decently inter it. For these services and outlays the sexton shall present his bill to the Common Council, to be audited and allowed by the same. Poor to be buried at expense of city.

SEC. 9. Any person wishing to purchase a lot in the cemetery may do so by paying the Commission such sum as has been fixed for the same, and the Controller of the City of Saginaw is hereby authorized, after receiving a certificate from the Commission that said sum has been fully paid, to execute deeds for such lots under the seal of the corporation. Purchase of lots, how made.

SEC. 10. No person shall obstruct any road, walk or alley in the cemetery. Prohibitory provisions.

SEC. 11. No person shall commit any trespass by destroying, injuring or defacing any grave, vault, tombstone, monument, enclosure, building, fence, bridge, seat, tree, flower, shrub, or anything belonging to the cemetery.

Violations of this ordinance, how punished.

SEC. 12. Any violation, or failure to comply with the provisions of this ordinance, shall be punished by a fine not to exceed one hundred dollars and costs, and in the imposition of any such fine and costs, the court may make a further sentence, that in default of the payment thereof within a time to be fixed in such sentence, the offender be committed to the county jail for any period of time not exceeding six months.

SEC. 13. This ordinance shall take effect from and after its passage.

Adopted May 19, 1868.

A. F. R. BRALEY, Mayor.

ROBERT MCQUEEN, Recorder.

[*Record Ordinance Book, page 85.*]

---

*An Ordinance relative to the prevention of fire.*

*It is hereby ordained by the Common Council of the City of Saginaw:*

Board of Fire Wardens.

SECTION 1. The fire wardens of the City of Saginaw shall constitute a Board, of whom the majority shall be a quorum, for the purpose of considering the most efficient and prompt means of discharging the duties imposed upon them by the laws and ordinances of this city.

Duties of.

They shall choose from their number a chief and clerk, at such time and in such manner as they may designate. The fire wardens shall notice and correct any infractions of the laws and ordinances made for the protection of the city from fire, in their own ward particularly, and in the city generally, and shall make reports by their chief, to

Reports made first Mondays of June and December.

be by them respectively chosen, of the state and police of the city as respects dangers from exposures to fires, on the first Mondays of June and December of each year, to the Common Council; and the Board may impose such fines upon the members as in their judgment may best secure the performance of the duties of said fire wardens, both at fires and in visiting buildings, and in other duties in the city, and for non-attendance at regular and special meetings of the wardens; and disobedience to such rules shall be reported to the Common Council, and shall subject the fire wardens so disobeying to fine and removal by the Common Council. Board may impose fines on members

SEC. 2. It shall be the duty of the fire wardens, or either of them, in this city, twice in each year, to wit: in the months of May and November, and as much oftener as may be deemed proper, between sunrise and sunset, to enter into any house or building, lots, grounds or premises in said city, and examine the fire-places, hearths, chimneys, stoves, and pipes thereto, ovens, boilers, and other apparatus likely to cause fire; also the places where ashes may be deposited, and all places where any gunpowder, hemp flax, tow, hay, straw, rushes, shingles or other combustible materials may be lodged, and the said fire wardens shall give such direction in regard to the several foregoing matters as they or any of them may think expedient, either as to the removal or alteration or better care and management thereof, which directions shall be obeyed and complied with by the person or persons directed in that behalf and at their expense. Wardens to examine fire places, etc., in the city. To give directions.

SEC. 3. The said fire wardens shall also have authority to cause chimneys to be burned out, or otherwise cleaned, whenever they shall deem it necessary, and to require tenant or tenants, owner or owners of any blacksmith's shop, so to alter or construct (as the case may require) the chimneys of such shops so as to prevent sparks of fire from passing into the open air, and re- Auth'ority to give certain directions for prevention of fire.

quire the ceiling, or sides, if any, or any part thereof, to be plastered.

Penalty for obstructing fire wardens and otherwise offending.

SEC. 4. If any person or persons shall neglect or refuse so to comply with any such direction as any of the said fire wardens may give in the premises, or shall obstruct or hinder any fire warden, or his assistants, in the performance of his duty, the person so offending shall forfeit, and for such neglect, non-compliance, or hindrance, a sum not exceeding fifty dollars ; and for every day which shall elapse after the time allotted for such removal, alteration, better care or management, without compliance with such directions, the said person shall forfeit and pay a further and additional sum of five dollars ; and all the expense caused in carrying into effect the directions of the fire wardens shall, in the first instance, be paid by the occupant of the premises, and shall be deducted from the rents payable by him, her or others, unless such directions were rendered necessary by the act or default of such occupant, or there be a special agreement to the contrary between the landlord and said occupant. And it shall be the duty of the fire warden to ascertain whether or not these directions are duly complied with, and in case of non-compliance, or in case of any violation of this ordinance, to report the names of all offending, with the particular circumstances, to the Common Council, who may thereupon cause such offenders to be prosecuted for the penalties incurred by them.

Stove pipes.

SEC. 5. No pipe of any stove shall be put up, or suffered to remain in any house or building, unless it be conducted into a chimney of brick or stone, nor shall any person at any time set fire to any chimney, for the purpose of cleaning the same, unless during a rain or

Cleaning of Chimneys.

snow storm, or while the roof of the building in which said chimney may be is covered with snow, without previous consent of one of the fire wardens of said city. Any person putting up, or procuring to be put up, or maintaining the pipe of any stove, or doing any other act contrary to this section, shall for every offense forfeit the sum of five dollars, and the further sum of one dollar for every twenty-four hours the same shall remain so put up after notice by any fire wardens to alter the same. Penalty.

SEC. 6. Every chimney hereafter to be erected, and all chimneys whatever, shall be plastered with lime and sand on the inside thereof, under a penalty of twenty-five dollars, and a further penalty of ten dollars for every fifteen days' neglect to alter or take down the same, after a notice by any fire warden, for that purpose. It shall be the duty of the engineers or fire wardens to take notice of all chimneys, when the same are being constructed, and ascertain whether the same are in conformity with the requirements of this ordinance, and if not, make a report of the same to the Common Council. Chimneys. Penalty.

SEC. 7. No ashes, except manufactories, where ashes are used, shall be kept or deposited in any part of this city, unless the same be in a close and secure metallic or earthen vessel, or brick or stone ash room, under a penalty of one dollar for every twenty-four hours the same shall remain after notice from a fire warden to remove the same. Ashes. Penalty.

SEC. 8. Every dwelling house, or other building, more than one story in heighth, within this city, shall have a scuttle through the roof, a convenient and suitable stairway or ladder leading to the same, and any one constructing such dwelling house or building without Every building over two stories high to have scuttle, etc.

such scuttle, and every owner of such house or building now erected (not having other permanent and convenient means of access to the roof) neglecting to comply with the requisition of this section, for the space of thirty days after notice by a fire warden, shall forfeit twenty-five dollars, and the further sum of five dollars for every ten days the non-compliance shall continue to exist.

Penalty.

Shavings, etc., not to be burned, except by permission.

SEC. 9 It shall not be lawful to burn any shavings, edgings, or other combustible matter, in any street, road, lane or alley, or on any wharf in this city, except on a written permission from a fire warden, under a penalty not exceeding ten dollars for each offense, to be recovered from any person so offending, and against any person or persons aiding or assisting therein.

Gunpowder.

SEC. 10. If any person, during a fire, and in the vicinity thereof, shall discover in any building a greater quantity than twenty-eight pounds of gunpowder, it shall be lawful for him to seize, without warrant from any magistrate, and convert the same as forfeited to the use of said city.

Edgings, etc., not to be placed in streets, etc., or on any premises.

SEC. 11. It shall not be lawful for any person or persons to place upon any street, lane or alley in this city any edgings or other combustible matter, nor shall it be lawful for any person to place or keep any edgings on any premises within said city, unless the same is cut into four feet lengths, or less, and piled in a suitable manner into racks, under a penalty of ten dollars for each and every offense. *Provided*, however, that no penalty shall be enforced under this section if the person or persons so offending shall remove the same within twenty-four hours after notice to remove the same from the Marshal.

Penalty.

Proviso.

SEC. 12. There shall not be kept within the limits of this city, within 300 feet of any dwelling, at any one time, in any one building, or its appurtenances, any greater quantity of gunpowder than twenty-eight pounds, and the gunpowder shall be well secured in metal canisters, with metal stoppers or covers. All gunpowder which shall be kept in this city contrary to the meaning and provisions of this ordinance shall be forfeited by the person or persons so keeping the same, and it shall be lawful for any fire warden to seize the same without warrant and convert the same as forfeited to the use of the city; and the person or persons so offending shall also forfeit the sum of one hundred dollars for every one hundred pounds of gunpowder, and in that proportion for a greater or less quantity so kept contrary to the true intent and meaning of this ordinance, to be recovered with costs of suit.

Gunpowder. Not more than 28 lbs. kept in one building. How secured. Forfeiture. Penalty.

SEC. 13. It shall be the duty of the Chief Warden and Marshal to dispose of all the gunpowder forfeited and seized as provided in the preceding sections, and pay the proceeds arising therefrom to the Treasurer of said city, taking his receipt therefor, and report the same to the Common Council.

Chief Warden and Marshal to dispose of gunpowder.

SEC. 14. No steamboat or propeller shall land or haul alongside of any wharf, dock or bank within this city, or nearer than one hundred feet to any such wharf, dock or bank, unless such boat or propeller has a sufficient spark-catcher covering the smoke-pipe of such boat or propeller, so as to prevent any sparks passing from the fire on said boat or propeller, under a penalty of not less than twenty nor more than two hundred dollars for each and every offense, and the master of such

Boats, etc., to have spark catchers. Penalty.

boat so offending shall also be liable to be imprisoned, until the same is paid, not exceeding ninety days.

Lighted candles not to be used in livery stables.

SEC. 15. No owner or occupant of any livery or other stable within this city, or any person in the employment of such owner or occupant, shall use therein any lighted candle or light, except the same be kept within a horn, tin or glass lantern, under a penalty of not exceeding ten dollars for each offense, to be recovered with costs of suit.

Comubustibles to be removed from fire-places, etc.

SEC. 16 No person shall have, put or keep, within the said city, any hay or straw, hemp, flax, tow, shavings or rushes, in any stable or building which is or shall be within such distance from any chimney, hearth or fireplace, or place for depositing ashes, nor in any dwelling house whatever, as may be deemed unsafe or dangerous by the fire wardens of the city, under a penalty not exceeding twenty-five dollars for each and every offense, to be recovered with costs of suit, and the further sum of ten dollars for every twenty-four hours the same shall so remain after due notice given in writing to the offender by any fire warden.

Penalty.

Ordinances repealed.

SEC. 17. All ordinances, or parts of ordinances, heretofore passed by the Common Council of this city, contravening the provisions of this ordinance, be and the same are hereby repealed.

Passed April 26, 1865.

STEWART B. WILLIAMS, Mayor.

A. F. R. BRALEY, Recorder.

[*Record Ordinance Book, page 44.*]

*An Ordinance establishing fire limits in the City of Saginaw, as amended September 22, 1868.*

*It is hereby ordained by the Common Council of the City of Saginaw:*

SECTION 1. The following boundaries shall constitute and be known as the fire limits of the City of Saginaw, to-wit: Commencing at the center of the foot of Jackson street, thence along the center of said street to the center of Fayette street, thence along Fayette street to the center of Mackinaw street, thence along the center of Mackinaw street to the center of Washington street, thence along the center of Washington street to the center of Madison street, thence along the center of Madison street to the river, thence along the river to the foot of Mackinaw street, thence along the west line of the bayou to the place of beginning. **Fire limits.**

[*Journal No. 3, page 272, May 13, 1870.*]

SEC. 2. No person shall erect or place any building, or any part of a building, within said fire limits, unless the same shall be constructed of stone, brick, or iron. **Buildings prohibited.**

SEC. 3. Nothing contained in the preceding section shall be construed to prohibit the erection within said fire limits, of any wooden building not more than eight feet square. **Exception.**

SEC. 4. No person shall, within said fire limits, except as provided in the next section, repair any wooden building, which has been partially destroyed by fire or otherwise, or remove any wooden building from one lot in said fire limits to another. **Not to repair wooden buildings.**

SEC. 5. When any wooden building, within the fire limits, shall be partially destroyed by fire, or otherwise, **Exception.**

and the damage thereto shall not exceed one-half its value at the time of such partial destruction, such building may be repaired, and not otherwise.

In case of partial destruction by fire, proceedings necessary to enable repair.

SEC. 6. In case of the partial destruction, by fire or otherwise, of any such building within said fire limits, it shall be the duty of the Marshal of said city, with a person to be selected by the owner of said building, to proceed at once to estimate the amount of damage thereto, and if they shall be unable to agree, they shall select a third disinterested person, and the estimate of any two of them shall be binding on the city as well as on the owner of said building. If the amount of the damage, so ascertained, exceed that provided in section five, such building shall not be repaired: but if the damage does not exceed the amount provided in said section, the Marshal shall report the same to the Common Council, who shall thereupon enter upon their records a permit to said owner to repair his building.

Any block in the city may be included in fire limits by application, etc.

SEC. 7. On the application, in writing, of the owner or owners of the greater part of the grounds in any block in said city, not included within the fire limits, the Common Council may, by resolution, include the same within the fire limits, and the provisions of this ordinance shall be thereby extended over such block.

Resolution to be published.

SEC. 8. Every such resolution shall be published for two successive weeks in a newspaper of the city.

Every week building remaining contrary to this ordinance a distinct offense

SEC. 9. For each and every week which a building erected, placed, removed or repaired contrary to the provisions of this ordinance, shall be allowed to remain, the owner of such building may be complained of as for a distinct offense, and punished as hereinafter provided.

SEC. 10. Any person who shall violate any of the provisions of this ordinance shall be punished by a fine not exceeding one hundred dollars, with the costs of prosecution ; and it shall be the duty of the Marshal to prosecute for all penalties incurred under this ordinance. **Penalty for violation of this ordinance.**

Adopted September 22, 1868.

A. F. R. BRALEY, Mayor.

JOHN B. SCHICK, Recorder.

[*Record Ordinance Book, page 90.*]

---

*An Ordinance relative to licensing public exhibitions.*

*It is hereby ordained by the Common Council of the City of Saginaw :*

SECTION 1. No itinerant person or persons shall exhibit in the City of Saginaw any natural or artificial curiosities, or any circus, caravan or menagerie, or any theatrical representation, concert or musical entertainment, or any sleight of hand, juggler or legerdemain tricks, or other public exhibition or show, demanding and receiving any sum for admission thereto, without having first obtained a license therefor, as hereinafter provided. **Exhibitions that require license.**

SEC. 2. No person or persons shall be entitled to a license for any of the purposes mentioned in the first section of this ordinance, until he or they shall have paid into the city treasury, for the use of said city, the sum of money by this ordinance provided therefor, and shall have the receipt of the City Treasurer showing the fact and purpose of such payment. **License fee must be paid before license issues.**

SEC. 3. The money to be paid by any person or persons, for a license for any of the above purposes mentioned in the first section, shall be as follows, viz :

Circus, etc. 1st. For any circus, caravan or menagerie, fifteen dollars ($15).

Circus and caravan combined. 2d. For a circus, and caravan or menagerie combined, and exhibiting at the same time and under the same canvass, twenty dollars ($20).

Curiosities. 3d.. For the exhibition of any natural or artificial curiosities, or the same combined and exhibited at the same time and place, or for the exhibition of any side show or performance of any kind, traveling with any circus, caravan or menagerie, five dollars ($5).

Theater, concert, musical entertainment. 4th. For the performance of any theatrical representation, concert, or musical entertainment, three dollars ($3).

Juggler, etc. 5th. For the exhibition of any sleight-of-hand, juggler, or legerdemain tricks or performance, five dollars ($5).

Other shows. 6th. For the exhibition of any other show or performance, not otherwise provided for, the sum of three dollars ($3).

Refreshment stand. 7th. For the keeping of any refreshment stand, or other place for the sale of any article whatever, on the same grounds or contiguous to the grounds occupied by or for the exhibition of any circus, caravan or menagerie, or other exhibition, when kept by a resident of the city, two dollars ($2); and when kept by any non-resident, three dollars ($3).

Duration of license. SEC. 4. No such license shall be issued, or be in force and valid, for a longer time than one day, except a license for a theatrical representation, concert or musical entertainment, which may be issued, and be in force and valid, for a period of ten days, in which case the money to be paid therefor shall be ten dollars ($10)

SEC. 5. Upon presentation to the Recorder of said city, of a written application, signed by any person or persons, his or their agent, desiring a license for any of the purposes mentioned in the third section of this ordinance, and the receipt of the City Treasurer, showing the payment to him of the money required by this ordinance therefor, and upon payment to the said Recorder of a fee of fifty cents, the Recorder shall issue to such person or persons the desired license, under his official signature and the seal of said city, which license shall be in force and authorize the person or persons therein named, to give the exhibition, representation, entertainment or performance, or keep the stand therein mentioned, on the day and for the time therein specified. And the said Recorder shall, within five days thereafter, deliver such receipt to the Comptroller, who shall thereupon charge the Treasurer with the amount.

License, how obtained.

Recorder's fees.

Recorder's duty.

Comptroller's duty.

SEC. 6. Any person who shall, within the limits of said city, open, commence, carry on, or give any exhibition of any natural or artificial curiosities, or any circus, caravan, menagerie, or any theatrical representation, concert or musical entertainment, or the exhibition of any sleight-of-hand, juggler or legerdemain tricks, or other show or performance, or keep any stand for which a license is by this ordinance required, without a license therefor (except as provided in the seventh section), or having the license (required) therefor, shall refuse on demand to show the same to any officer of said city, and any person who shall assist at, in or about any unlicensed exhibition or performance, representation, entertainment or show, for which a license is by this ordinance required, shall, upon conviction thereof, be punished by a fine of

Penalty.

Refusal to show license.

Liability of persons aiding in unlicensed show

Fine. not less than five dollars and not more than twenty-five dollars, with costs of prosecution ; and the court having jurisdiction thereof may make a further sentence, that in default of the payment of such fine and costs, within a time to be fixed in such sentence, the person so Imprisonment. convicted be committed to the county jail of Saginaw County for a period of time not exceeding forty days. And the person so convicted and sentenced shall forthwith be committed, by the court making such sentence, to the custody of the Marshal, or some constable or policeman of said city, during the time fixed for the payment of such fine.

No license required of amateur exhibition. SEC. 7. The provisions of this ordinance shall not apply to any amateur theatrical representation, concert, or musical entertainment, or other exhibition, the proceeds whereof are intended and shall be applied for the benefit of any religious, charitable, benevolent or literary society or association organized or existing in this State, nor be so construed as in any manner to authorize the exhibition of any immoral or indecent performance, exhibition or show.

Marshal shall arrest without process for violations of this ordinance. SEC. 8. The Marshal and all policemen of said city, are authorized and directed to arrest without process, any person found violating any of the provisions of this ordinance, and forthwith to convey the person so arrested before the Recorder, or some Justice of the Peace May detain the person arrested. of said city, to be dealt with therefor. And in case the Recorder, or no Justice of the Peace can be found in his office, then safely to detain the person so arrested in his custody until the said Recorder or some Justice of the Peace may be found in his office; but such detention shall in no case exceed forty-eight hours.

Adopted May 5, 1870.

WILLIAM H. SWEET, Mayor.

JOHN B. SCHICK, Recorder.

[*Record Ordinance Book, page 107.*]

---

*An Ordinance relative to lighting the streets of the City of Saginaw with gas.*

WHEREAS, the Saginaw Gas Light Company have made a proposition to the Common Council of said city, in words and figures following, to-wit:

"The Saginaw Gas Light Company will furnish gas "for public street lamps, at the rate of three dollars and "fifty cents, metre measurement, per thousand cubic "feet, and the government tax, will light, extinguish "and clean them at the rate of six dollars per post per "year, payments to be made quarterly, viz: On the "first days of April, July, October and January of each "year, and if not paid within thirty days of the time "when each payment becomes due, interest shall be "added at the rate of ten per cent. per annum, until "the same be paid. **Proposition of Gas Co.**

"This proposition, if accepted, to remain in force "until the first day of January eighteen hundred sev-"enty-three, and to be considered as renewed from year "to year, unless either party gives notice to the other of "their desire to terminate the same, not less than thirty "days previous to the first day of January of any year.

"Will furnish posts and lamps of any pattern or de-"sign the city may desire, and erect the same at net "cost."

"D. L. C. EATON, Secretary."

*Therefore, It is hereby ordained by the Common Council of the City of Saginaw :*

Proposition accepted.

SECTION 1. That said proposition be and the same is hereby accepted, to take effect and be in force from and after the eighth day of July, A. D. 1871. *Provided,* the said Gas Light Company shall cause their assent to be endorsed upon the record book of ordinances of said city, on or before that date, by their Secretary, which assent shall be and become a part of this ordinance ; and this ordinauce shall be construed as a contract between said city and said Saginaw Gas Light Company.

Proviso.

Assent of Gas Co. required.

Council to designate location of lamp posts, etc.

SEC. 2. That the Common Council may from time to time designate the location, kind, number and size of posts and lamps to be used in lighting the streets of said city, and shall have the general direction and control of the same, together with all service pipes connecting therewith, and may require from said company reports of the condition of said property, the cause of any breakage, stoppage, leakage, overcharges, defect or neglect on the part of said company, its officers or employes, affecting the lighting of said city, or its interests and rights under this ordinance. And in case of any protracted or willful neglect of said company, its officers or employes, and upon the failure of said company, after five days' notice from the Common Council to remove the cause of objection, said Council shall have the right, by a majority vote of all its members elect and qualified to vote, to rescind this ordinance, or in

Council may require report from Gas Co.

Right to rescind this ordinance reserved.

connection with said company to make other or new stipulations thereto, as the interests of said city may require.

Gas Co. to care for post, lamps, etc.

SEC. 3. That for the purpose of more perfectly and securely providing for the lighting of the streets of said city, and the better protection of its property used therefor, said company shall be charged with the care and supervision of the posts, lamps and pipes belonging to said city and used for the purpose aforesaid, to repair and keep the same in order, but at the expense of said city. *Provided*, That in all cases where such repairs shall exceed five dollars ($5) per week, a written order shall first be obtained from the Mayor, Controller, or Chairman of the Committee on Gas, authorizing such repairs to be made.

To keep lamps in order.

Repairs, how ordered.

Liability of Gas. Co.

SEC. 4. Said company shall be liable for all loss of gas or other property, and damage thereto, caused by the neglect or fault of said company, its officers or employes, and for all damages to individuals, or to said city, arising from a failure to comply with the lawful orders or requirements of the Common Council, relative to lighting the streets of said city with gas.

Bills of Gas Co. vs. City must be verified by an officer of the company.

SEC. 5. All bills of said company for claims and charges arising under this ordinance against said city, shall be verified by the oath of some officer of said company, in the usual form, and shall set forth all the items charged for, and be accompanied by the order of the Mayor, Controller or Chairman of the Committee on Gas, in the matters hereinbefore mentioned, which require such order. Payment of all such bills shall be made quarterly in orders on the contingent fund. The measurement of gas used by said city, under this contract, shall be by the use of two standard meters, se-

Repair bills, when paid.

Measurement of gas.

lected, stationed and controlled jointly by said Gas Light Company and said Committee on Gas, and the members of said committee shall have free access to said meters at all times, and may require the same to be tested, changed or moved, as the interests of said city may require.

Committee on gas.

SEC. 6. Said lamps shall be lighted by said company according to the American Meter Company's time table, and extinguished at one o'clock each night, or at such other hour as the Common Council may from time to time direct; and said Common Council may require said Company to light said lamps, or a portion thereof, during nights, and certain hours thereof not designated in said time table.

Lamps, how lighted.

SEC. 7. Nothing in this ordinance contained shall be construed so as to release said Gas Light Company from the operation, effect and obligations of an ordinance of said city, adopted April 2d, 1868, entitled, "An ordinance to provide for the establishment and maintenance of gas works in the City of Saginaw."

Adopted July 6, 1871.

GEORGE F. WILLIAMS, Mayor.

JOHN B. SCHICK, Recorder.

D. L. C. EATON,
Secretary Saginaw Gas Light Company.

[*Record Ordinance Book No. 1, page 113.*]

---

*An ordinance to provide for the establishment and maintenance of Gas Works in the City of Saginaw.*

WHEREAS, it is desirable that this city shall be lighted with gas, and in order to induce any company to erect Gas Works therein, and lay down gas pipes in the streets thereof, and to furnish a supply of gas for private and

Preamble.

public use therein, it is necessary to grant and secure to such company certain exclusive rights and privileges, subject to certain restrictions and conditions to protect the rights of the city, of its citizens and of such company; therefore,

*It is hereby ordained by the Common Council of the City of Saginaw:*

Rights granted to certain persons to operate and maintain Gas Works.

SECTION 1. That the exclusive right and privilege of erecting, maintaining, continuing and operating Gas Works within this city and of laying down and continuing gas pipes along, across, under and through any and all of the streets, sidewalks, alleys, lanes and public grounds in said city, and in like manner in the territory which may be hereafter added to the corporate limits of said city, for conveying gas for supplying said city and the inhabitants thereof with gas lights, and the exclusive right and privilege of manufacturing gas in said city for sale for lights, and of selling the same, and of supplying the inhabitants of said city, and said city and the buildings and streets therein with gas for lighting the same, be and is hereby granted and secured to ALEX. SWIFT, of Cincinnati, Ohio; EDWIN SWIFT, of Cincinnati, Ohio; N. S. LOCKWOOD; DANIEL L. C. EATON and THOMAS MERRILL, of the City of Saginaw, County of Saginaw and State of Michigan and their associates, successors and assigns for thirty years: *Provided*, however, and this grant is made subject to the following conditions and restrictions:

Within what time said persons to organize under act of Legislature, and accept the provisions of this ordinance.

SEC. 2. That said Alexander Swift, Edwin Swift, Nathan S. Lockwood, Daniel L. C. Eaton and Thomas Merrill and their associates, successors and assigns shall within thirty days after the passage of this ordinance, organize under the act of the Legislature of this State, entitled "an act to authorize the formation of Gas Light Companies," and file with the Recorder of this city, a copy of their articles of association, and their acceptance of this ordinance, and agreements to perform on their part according to the terms and conditions thereof, to supply the said city and the inhabitants thereof, gas for lights, and shall within one year and six months, erect good, permanent and sufficient Gas Works in said city, and lay down in the streets thereof at least nine thousand feet of main pipe and supply and continue to supply all persons along the line of said main pipe, who shall suitably supply their premises with surface pipes and fixtures for receiving and burning gas, and who shall sign the rules and regulations of said Gas Company (such as are usual with such companies), and who shall require gas and pay for the same at a rate not exceeding, exclusive of a reasonable rent for meters, four dollars per thousand cubic feet for private lights, and to this city for public lamps at a rate not exceeding three dollars and fifty cents per thousand cubic feet, and that after said year and six months as other parts of the city may become more compactly built so as to afford responsible applicants or consumers of gas in fifteen different buildings, who shall agree to take and continue to use and pay for gas lights therein on foregoing terms and conditions for each additional one thousand feet of main pipe, the said company, their successors and assigns, shall within a reasonable time after such application, lay down and extend gas pipes and furnish gas to such applicants on said terms. The office of said company shall be in the city of Saginaw, and one or more directors of the company shall at all times be residents of this city.

Within what time to erect gas works, etc.

Rate of purchasing gas exclusive of rent of meters not to exceed $4.00 per cubic ft. private use, and $3.50 for public use.

Location of office and residence of at least one director in the City of Saginaw.

SEC. 3. Said company before digging for and laying down, relaying and continuance of gas pipes along, across, under and through any and all the streets, lanes, alleys, sidewalks and public grounds of said city, shall give one day's notice to the Street Commissioner or other proper authorities of their intention to so do, and in digging for the repairs of said pipes, take care not to unnecessarily obstruct or injure any such street, lane, alley, sidewalk or public ground and water pipes, and shall with reasonable diligence, return such street, lane, alley, sidewalk or public grounds to as good a state of repair and condition as the same was before disturbed by said company, and shall in all respects fully indemnify and save harmless this city from and against all damages or costs, which the city shall be put to or sustain by virtue of such digging.

Notice of laying pipes etc., to be given to St. Commissi'r or other Officer.

Not to obstruct str'ts etc.

To save city harmless from damages.

SEC. 4. If said company shall not comply with the conditions of this ordinance, and shall at any time fail, to keep their said works, pipes and meters in good repair or shall fail to supply said city or the inhabitants thereof with the requisite quality and a good article of burning gas, to wit: Of as good quality as is furnished by other companies to cities similarly situated, which quality shall be subject to inspection by three competent persons, one appointed by the Common Council, one by the Gas Company, and a third by the two already chosen, said company shall thereby forfeit all rights and privileges within this ordinance. But nothing in this act shall be construed to prevent the cutting off or refusing the usual supply of gas from or to any person or persons on account of any neglect or refusal to pay for the same, or on account of any necessary repairs or alterations of said gas pipes or mains: *Provided*, That when gas

Forfeitures of conditions by said Co.

Proviso.

shall be shut off to make repairs or alterations as aforesaid, it shall only be for such time, as by reasonable diligence said repairs or alterations can be made, and each exemption from liability only in cases of accident to the works, or pipes or necessary repairs.

Renewal of this ordinance by city at expiration of 30 years, or to purchase gas works, &c.

SEC. 5. At the end of thirty years, this city shall renew and extend this ordinance for a like term of time, or purchase of said company, their successors or assigns, their gas works, pipes, fixtures, materials, apparatus, tools and meters as the city shall elect ; and if the city elects to purchase and the parties are unable to agree as to the value of the property, or the terms of payment, then the same shall be determined as follows : The city shall appoint two disinterested persons, and said company shall appoint two disinterested persons, and these four persons shall agree upon a fifth, and said five persons shall determine the value of said property, and terms of payment, and the decision of the said five persons or a majority of them, made in writing, shall be binding upon and performed by the parties respectively, and until such decision so made and given, said company shall continue their said work and supply of gas with all the rights and privileges, and subject to all the conditions in this ordinance contained.

Terms, how determined.

Price of gas to be fixed at certain periods.

SEC. 6. At the end of ten years from the date of the passage of this ordinance, and at the end of every five years thereafter, during the time this ordinance shall remain in force, the price of gas to be furnished to the city and the inhabitants thereof, under the grants of this ordinance shall be fixed for the ensuing five years, at the request of the Common Council of this city, by five disinterested persons chosen in the manner provided in section five, who shall in making their decision be governed by the price of gas in neighboring cities, similarly situated with regard to the cost of production, the written decision of a majority of whom shall be final.

Adopted April 22, 1868.

A. F. R. BRALEY, Mayor.

ROBERT McQUEEN, Recorder.

[*Record Ordinance Book, page 81.*]

There is on file in the Recorder's office, the following acceptance: [*See Ordinance Book, page 81.*]

"ROBERT McQUEEN, Recorder:

"The ordinance to provide for the establishment and "maintenance of Gas Works in the City of Saginaw, "passed April 22d, 1868, with all its provisions and con- "ditions, is hereby accepted and agreed to."

"May 20, 1868.

"N. LOCKWOOD,

"For himself and associates."

[*See Record Ordinance Book, page 81.*]

---

*An Ordinance relative to the disposition of fines, forfeitures and penalties, and moneys received for granting of license, collected or received, by virtue of any ordinance or by-law of the City of Saginaw City.*

*Be it ordained by the Mayor, Recorder and Aldermen, of the City of Saginaw City, in Common Council convened:*

Moneys collected by city officers to be paid to City Treasurer.

SECTION 1. Whenever any Justice of the Peace of said city, or City Attorney, or any other person or persons, shall collect or receive any fine, penalty or forfeiture incurred by the violation of any ordinance or bylaw of said city, or whenever the Mayor, Recorder, or

City Attorney, or any other person or persons shall receive any money for the granting of any license, they shall pay the same over to the Treasurer of said city and take his receipt therefor, within thirty days after the same shall have been collected and received.

Treasurer to give receipt and place the amount to credit of Contingent Fund.

SEC. 2. The said Treasurer shall upon the receipt of any money paid to him as a fine, penalty, or forfeiture, or as money received for the granting of any license, give the person paying the same, a receipt for the amount so received, stating the name of the person or persons of whom the same was recovered or received from, and shall forthwith place the amount so received to the credit of the general fund for the payment of expenses.

Penalty for refusing to pay over moneys.

SEC. 3. If any person or persons shall neglect or refuse to pay over to the Treasurer of said city, any money collected or received as a fine, penalty or forfeiture, or any money received for the granting of any license in violation of the first section of this ordinance, he or they so offending shall forfeit or pay twice the sum so collected or received and not paid over to the Treasurer within the time therein specified, together with costs of prosecution.

Adopted October 18, A. D. 1857.

GARDNER D. WILLIAMS, Mayor.

C. GARRETT, Recorder.

[*Journal of 1857, page 69. Record Ordinance Book, page 16.*]

*An Ordinance relative to a capitation or poll tax.*

*It is hereby ordained by the Common Council of the City of Saginaw, as follows :*

SECTION 1. The City of Saginaw shall be and the same is hereby constituted a highway district. Highway district.

SEC. 2. It shall be the duty of the Street Commissioner, between the second Monday of April and the first Monday of May of each year, to make out and deliver to the Recorder a list of the names of all persons residing or being in the city, liable to pay a poll tax under the provisions of section twenty-one of an act to revise and amend the charter of the city of Saginaw. Duty of Street Commissioner.

SEC. 3. There shall be assessed against and collected from each male inhabitant of said city, over twenty-one and under fifty years of age, (except idiots, paupers and lunatics,) an annual capitation or poll tax of one dollar, the proceeds of which shall be expended upon the streets and highways in said city : *Provided*, That any person liable to pay the said tax shall have the right, in lieu of paying one dollar, to work one day upon said streets and highways under the direction of the Street Commissioner. Poll tax, who liable to pay.

[*Ordinance Book, page 191.*]

SEC. 4. For the purpose of assessing and collecting such tax, the Recorder shall, between the first Monday of May and the first day of June in each year, prepare duplicate assessment rolls, which shall contain in one column, alphabetically arranged, the names of all persons liable to a poll tax as herein prescribed, and in another column the amount of poll tax assessed against each person. Poll tax roll

SEC. 5. One of said rolls shall be filed in the Recorder's office, where it shall remain open to the inspection and examination of all persons interested. To the other roll shall be annexed a warrant, signed by the Mayor and Recorder, or one of them, and sealed with the corporate seal of the City of Saginaw, directed to the Street Commissioner, commanding him to require the several persons in such roll named to perform, under the direction and superintendence of such Street Commissioner, each one day's labor on the streets and highways or pay the amount of money set opposite their respective names in said roll, and in default thereof, further commanding said Street Commissioner to levy the same on the goods and chattels of such persons, and that such Street Commissioner make return of his doings to the Common Council on the first Monday of September next after the date of said warrant, which roll, with warrant annexed, when so prepared and signed, shall be delivered to the Street Commissioner of said city.

Report of Commissioner.

SEC. 6. The Controller shall open an account with such Street Commissioner and charge him with the amount of tax contained in his roll, and when he shall report his doings under said roll, the Controller shall make entries of and audit the same as justice requires.

Names omitted to be inserted by Street Commissioner.

SEC. 7. The names of persons left out of said roll, which ought to have been inserted, and of new inhabitants of said district who have not been assessed previously the said year, and who are subject to a poll tax, shall be added to the assessment roll by the Street Commissioner, subject to an appeal to the Common Council.

SEC. 8. The Street Commissioner shall, by notice, require each person assessed on the roll delivered to him, at a time and place to be designated by him, and not to be less than twenty-four hours from the time of giving such notice, to appear and perform one day's labor on the streets or highways or to pay within the same time to such Street Commissioner the amount assessed against such person on said roll, which notice shall be, either personal or in writing, left at the usual residence of the person notified. The Street Commissioner, in giving such notice, shall designate the implements with which such work is to be done, and may require a team, wagon, plow or scraper to be furnished by any person having the same within his district. Any person furnishing a team shall be allowed therefor the same as for an able-bodied man; for a wagon, plow or scraper, one-half as much.

Notice to persons liable to pay poll tax.

Team work.

SEC. 9. Every person assessed and required to work on the streets or highways as aforesaid, may, within the time designated, pay the Street Commissioner the sum assessed against him on said roll, or may at his option appear and perform the required labor in person, or by a faithful and able-bodied man as a substitute, and the person or substitute so appearing shall actually work eight full hours under the direction of the Street Commissioner, under a penalty of twenty cents for every hour and a proportionate sum for any less time that such person or substitute shall be in default, to be imposed by a fine on the person assessed.

Payment of poll tax, how made.

SEC. 10. Every person or substitute who, after appearing to work, shall remain idle, or not work faithfully, or hinder others from working, shall for each offense forfeit and pay the sum of one dollar, with costs of prosecution.

Penalty.

Collecting of poll tax by levy, etc.

SEC. 11. In case any person shall not peform the labor, or furnish the teams or other implements required by the Street Commissioner, nor pay the amount assessed against him on said roll within the time designated by the Street Commissioner, the said Street Commissioner shall, as soon as may be, levy the amount of the assessment by distress and sale of any goods and chattels of such person wherever the same may be found in said city.

Notice of sale.

SEC. 12. The said Street Commissioner shall give public notice of the time and place of sale, describing the property to be sold, at least five days previous to the sale, by a printed or written notice, to be posted up in at least three public places in said city, one of said notices to be posted on or by the side of the door of the postoffice in this city. The sale shall be by public auction, and out of the proceeds the Street Commissioner shall retain the amount of the assessment for which said sale shall have been made, and of his fees in making such distress and sale, and shall pay over the surplus of said proceeds, if any, to the owner of the property so sold.

Proceeds of sale.

When city may sue for poll tax.

SEC. 13. If the Street Commissioner shall not be able to find any goods and chattels whereon to levy to satisfy said assessment, the person liable therefor may be sued for the same in the corporate name of the City of Saginaw.

Moneys to be delivered to Treasurer.

SEC. 14. The Street Commissioner shall deliver to the Treasurer of the City of Saginaw all moneys received by him on account of any assessment on said assessment roll, and take his receipt therefor and file the same with the Recorder on or before the return day of the warrant annexed to the assessment roll.

Returns of Street Commissioner.

SEC. 15. On or before the first Monday of September, in each year, the Street Commissioner shall return an account in writing, verified by his oath, and containing,

1st. The number of names originally contained in the assessment roll.

2d. The number of names added by him to the assessment roll.

3d. The names of all who have worked on the streets or highways, with the length of time they have worked.

4th. The names of all those who have been fined, with the amount of each fine.

5th. The names of all those who have paid, and of all those of whom he has collected the assessment against, and the sums so collected.

6th. The names of all those of whom he has not been able to collect their tax.

7th. The number of days said Street Commissioner shall have actually worked on the streets or highways, together with the dates: *Provided*, That the Common Council may at any time require the Street Commissioner to report his doings under this or any other ordinance.

Penalty for neglect to make returns.

SEC. 16. If the Street Commissioner shall refuse or neglect to render an account, as in this last section specified, he shall forfeit and pay a penalty of twenty-five dollars, with costs, and shall also be liable to pay the amount due on the assessment roll delivered to him, as shall appear from the books of the Recorder, in case no return is made as herein required, of the balance remaining in his hands, as the case may be; and if the Street Commissioner shall neglect to pay to the Treasurer the money received by him, or to file the Treasurer's receipt therefor with the Recorder, as required in section fourteen of this ordinance, he shall forfeit and pay a fine not exceeding fifty dollars, with costs, and be liable to prosecution for all moneys received by him and not delivered to the Treasurer; and if the Street Commissioner shall neglect to perform the duties enjoined by this ordinance, or do any act contrary to the provisions thereof, he shall for every such offense, where no penalty is otherwise prescribed, forfeit and pay a sum not exceeding fifty dollars, and costs of prosecution.

Passed April 26, 1865. [See section 5, page 132.]

STEWART B. WILLIAMS, Mayor.

A. F. R. BRALEY, Recorder.

[*Record Ordinance Book, page 39.*]

---

*An Ordinance relative to the duties of Supervisors, Justices of the Peace, School Inspectors and Directors of the Poor.*

*Be it ordained by the Mayor, Recorder and Aldermen, of the City of Saginaw, in Common Council convened:*

Duties of certain officers defined

SECTION 1. That the Supervisors, Justices of the Peace, School Inspectors and Directors of the Poor of the city of Saginaw City, shall perform, in and for said city of Saginaw City, like duties to those required to be performed by the corresponding township officers in the several townships or this State, except as is otherwise provided by the "Act to incorporate the City of Saginaw City," and as may be provided by the by-laws and ordinances of the Common Council; and the Recorder of said city shall perform, in and for said city, like duties to those required of Township Clerks in this State, except as is provided in the "Act to incorporate the City of Saginaw City," and as may be provided by the by-laws and ordinances of said city.

Adopted May 13, 1857.

GARDNER D. WILLIAMS, Mayor.

C. GARRETT, Recorder.

[*Journal of 1857, page 29.*]

---

*An Ordinance relative to the duties of Comptroller.*

*Be it ordained by the Common Council of the City of Saginaw:*

SECTION 1. The Comptroller shall constitute the chief financial officer of the corporation, and, as such, shall countersign all bonds which the corporation or Common Council are authorized to issue, pledging the faith and credit of said city, and to countersign all orders drawn on the Treasurer by the Recorder. Comptroller chief financial officer, to countersign all bonds, orders, etc.

SEC. 2. All claims and demands against said city which may be referred to the Comptroller shall be examined by him in detail, and he shall present the same to the Common Council at the same or next regular meeting thereof, or as soon thereafter as practicable, together with a communication in writing, setting forth the facts in relation to such claims and demands, and his opinion in regard to the allowance and payment thereof. Claims and demands against city shall be examined by Comptroller and reported to the Common Council.

SEC. 3. The Comptroller shall, under the direction of the Common Council, make all purchases of personal property, supplies and materials required for the use of the city in its various departments, and to report his action thereon, from time to time, to the Common Council, as may be required by said Common Council. Comptroller to make all purchases of personal property, etc., and report.

To examine reports of Treasurer and other officers, involving expenditures, etc.

SEC. 4. The Comptroller shall examine the reports and returns of the Treasurer, Street Commissioner, Recorder and Justices of the Peace, and of all other city officers, involving receipts or expenditures of moneys or value connected with the said city, and report in writing as to the correctness of the same to the Common Council, from time to time, or as may be required by said Common Council.

To keep set of books of account, exhibiting financial condition of the city.

SEC. 5. The Comptroller shall keep a complete set of books, exhibiting the financial condition of said city in all its various departments and funds, its resources and liabilities, with a proper classification thereof. When any funds or appropriations have been exhausted by warrants already drawn thereon, or by appropriations, liabilities debts and expenses actually made, incurred or contracted for, and to be paid out of such funds or appropriations, the Comptroller shall advise the Common Council of the situation thereof at its next meeting. He shall open accounts with the City Treasurer, charging him with the amounts of taxes, general and special, levied in said city, specified in tax rolls delivered to him; also with the Street Commissioner, charging him with the poll tax levied in said city. He shall also open an account showing the whole amount in detail of all bonds, notes and mortgages and moneys receivable of the said city. He shall also open and keep proper accounts with all salaried officers of said city, and with all persons rendering services or making claims under and by virtue of general or special contracts with said city. He shall also keep a list of all the property, real, personal and mixed, belonging to said city, and of all its debts and liabilities, to the end that the assets and liabilities of said city may at any time be known at the Comptroller's office.

To keep list of all property belonging to city.

SEC. 6. The Comptroller shall open accounts with the Treasurer, in which he shall charge him with all moneys appropriated, raised and received for each of the several funds of the said city, and credit him with all warrants drawn thereon, keeping a separate account of debt and credit for each fund, charging every warrant drawn to the account of the particular fund created for the specific purpose for which such warrant is drawn, in order that the condition of each fund may at all times be known at the Comptrollers office. He shall also make and extend all assessment rolls for special assessments and public improvements which may be ordered by the Common Council, and shall perform such other duties, not inconsistent with the charter of said city and the laws of this State, as the Common Council may from time to time require.

Manner of keeping account with Treasurer.

Comptroller to make and extend all assessment rolls.

Other duties.

SEC. 7. All ordinances, or parts of ordinances, heretofore passed, contravening the provisions of this ordinance, be and the same are hereby repealed.

Adopted May 5, 1858.

A. F. R. BRALEY, Mayor.

ROBERT MCQUEEN, Recorder.

[*Record Ordinance Book, page 82.*]

---

*An Ordinance relative to public decency.*

*It is hereby ordained by the Common Council of the City of Saginaw as follows:*

SECTION 1. If any person or persons shall expose his, her or their naked bodies within the limits of said city, between the hours of four o'clock in the forenoon and nine o'clock in the afternoon, he, she or they shall, on conviction thereof, pay a fine of not less than one

Indecent exposures.

Penalty.

dollar nor more than twenty dollars, and in default of payment of said fine, may be imprisoned in the county jail for not less than one day nor more than twenty days.

Firing of guns, etc., prohibited on Sunday, and on other days within certain limits.

SEC. 2. It shall not be lawful for any person on the first day of the week, called Sunday, to fire any gun, rifle, cannon or pistol, within the limits of said city, nor shall it be lawful for any person or persons to fire any gun, rifle or pistol, on any other day of the week within the boundaries embraced within the following limits of said city, to wit: Farley street, Bond street, Emerson street, and the Saginaw River, except for the destruction of noxious animals or birds of prey; and whoever shall violate this, or the preceding section of this ordinance, shall be liable to the penalty imposed in section one of this ordinance for every such offense, and upon a trial for such offense, proof of the firing of any cannon, gun, rifle or pistol shall be *prima facie* evidence of a violation of this ordinance, but no punishment or fine shall be inflicted for a violation of this section, provided the person accused shall make it satisfactorily appear, by his own affidavit or otherwise, that such firing was for the destruction of animals or birds above excepted.

Exceptions. Penalty. Proviso.

Ordinances repealed.

SEC. 3. All ordinances or parts of ordinances, heretofore passed by the Common Council of this city, contravening the provisions of this ordinance, be and the same are hereby repealed.

Passed April 26, 1865.

STEWART B. WILLIAMS, Mayor.

A. F. R. BRALEY, Recorder.

[*Record Ordinance Book, page 33.*]

*An Ordinance relative to shade trees.*

*It is hereby ordained by the Common Council of the City of Saginaw, as follows :*

SECTION 1. All shade trees hereafter to be set out, outside the walks on Court street and Washington street, shall be set fifteen feet from the line of lots, and all trees on said streets which may be set inside the walks on said streets, shall be set two feet from the line of lots, and shade trees to be set out on other streets in said city, outside the walks, shall be set nine feet from the line of lots, and all trees on lots last aforesaid, which may be set inside the walks, shall be set one and a half feet from the line of said lots. **Shade trees, how set out.**

SEC. 2. If any person shall set out trees at other distances than those above mentioned, he shall be liable to pay a fine sufficient in amount to defray the expense of removing said trees, and also the sum of five dollars in addition, to be collected before the Recorder or any Justice of the Peace in this city. **Penalty.**

SEC. 3. No person shall tie, or hitch, to any ornamental or shade trees standing or growing within the streets of this city, any horse, horses, team or teams, or any animal whatever, under a penalty of five dollars for each offense, to be recovered on the complaint of any person before the Recorder or any Justice of the Peace of said city. **Horses, etc., not to be tied to shade trees, etc.** **Penalty.**

SEC. 4. Any person who shall wrongfully take and carry away from any place any fruit trees, or ornamental trees, shade trees, ornamental shrub, or any plant, vine, bush or vegetable there growing, standing or being, with intent to deprive the owner thereof, or who shall, with- **Removing trees, etc., wrongfully.**

out right and with wrongful intent, detach from the ground or injure any fruit trees, or ornamental trees, shade trees, ornamental shrub, or any plant, vine, bush or vegetable, shall be guilty of a misdemeanor, and, on conviction thereof, shall be punished by imprisonment in the county jail not more than thirty days, or by a fine not exceeding one hundred dollars, or by both fine and imprisonment, in the discretion of the Court.

Penalty.

Adopted April 26, 1865.

STEWART B. WILLIAMS, Mayor.

A. F. R. BRALEY, Recorder.

[*Record Ordinance Book, page 34.*]

---

*An Ordinance to prevent the existence of houses of ill-fame.*

*Be it ordained by the Common Council of the City of Saginaw, as follows:*

Prohibition

SECTION 1. No occupant or owner of any premises within said city, shall keep, or suffer to be kept on said premises, a house of ill-fame.

Prohibition.

SEC. 2. No person shall reside in a house of ill-fame, or visit such house, for the purpose of prostitution.

Evidence.

And if any person shall be found visiting any house of ill-fame, it shall be *prima facie* evidence of having visited for that purpose, but such person may exculpate himself or herself by reasonable proof.

Reputation.

SEC. 3. If it shall appear on the trial of any case under this ordinance, that the general reputation of a house is that of a house of ill-fame, it shall be *prima facie* evidence that such a house is a house of ill-fame within the meaning of this ordinance; but any person may exculpate himself or herself by reasonable proof.

SEC. 4. Any person who shall violate the provisions of this ordinance, shall, on conviction thereof, be punished by a fine not exceeding one hundred dollars and the costs of prosecution, or by imprisonment in the Detroit House of Correction, for not less than sixty days, and not exceeding three months, and in the imposition of such fine, the court may make a further sentence, that in default of payment of such fine and costs, such offender be imprisoned in the Saginaw County jail for a period not exceeding three months. Fine, $100. Imprison'd.

[*Record Ordinance Book, page 157, June 19, 1873.*]

SEC. 5. The Marshal and police force of the city of Saginaw, are empowered to arrest without process, all persons found offending against any of the provisions of this ordinance. Arrest without process.

SEC. 6. It shall be the duty of the Marshal to see that the provisions of this ordinance are carried into effect, and to give notice to the attorney for the city, of all violations thereof. Duty of Marshal.

SEC. 7. This ordinance shall take immediate effect.

Adopted December 28, 1871.

GEORGE F. WILLIAMS, Mayor.

JOHN B. SCHICK, Recorder.

[*Record Ordinance Book, page 130.*]

---

*An Ordinance relative to vagrants.*

*Be it ordained by the Common Council of the City of Saginaw :*

SECTION 1. All persons within the city of Saginaw, who, not having visible means of support, are found loitering or rambling about, or lodging or loitering in drinking saloons, tippling houses, beer houses, houses Vagrants. Who are vagrants.

of ill-fame, houses of bad repute, vessels, sheds or barns, or in the open air, and not giving good account of themselves, or begging in the streets or elsewhere, all

Keepers of gambling tables, etc.

keepers or exhibitors of any gambling table or device, and all persons who for the purpose of gaming or for the purpose of watch-stuffing, travel about or go from place to place, and all persons upon whom may be found any instrument or thing used for the commission of burglary, larceny, or for the picking of pockets or locks, or anything used for obtaining money under false pretences, and who cannot give a good account of their possession

Fortune tellers.

of the same, and all fortune tellers, shall be deemed vagrants, and upon conviction thereof, shall be punished

Fine, $100.

by a fine not exceeding one hundred dollars and costs of prosecution, and in default of the immediate payment

Imprison'd.

thereof, shall be committed to the Detroit House of Correction until such fine be paid: *Provided*, such time of imprisonment shall not exceed the period of one year.

Marshal's duty to arrest without process.

SEC. 2. It shall be the duty of the Marshal, deputy Marshals, and police officers of the city of Saginaw, to arrest without process, any person by them or either of them found violating any of the provisions of this ordinance.

SEC. 3. This ordinance shall take immediate effect.

Adopted August 17, 1871.

GEORGE F. WILLIAMS, Mayor.

JOHN B. SCHICK, Recorder.

[*Record Ordinance Book, page 133.*]

*An Ordinance relative to the appointment of an Inspector, and the measurement of fire-wood.*

*It is hereby ordained by the Common Council of the City of Saginaw:*

SECTION 1. There shall hereafter be one officer in and for said city of Saginaw, to be denominated Inspector of fire-wood, to be appointed by the Common Council, to hold his office for one year, or until his successor is appointed and qualified, and who shall possess and exercise the powers and duties hereinafter provided. **Inspector, how appointed.**

SEC. 2. The Inspector shall, before entering upon the duties of his office, execute a bond to the city of Saginaw City, with one or more sureties conditioned for the faithful performance of the duties of his office, and shall also subscribe the usual oath subscribed by other officers of said city. **Inspector to give bond** **Oath of office.**

SEC. 3. The Inspector shall keep an office at or near the corner of Hamilton and Court streets in said city, and the same shall be open each day (Sundays excepted) between the hours of 7 A. M. and 6 o'clock P. M. **Inspector to keep an office.**

SEC. 4. The Inspector shall receive for his services the following compensation, and no more: For measuring a load drawn by one horse or other animal, five cents; a load drawn by two or more horses or other animals, ten cents; for measuring wood brought to the city in boats or other water craft, or by cars, as follows: For ten cords or under, ten cents per cord, and five cents for each additional cord. **Fees of Inspector.**

SEC. 5. No person shall sell or offer to sell any fire-wood by the wagon, cart, sled, boat, or other water craft, or car-load, unless the same has been measured by said **Wood must be inspected before sale.**

Inspector ; and if necessary to the more accurate measurement of wood brought to said city by boat or car, the owner or person in charge thereof shall, on request of the Inspector, cause it to be piled in a convenient place for that purpose.

Inspector to give certificate.

SEC. 6. On the receipt of his legal compensation, the Inspector shall deliver to the person employing him a certificate, stating the number of feet contained in the load measured by him, or the number of cords or parts of cords contained in any boat or water craft, or car or pile measured by him ; and in making his measurement, he shall examine carefully the manner in which the wood is piled in the vehicle, boat, craft, car or pile, and make a reasonable and fair deduction for improper or unfair piling, or for the crookedness or unevenness of the wood. The Inspector shall keep a receipt book in which he shall enter, in ink, the names of the owners of wood and the amount of the same, measured by him. The entry shall be made upon the margin of the book, together with the date and the hour when such measurement was made. The owner of the wood must, in every instance, surrender to the purchaser of the wood the certificate received by him from the Inspector.

Purchaser entitled to the certificate.

Penalty for taking illegal fees.

SEC. 7. If said Inspector shall be guilty of taking or demanding more compensation for his services than is prescribed by this ordinance, or shall be guilty of any fraud in his office, he shall, in addition to the punishment hereinafter prescribed, be removed from office by the Common Council of said city.

Penalty for violation of this ordinance.

SEC. 8. Any violation of, or failure to comply with the provisions of this ordinance, shall be punished by a fine not to exceed one hundred dollars and the costs of prosecution ; and in the imposition of any such fine or costs, the court may make a further sentence, that the offender be committed to the county jail of Saginaw County until the payment thereof, for any period of time not exceeding three (3) months.

SEC. 9. Every wagon, cart, sleigh, boat, vessel or car load of fire-wood brought to said city for sale, before the same shall be offered for sale, shall be subject to measurement by the Inspector of fire-wood in and for said city ; and in case of a refusal of the person or persons in charge of said wood, to have the same measured and to pay the Inspector his lawful fees therefor when demanded, he or they shall be liable to the pains and penalties mentioned in the last preceding section of this ordinance.

All wood must be inspected before sale.

Refusal to have wood inspected, $100 fine.

Adopted January 16, 1872.

GEORGE F. WILLIAMS, Mayor.

JOHN B. SCHICK, Recorder.

[*Record Ordinance Book, page 131.*]

---

*An Ordinance to provide for the appointment of Commissioners to take charge of the construction and have the management of the Water Works of the city of Saginaw.*

*It is hereby ordained by the Common Council of the City of Saginaw :*

SECTION 1. That David H. Jerome, Ezra Rust, William Binder, Dan P. Foote and George L. Burrows be and they are hereby named and constituted as a Board of Commissioners of the Saginaw Water Works, who, and their successors in office, shall be known by the name and style of the Board of Commissioners of the Saginaw Water Works.

Commis'rs.

Term of office of original Commis'er.

SEC. 2. The said Commissioners shall hold their offices respectively one, two, three, four and five years from the 7th day of December, A. D. 1871, and until their successors are appointed and qualified, and said Common Council shall, on the last regular meeting previous to the 7th day of December of every year hereafter, appoint a citizen of said city, being a qualified voter and freeholder, as a Commissioner who shall hold his office for five years from the said 7th day of December: *Provided*, That this section shall not be construed to disqualify any member of said Board for reappointment; and in case of death or resignation, or removal from the city of any of said Commissioners, the Common Council shall, as soon thereafter as practicable, fill such vacancy for the remainder of the term by appointing some citizen of said city, being a qualified elector and freeholder.

Commis'er appointed.

Proviso.

Term of office determined.

SEC. 3. Said Commissioners shall, within ten days after the passage of this ordinance, decide by lot their respective terms, which decision shall be certified in writing to the Common Council of said city, and the same be entered of record on the books of the said Common Council.

President of the Board.

SEC. 4. The Commissioners shall choose one of their members as President, who shall hold his office at the pleasure of the Board, and in case of his death, resignation or removal from the city, the Board shall have power to fill the vacancy so caused.

[*Record Ordinance Book, page 173.*]

Commiss'rs may make by-laws.

Proviso.

SEC. 5. Said Commissioners may, from time to time, make and adopt such by-laws, rules and regulations as they shall judge proper for their own and the government of their officers and employes: *Provided*, That such by-laws, rules and regulations shall first be submitted to the Common Council and approved by that body.

SEC. 6. The Treasurer of the city of Saginaw shall open and keep a Water Works account, which shall exhibit all amounts paid into said fund, either loans, water rents or taxes, and also all amounts expended on account of said fund, and he shall in addition to his other duties, collect all water rents under the direction of said Commissioners, and shall give a bond to said city in such sum, and with such sureties, as said Common Council may require, conditioned on the faithful performance of his duties as such collector. Treasurer to keep accounts.

SEC. 7. It shall require a majority of said Commissioners to constitute a quorum for the transaction of business, though a minority may legally adjourn any meeting thereof. Quorum.

SEC. 8. As soon after the passage of this ordinance as possible, said Board of Commissioners shall examine and consider all matters relative to supplying the city of Saginaw and its inhabitants with a sufficient quantity of pure, wholesome water, to be taken from the Tittabawassee river or such other source as may be deemed expedient for such purpose, and for this purpose may employ in the name of the city, engineers, surveyors and such other persons as in their opinion may be necesary to enable them to perform their duties under this ordinance, and to fix their compensation ; but said Commissioners shall not, directly or indirectly, receive any compensation for their own services. Duty of Board.

SEC. 9. The said Commissioners shall devise a general plan of supplying the city with water, which plan Plan to be devised.

shall embrace the system of hydraulic works to be purchased, and all other matters they may think proper to include in said plan, and shall submit said plan to the Common Council of said city. Upon such plan being confirmed and adopted by the Common Council, it shall be certified to by the Recorder of said city and filed in the office of the Board of Commissioners of the Saginaw Water Works, and shall from the time of its adoption be and become the permanent plan of supplying the city with water, subject to alteration only on the recommendation of at least four members of said Board and the approval, by at least two-thirds of the members elect of the Common Council, certified and filed as hereinbefore provided.

Plan to be confirmed.

Alterations of plan.

[*Record Ordinance Book, page 124.*]

SEC. 10. The said Board shall, upon the filing of said plans, recommend and report to the Common Council the construction of such hydraulic works, the purchase of such real estate upon which to erect such works, the laying and construction of such distribution pipes, the purchase of such machinery and material, and the doing of such work connected therewith, as said Board shall deem necessary, and shall accompany such recommendatory report with careful estimates in detail of the probable cost and expense of whatever they recommend.

Power of Board as to purchase of land and construct Water Works.

SEC. 11. Upon the adoption of said report in whole or part, said Commissioners are hereby authorized, and it is made their duty for and in behalf of said city of Saginaw City, and as the lawfully authorized agents of said city, to purchase such lands, machinery and material, and to provide for the doing of such work, and the erection and construction of such buildings and reservoirs as shall be mentioned and approved of by the said Common Council in the report provided for in the last preceding section: *Provided*, That the job of laying the distributing pipes and the establishment of hydrants, and the furnishing of materials for, and the construction and erection of all buildings shall be let to the lowest responsible bidder or bidders, who shall give security for the faithful performance of their contract to the satisfaction of said Board, ten day's public notice of the letting of said work being first given in such a manner as the said Commissioners shall deem most expedient.

**Proviso.**

**Public notice of letting work.**

SEC. 12. No Commissioner or member of the Common Council shall be directly or indirectly interested in any contract relating to the furnishing of materials for, or the work of constructing said Water Works, nor shall they or any of them become surety on the bond of any person contracting to do any work or furnish any materials to be used therein.

**Prohibition.**

SEC. 13. Said Board of Commissioners are hereby charged with the control and supervision of said work, and the erection and establishment of said Water Works, and themselves and all others acting under their authority shall have the right to enter upon any land or water for the purpose of making surveys, and may make any and all excavations in said city that may be necessary in the prosecution of said work of putting in said Water Works, but shall guard such excavations in the manner provided for in the existing ordinances of said city, and shall cause the surface of the ground to be restored to its usual condition, and all damages done thereto and to sidewalks, paving and planking to be repaired.

**Commiss'rs to have control of Works.**

**May enter upon lands, etc.**

Board to certify am't due on contracts, etc.

SEC. 14. Said Board shall certify to the amount due upon all contracts, and for all materials furnished and labor performed in constructing or repairing said Water Works, and all bills and accounts thus certified shall be audited by the Comptroller of said city and presented by him to the Common Council in the same manner as other bills and accounts against said city, and shall be paid out of said Water Works fund.

Comptroller to audit accounts, etc.

SEC. 15. Said Board of Commissioners shall have charge and management of said Water Works during the construction and after the completion thereof, and it shall be their duty as soon as practicable to recommend to the Common Council such rules, regulations and ordinances relating to the fixing and establishing of water rates or rents and the duties and rights of plumbers, as shall in their judgment be proper and necessary.

Board after April, 1875, how constituted and appointed.

SEC. 16. From and after the fifteenth (15th) day of April, 1875, the Board of Water Commissioners shall consist of the City Comptroller and four other members, who shall be resident tax-payers of said city, appointed by the Common Council, one of whom shall be appointed for one year, one for two years, one for three years, and one for four years; and after the first appointments made by the Council under this section, the Common Council in the month of April of each year, shall appoint one Water Commissioner who shall hold his office for four years. The Common Council shall fill by appointment any vacancies that may occur in said Board; and the Commissioners who qualify and enter upon the discharge of their duties, shall hold their offices for the terms for which they were appointed, and until their successors shall be appointed and qualified. The Comptroller shall be Secretary of the Board, and shall keep a complete and

Appointment, when made.

Vacancies, how filled.

Secretary of Board.

correct record of its doings, which record shall be authenticated by his signature and the signature of the President of the Board, and shall be *prima facie* evidence of the matters there recorded. The Comptroller under the direction of the Board of Water Commissioners, shall purchase all materials and supplies required for the use of the Water Works, and he shall keep a book wherein he shall enter an account of all material and supplies by him purchased for the purpose aforesaid, showing when, of whom purchased, and the cost thereof. The Comptroller shall also keep an account with all consumers of water, and all applications to use water shall be made to him.

To keep record.

Comptroller to purchase supplies.

Account with consumers.

[*Record Ordinance Book, page 193.*]

SEC. 17. The Board of Water Commissioners shall have power, and it shall be the duty of said Board to take the care, charge and management of the city Water Works, and at all times to control, manage and direct the same except as provided for in section eighteen of this ordinance. The Board shall appoint and employ all engineers, firemen, laborers and other persons necessary to be employed in and about the Water Works in the ordinary operation thereof and in the repair and extension thereof (when the same shall be lawfully extended), and subject to the approval of the Common Council, may fix the compensation of all persons so appointed and employed, and, subject to the like approval, change the same from time to time; and may discharge such appointees and employes at pleasure. The appointment or employment of any person by the Board shall at once be reported to the Common Council by the Secretary of the Board. The power conferred upon said Board by this ordinance shall at all times be exercised subject to

Power and duties of Board.

Board may appoint employes subject to approval of Council.

Board may fix pay.

and in compliance with the by-laws and ordinances of the city; and the said Board shall not have power to alter, vary or modify the present plan or system of water works. There shall be no alteration or addition to, or extension of, the water pipes as heretofore established and now existing, except in the manner and upon the conditions provided for in section nine (9) of this ordinance.

[*Record Ordinance Book, page 193.*]

When Chief Engineer of Fire Dep't may have charge of Water Works.

SEC. 18. Whenever an alarm of fire shall be given, the Chief Engineer of the Fire Department of the city, or the person lawfully acting in his place, may take charge of and have the full and entire control of the Water Works, its machinery, hydrants and appurtenances, and all persons employed as engineers or firemen, or in any other capacity about the Water Works, shall be subject to his lawful orders during the time his authority may continue; and he shall have like control over the Water Works and all persons employed about the same, whenever in his judgment it is for the public interest to exercise the firemen or to use the Water Works for any of the proper purposes of the Fire Department.

Duration of such authority.

The authority here given to the Chief Engineer and to the person lawfully acting in his place, shall continue during the existence of any fire and until the occasion for calling out the firemen has wholly ceased; and also during the time he may deem it necessary to exercise the firemen as above provided for, or to use the Water Works for the proper purposes of the Fire Department. Any person employed in or about the Water Works who shall refuse to obey any lawful order of the Chief Engineer of the Fire Department, or the person lawfully acting in his place, or the Water Commissioners, shall, on conviction thereof, be fined not less than ten and not more than one hundred dollars and costs of prosecution ; and the person so convicted may be imprisoned in the Saginaw county jail until such fine and costs are paid, but such imprisonment shall not exceed sixty days. [*Record Ord. Book, page 193.*]

Approved December 7, 1871.

GEORGE F. WILLIAMS, Mayor.

JOHN B. SCHICK, Recorder.

[*Record Ordinance Book, page 119.*]

---

*An Ordinance in relation to cross-walks.*

*Be it ordained by the Mayor, Recorder and Aldermen, of the City of Saginaw City, in Common Council convened:*

SECTION 1. That all cross-walks hereafter to be laid in this city shall be made of the width of the sidewalks of which they form a part, and be constructed of sound pine, hemlock, or oak plank, square-edged, and not less than three inches in thickness, and to be laid according to the directions of the Street Commissioner, unless otherwise ordered by the Common Council.

Adopted August 21, A. D, 1858.

GARDNER D. WILLIAMS, Mayor.

NEWTON D. LEE, Recorder.

[*Record Ordinance Book, page 106, Journal of 1858, page 143.*]

## *An Ordinance relative to the Public Health.*

*It is hereby ordained by the Common Council of the City of Saginaw:*

Organizat'n of Board of Health.

SECTION 1. The Common Council may immediately on the passage of this ordinance and at the regular meeting of said Common Council next preceding the ninth day of February in each year hereafter, appoint four suitable persons, residents of said city, who shall be and are hereby constituted a "Board of Health" in and for the city of Saginaw, with powers and duties hereinafter prescribed, and a majority of said Board shall constitute a quorum for the transaction of business.

Quorum.

City Physician.

SEC. 2. The City Physician shall by virtue of his office, be *ex-officio* member of said Board.

President.

SEC. 3. At the first meeting of said Board they shall select from their number a President, to hold his position during the pleasure of said Board. The Recorder of said city shall be the Clerk of said Board, and keep regular minutes of their proceedings in a book to be provided for that purpose.

Recorder to be Clerk of the Board.

Powers of Board.

SEC. 4. The Board of Health shall have power and it is hereby made their duty:

1st. To make, and to direct to be made, diligent inquiry with respect to all nuisances of every description in said city, which are, or may be, injurious to the public health, and abate the same.

2d. To stop, detain and examine, or direct to be stopped, detained and examined, every person coming from a place infected with a pestilential or infectious disease, in order to prevent the introduction of the same into this city.

3d. To cause any person, not a resident of this city, who is infected with any infectious or pestilential disease, to be sent back to the place from whence he or she came, or to the pest-house or hospital. May remove non-residents.

4th. To cause any person, a resident of this city, who is infected with any pestilential or infectious disease, to be removed to the pest-house or hospital, if, in the opinion of the Board, the removal of such person is necessary for the preservation of the public health: *Provided, however*, That such removal can be effected with safety to the patient. May remove residents.

5th. To destroy any furniture, wearing apparel, goods, wares or merchandise, or articles, or property of any kind, which shall be exposed to or infected with a contagious or infectious disease: *Provided, however*, That such property shall be appraised by two disinterested persons, in order that remuneration may be made therefor by the Common Council. May destroy infected property.

6th. To rent or construct proper houses, to be used for pest-houses and hospitals. May rent pest-house.

7th. To employ such nurses, officers, agents, servants or assistants, and provide the necessary furniture, medicines, articles and necessaries, for the uses of the pest-houses or hospitals, and the persons therein confined, as may be deemed necessary. May employ nurses.

8th. To require the occupant of any dwelling house store, shop, or other building in which there shall be any person sick with small pox, or varioloid, to put up and maintain in a conspicuous place, on the front of said dwelling house, store, shop, or other building, a card or sign, to be furnished by the Board, on which shall be Small pox card. May require occupant to put up.

written or printed, in large letters, the words "Small Pox:" and in case of the neglect or refusal of any person to comply with such requirement, to remove the patient therein to the pest-house or hospital.

To make rules.

9th. To make any order requiring any steamboat, or other vessel or craft, having on board any infected or diseased person or property, not to stop at any dock in said city, or to remove therefrom.

To make recommendations to Council.

10th. To exercise a general supervision over the health of the city, and to make from time to time, such recommendations to the Common Council as they deem proper, to promote the cleanliness and salubrity of the city.

To make rules.

11th. To make and determine the rules of its own proceedings.

May divide city.

12th. The Board of Health shall annually, and oftener if they deem it necessary, divide the city into health districts.

Small pox cards.

13th. The Board of Health shall provide and keep on hand a supply of cards marked "Small Pox," to be put upon any house in which there may be a person sick of that disease or the varioloid; and such cards, upon application, shall be furnished without charge.

May take possession of buildings when a nuisance.

14th. Whenever in their judgment it shall be necessary for the public health, to at once take possession of any building, factory, hotel, dwelling house, out house, premises or grounds, upon which in their judgment, there exists any nuisance prejudicial to the public health, and if the owner or occupant shall refuse or neglect to forthwith abate such nuisance in the manner directed by said Board, said Board may cause the same to be abated forthwith in such a manner as they may deem proper, and all expenses incurred shall be a legal claim against the owner and a lien upon the premises, to be collected in the same manner as other special assessments. The said Board may also, when they deem it requisite for the public health, at once, and by force if necessary, close up such houses, buildings, hotels and premises, and exclude all occupants therefrom until such nuisance be fully abated and the air of such building or premises is thoroughly purified. Any person who shall resist the action of the Board, or their agents under this subdivision, shall be liable to the penalty provided for in section sixteen of this ordinance.

May close certain places.

15th. And said Board are further authorized to adopt such measures as shall in their judgment be necessary to secure the inhabitants of said city from contagious, malignant and infectious diseases, and for that purpose may enforce vaccination throughout said city; and any and all persons resisting any lawful order of said Board shall be liable to the penalties provided for in section sixteen of this ordinance.

May adopt measures for security of inhabitants.

SEC. 5. The keeper of any tavern, boarding or public house, in which any inmate thereof shall be sick with small pox, varioloid, or other infectious or pestilential disease, shall forthwith report the same to the Board of Health, or to some member, or to the Clerk thereof; and the keeper or keepers aforesaid, if required by the Board, shall close such house immediately, and keep it closed against all lodgers and customers, until the patient is removed, and such house is thoroughly cleansed and ventilated.

Duties of keepers of public houses.

Duties of physicians.

SEC. 6. Every physician, or person acting as such who shall have a patient sick of the small pox, varioloid, or other infectious and pestilential disease, shall forthwith report the fact, in writing, to the President of the Board of Health, together with the name and place in said city, where such patient is treated, and the President shall report the same at the next meeting of the Board.

Duty of occupant of house where small pox exists.

SEC. 7. It shall be the duty of the occupant of any dwelling house or other building, in which there shall be small pox or varioloid, to put up and maintain, in a conspicuous place, on the front of such building, a card or sign, to be furnished by the Board of Health, on which shall be written or printed the words "Small Pox," and such sign or card shall be kept on such building during all the time any person so diseased shall remain therein, and no person shall take take down, injure or deface such card or sign.

Persons having small pox may be kept confined.

SEC. 8. All persons having small pox, varioloid, or other contagious or infectious disease, are hereby required to be kept closely confined within their respective dwellings or places of abode; and no person who has been confined with such disease, shall leave his or her place of abode and go about the city, until, in the opinion of his or her physician, it can be done without danger of communicating the disease to others.

Prohibition

SEC. 9. No person having the small pox, varioloid, or other contagious disease, shall go about the city.

Board and members thereof may enter houses for examination.

SEC. 10. It shall be the duty of said Board or some authorized member thereof, in said city, to enter upon the premises and into the house of every person in the city as often as they shall deem necessary, and to examine into the health, cleanliness, and number of persons inhabiting such house, and inspect the cellars, vaults, privies and sewers on said premises.

SEC. 11. Said Board shall have the authority to incur such indebtedness as shall be necessary for the proper execution of its powers granted in this ordinance, which shall be submitted to the Common Council for audit and allowance in the same manner as other demands against the city, and shall be paid out of the Contingent Fund accordingly. Board may incur indebtedness. Debts of Board to be paid by city.

SEC. 12. All debts lawfully contracted by the Board of Health, shall be paid by the city, in the same manner that other claims and demands against said city are paid. Debts of Board to be paid by the city.

SEC. 13. No person shall bring, or cause to be brought into the city of Saginaw, any person infected with the small pox, varioloid, or any other infectious or pestilential disease. Infected persons excluded.

SEC. 14. The Board of Health, through its President, shall, on the first Tuesday of each month, and oftener if required, make a report to the Common Council, giving any information in their power in respect to the health and salubrity of the city, and also a detailed statement of what money has been expended by them, and for what purpose the same has been expended. Board to make monthly reports to Common Council.

SEC. 15. The pest-houses and hospitals of the city shall be under the control and direction of the Board of Health. Pest houses and hospitals.

Penalty for a violation of this ordinance.

SEC. 16. Any violation of or failure to comply with the provisions of this ordinance, or failure or neglect to comply with any of the requirements of the Board of Health, shall, on complaint to the Recorder or any Justice of the Peace of said city, be punished by a fine not to exceed one hundred dollars and costs ; and in the imposition of any such fine and costs, the court may make further sentence that the offender be imprisoned in the county jail until such fine and costs be paid : *Provided, however,* That the term of such imprisonment shall not exceed the period of six months.

Proviso.

SEC. 17. This ordinance shall take immediate effect.

When nuisance to be abated.

How the Board shall proceed in relation thereto.

Copy of resolution to be served on occupant.

SEC. 18. Whenever the Board of Health shall determine by a resolution, to be entered at length upon the record of its proceedings, that there exists any nuisance prejudicial to the public health, upon any lot, lots or premises (describing the same), and pointing out the nature and character of such nuisance, and shall have caused a copy of such resolution to be served upon the owner or occupant of such lot, lots or premises, together with a notice forthwith to abate and remove such notice, it shall be the duty of the owner or occupant of such lot, lots or premises, to cause such nuisance to be forthwith abated and removed ; and any owner or occupant of any lot, lots or premises, described in such resolution, who shall omit, neglect or refuse, after such notice aforesaid, forthwith to abate or remove such nuisance, shall, on conviction thereof, be punished by a fine of not less than ten dollars and not more than one hundred dollars and costs of prosecution : and the court imposing such fine may make a further sentence, that the person so fined be imprisoned in the Saginaw County jail until such fine

Duty of occupant on receiving notice, and penalty for failure to comply.

and costs be paid : *Provided, however,* That such imprisonment shall not exceed sixty days.

[*Record Ordinance Book, page 154.*]

SEC. 19. Whenever the Board of Health shall determine by resolution, as provided in section eighteen of this ordinance, that there exists in any alley in this city any nuisance prejudicial to the public health, the President or Secretary of said Board shall cause a copy of such resolution to be served upon the owners or occupants of the lots or premises adjacent to said alley, together with a further notice to abate the same ; and it shall be the duty of any owner or occupant of any lot or premises adjacent to such alley, upon whom such notice shall be served, forthwith to abate and remove the same adjacent to the lots or premises owned or occupied by him ; and in default thereof, such owner or occupant shall be punished as provided in section eighteen of this ordinance.

Duty of President and Secretary in relation to nuisances.

Duty of owner or occupant on receipt of notiee.

[*Record Ordinance Book, page 154.*]

SEC. 20. It shall be the duty of the Marshal of said city, forthwith to serve any and all notices delivered to him for service by the President or Secretary of the Board of Health. And this ordinance shall take immediate effect after publication. [*Rec. Ord. Book, p. 154.*]

Marshal to serve notices for Board.

Adopted February 9, 1872.

JAY SMITH, Mayor *Pro tem.*

JOHN B. SCHICK, Recorder.

[*Record Ordinance Book, page 138.*]

*An Ordinance to establish a market place for the sale of wood, hay and meat from wagons, sleighs and other vehicles.*

*It is hereby ordained by the Common Council of the City of Saginaw:*

Market place, wood, hay and meat. Established where.

SECTION 1. That a market place for the sale of wood, hay and meat, from wagons, sleighs and other vehicles, be and the same is hereby established on Court street, between Fayette street and Washington street.

Vehicles, how placed on th ket.

SEC. 2. All persons standing or waiting upon said market place, with any wagon, sleigh or other vehicle, having wood, hay or meat thereon, shall cause such wagon, sleigh or vehicle to be placed lengthwise with said Court street, and parallel with the line thereof, and not more than twenty feet from the sidewalk, on one or the other side of said street.

Vehicles not to stand in the streets, etc.

SEC. 3. No person shall leave, wait or stand with, any wagon, sleigh or other vehicle, having wood, hay or meat thereon, in or upon any street, alley or public place within said city, other than the market place established by this ordinance.

Marshal, duty of. Notice by Marshal. Penalty for refusal to comply after notice.

SEC. 4. It shall be the duty of the City Marshal and his deputies, and of every policeman and constable of this city, to promptly and immediately notify all persons of this ordinance, who may by them, or by either of them, be found violating any of its provisions; and all persons who, after being so notified, shall violate any provision of this ordinance, or shall refuse, fail, neglect or omit to comply therewith, shall, upon conviction thereof, be punished by a fine not exceeding twenty dollars.

SEC. 5. This ordinance shall take immediate effect.

Adopted January 23, 1871.

WILLIAM H. SWEET, Mayor.

JOHN B. SCHICK, Recorder.

[*Record Ordinance Book, page 117.*]

---

*An Ordinance relative to the appointment and duties of Sealer of weights and measures.*

*It is hereby ordained by the Common Council of the City of Saginaw :*

SECTION 1. There shall be in and for the city of Saginaw, an officer to be denominated the Sealer of weights and measures, who shall be appointed by the Common Council of said city, shall hold his office during the pleasure of said Common Council, shall have the exclusive power to perform all the duties pertaining to his office, and shall, during the time he is directed by the Common Council to perform said duties, try and prove all scales, beams, weights and measures used in said city for the purpose of buying and selling; and such as he shall find conformable to the standards kept in his office, he shall stamp with the word "Approved," or the letter "M," and the year in which said inspection is made; and such as he shall find not to be conformable to said standard, he shall stamp with the word "Condemned," and the year in which the inspection is made.

Sealer of weights and measures.

Term of office.

Powers and duties of.

SEC. 2. The Sealer of weights and measures shall be provided by the city of Saginaw with a book, to be kept in his office, in which he shall register in alphabetical order the name of each person whose weights, measures, scales, beams or other instruments he has in-

To be provided with a book.

Contents of book.

spected, the number and size of the same, and what number of each was approved and condemned, with the time of inspection, and such book shall at all reasonable times be open to the inspection and examination of the public.

To make yearly inspection.

SEC. 3. It shall also be the duty of said Sealer of weights and measures, once in each year, and oftener if he deems it necessary, to inspect all wood boxes or measures used by wood dealers in said city, from which is sold or offered for sale, or delivered, sawed or sawed and split wood by the cord, half cord or less quantities; and all such boxes or measures found conformable to the standard (which standard shall not be less than one hundred and twenty-eight cubic feet for a cord) to be kept in his office, he shall stamp with the word "Approved," and the year in which each inspection is made.

All persons must exhibit their weights, etc.

SEC. 4. No person shall neglect or refuse to exhibit any weight, measure, scale, beam or other instrument used by him or her in weighing or measuring, or any box or measure from which is sold or offered for sale, or delivered, any sawed or sawed and split wood, in any quantity, to the Sealer of weights and measures, when demanded by him for the purpose of having the same inspected.

"Approved" weights and measures only to be used.

SEC. 5. No person shall use for buying or selling, any weights, measures, scales, beams or other instruments, or for buying, selling or delivering sawed or sawed and split wood, in any quantity, any box or measure, unless the same has been inspected and stamped "Approved," or with the letter "M," by the Sealer of weights and measures. And all boxes or measures from which sawed or sawed and split wood is sold, offered for sale or delivered, shall be bound by an iron band running around the upper edge thereof.

Penalty for non-compliance with this ordinance.

SEC. 6. Any person who shall neglect or refuse to exhibit his weights, measures, scales, beams or other instruments used for the purpose of weighing or measuring, to the Sealer of weights and measures, or neglect or refuse to exhibit to said Sealer of weights and measures, when demanded by him, any box or measure used for the purpose, sale or delivery of sawed or sawed and split wood as above provided, for the purpose of having the same inspected as hereinbefore provided, or who shall use in buying or selling, any weights, measures, scales, beams or other instruments used for weighing or measuring, or shall use for the purpose of buying, selling or delivering wood as aforesaid, any box or measure which shall have been inspected and condemned by the Sealer of weights and measures, or which not having been inspected and approved, shall not be conformable to the standards provided by law, shall be punished by a fine not to exceed one hundred dollars and costs of prosecution ; and the court may make a further sentence, that the offender be imprisoned in the jail of Saginaw County until the payment of such fine and costs : *Provided*, That such imprisonment shall not exceed the period of three months.

Fees of sealer.

SEC. 7. The Sealer of weights and measures shall, for inspecting and proving as herein provided, be entitled to demand and receive from the owner or possessor of such weights, measures, scales, beams or instruments, the following fees : For a hay, coal, cattle or depot scale, two tons or more, $2 ; for a platform scale, $1 ; for a beam scale, thirty-five cents ; for a counter, union counter or grocer's scale, twenty-five cents ; for a union counter platform scale, weighing from 160 to 200 pounds, forty cents ; for spring balance or butcher's scales, twenty-five cents ; for weights of seven pounds or more, three cents ; for a nest of weights of four pounds, twelve cents ; for a nest of weights of eight pounds or more, fifteen cents ; for comparing a bushel measure, fifteen cents ; for comparing a half-bushel measure, ten cents ; for comparing any dry measure less than a half bushel, five cents ; for comparing wine, ale and beer measures, containing three gallons or more, ten cents ; for any measure containing less than three gallons, five cents each ; for each yard measure and each sub-division, six cents each. [*Rec. Ord. Book, page 152.*]

Adopted August 17, 1871.

GEORGE F. WILLIAMS, Mayor.

JOHN B. SCHICK, Recorder.

[*Record Ordinance Book, page 139.*]

---

*An Ordinance relative to the protection of public lamps and lamp-posts.*

*It is hereby ordained by the Common Council of the City of Saginaw :*

Who to control lamps.

SECTION 1. The public lamps and lamp-posts in the city of Saginaw shall be under the supervision of the Saginaw Gas Light Company and the Committee on Gas.

Lamp posts not to be injured.

SEC. 2. No person shall willfully, maliciously or negligently injure, pull down, break, remove, or in any manner deface or injure any public lamp, lamp-post, crotchet, or gas light within the city of Saginaw.

SEC. 3. No person shall light or cause to be lighted, or extinguish or cause to be extinguished, any public lamp or gas light without authority either from the Common Council, Mayor, Comptroller, or the Saginaw Gas Light Company. Lamps to be lighted only by certain persons.

SEC. 4. No person shall hand or place any article or substance whatever upon, or place any box or other heavy material against, or hitch any horse or other animal to any public lamp or lamp-post in said city. Horses not to be hitched to posts.

SEC. 5. No person shall erect, place or suspend any lamp or lamp-post in any public street, lane or alley in said city without permission from the Common Council. Lamps to be placed only by order of Council.

SEC. 6. Any violation of the provisions of this ordinance shall be punished by a fine not to exceed the sum of twenty-five dollars and costs; and in the imposition of any fine and costs, the court may make a further sentence that the offender be imprisoned in the county jail for Saginaw County until the payment thereof, for a time not exceeding three months. Penalty.

Adopted August 17, 1871.

GEORGE F. WILLIAMS, Mayor.

JOHN B. SCHICK, Recorder.

[*Record Ordinance Book, page 146.*]

---

*An Ordinance to provide for planking the Saginaw City Street Railway.*

WHEREAS, it is deemed necessary, in order to protect the interests of the public using the streets of the city of Saginaw along which the street railway is laid, that the same should be planked within the track, and for two and one-third feet in width on each side without the track of said railway, therefore Preamble.

*It is hereby ordained by the Common Council of the City of Saginaw :*

Railway track to be maintained on grade of streets.

SECTION 1. That it shall be the duty of the Saginaw City Street Railway Company, its Superintendent, agents, officers, track-layers, and all persons engaged in maintaining, running, operating and repairing said railway, to maintain and keep the said railway track of said company on the same grade of the streets along which the same is laid, and to plank the same, within sixty days from the passage of this ordinance, from its terminus at Mackinaw street, its entire length to the city limits, and thereafter to keep and maintain the same as hereinafter provided.

To be planked on certain streets.

How planked.

SEC. 2. The entire width between the tracks, and for the width of two and one-third feet on each side immediately outside the track, and adjacent thereto, shall be well planked with good, sound planks, not less than three inches in thickness, and so laid that the upper surface inside the track shall not be more than three-fourths of an inch below the top of the rails between the same, and sloping away from the rail, on the outside, at an inclination of not more than ten degrees from horizontal on the side next the center of the street, and not more than fifteen degrees on the side next the gutter ; the edge of the plank next the rail to be not more than one-half an inch below the upper surface of the rail.

Penalty for violation of this ordinance.

SEC. 3. Any Superintendent, agent, officer or track-layer of said company, and any other persons, that shall violate any of the provisions of this ordinance shall, upon conviction thereof, be punished by a fine of not less than five nor more than fifty dollars, or by imprisonment in the common jail of the county of Saginaw not more than thirty days, or by both such fine and imprisonment in the discretion of the court before whom such conviction shall be had. And the Superintendent, and any other officer of said company, shall be subjected to a further penalty of twenty-five dollars for each and every twenty-four hours, after the expiration of said sixty days, that said railway track shall remain unplanked, as hereinbefore provided.

Adopted September 11, 1865.

STEWART B. WILLIAMS, Mayor.

A. F. R. BRALEY, Recorder.

[*Record Ordinance Book, page 55.*]

---

*An Ordinance relative to [the removal of the track of the Saginaw City] Street Railway [Company].**

Preamble.

Reference to ordinance of 1863.

WHEREAS the Mayor, Recorder and Aldermen of the City of Saginaw, by an ordinance for that purpose, adopted the sixth day of October, 1863, in Common Council convened, did grant to sundry persons the right to construct, maintain and operate a street railway upon and along parts of Water, Washington and Jefferson streets, in said city,

Franchises by virue of ordinance of 1863.

AND WHEREAS said rights and franchises are now held and owned by the Saginaw Street Railway Company, which, under such grant, has constructed its railway track, on Water street, from Mackinaw street to Jefferson street, on Jefferson street from Water street to Washington street, thence on Washington street from Jefferson street to the State Road, so called, thence on said State Road to the city limits, and for more than two years last passed has run its cars thereon,

*NOTE.—The title of this ordinance, as given in the Record Ordinance Book, does not fully express its object. The words included in brackets, in the title as here given, do not appear in the title as the ordinance is recorded in the Record Ordinance Book.

J. L. & S. R. R. Co.

AND WHEREAS the Jackson, Lansing & Saginaw Railroad Company are desirous of laying their track through and along Water street, in pursuance of an ordinance granting to said railroad company the right to pass through and along said street, and are also desirous to have the Saginaw Street Railway Company surrender their rights and franchises on said Water street, to avoid any trouble or difficulty that might arise from operating both of said roads on said street, therefore

*It is hereby ordained by the Common Council of the City of Saginaw:*

Right of company to operate street railway on certain streets.

SECTION 1. That, in consideration of the covenants and agreements hereinafter set forth, and to be executed by and on the part of the said Saginaw Street Railway Company, said company shall, for the period of thirty years from and after the sixth day of October, 1863, being the date on which the aforesaid ordinance was passed, have the exclusive right to build, maintain and operate a street railway in, along and upon Mackinaw street, from the west side of Hamilton street to the Saginaw River, or the eastern line of the city limits, also down Hamilton street from Mackinaw street to Jefferson street, thence up Jefferson street to Washington street, thence along Washington street and the State Road to the west line of the village of Florence, and also through Hamilton street to the northerly limits of the City of Saginaw, and also from Hamilton street to Washington street, on either Madison or Monroe street, as the said Saginaw Street Railway Company may elect, with all necessary switches, turn-outs, side tracks and appurtenances, and in case the said Jackson, Lansing & Saginaw Railroad Company shall at any time hereafter cease to occupy said Water street for railroad purposes, at any time during the life of the present charter of said Street Railway Company, then and in such case said Saginaw Street Railway Company shall have the right to lay and extend its track, and operate the same on said Water street on the same terms and conditions as said company is now operating its railway: *Provided* said Street Railway Company shall build its road and operate the same on said Water street within one year from service of written notice, by a two-third's vote of said Common Council, that a street railway is required on said Water street: *Provided*, That said company shall not be required, in order to secure its right to said Water street, to build its railroad on said Water street, without its consent, below or north of Throop street, in said city, and in case said company are required to build on said Water street, then it shall have granted to it the right to get from Water street to Washington street. *Provided*, always, that the Mayor, Recorder and Aldermen of said city shall have at all times the right, and such right is hereby expressly reserved, to grant the privilege to any railway company, either street or steam railway, that may hereafter be chartered and constructed, to cross the track of said Saginaw Street Railway Company at any point within the limits of said City. *Provided*, also, that the rights hereby granted and agreed upon shall be held, used and possessed by the said Saginaw Street Railway Company and its assigns, subject to the same control, on the part of the Common Council of said city, as is provided for in said ordinance, passed October sixth, 1863, and the amendments thereto, and as have been accepted by the said Street Railway Company.

Proviso.

Proviso.

Reserved rights of Common Council.

Rights of said company same as in ordinance of 1863 and amendme'ts thereto.

Consideration on part of Street Railway Company.

In consideration of and upon the conditions following, this ordinance is to be in force and effect, and not otherwise, that is to say :

To surrender right to Water St.

That the said Saginaw Street Railway Company agree to and do hereby surrender and give up its rights and franchises in and to said Water street, and to remove its railway track on such terms as to price for work in removing the same, to be paid by said railroad company, as may be agreed upon between said companies, from said Water street so soon or at such time as the said railroad company may desire said street for laying their track therein, or for preparing such street for that purpose, ten day's notice in writing to be given by said Jackson, Lansing & Saginaw Railroad Company of the time when it desires said street railway track to be removed. But, notwithstanding such surrender, no grant shall be made by the said Common Council to any other person or corporation of the right to construct, maintain or operate any street railway in or upon said Water street, north of Mackinaw street, until the said Saginaw Street Railway Company shall have forfeited all right to re-enter upon said street, as provided by this ordinance.

Common Council not grant rights to any other street railway, unless in case of forfeiture by said Saginaw Street Railway Company.

When this ordinance to become obligatory.

When the said Saginaw Street Railway Company shall have assented to the foregoing terms and conditions and have filed with the Recorder of said city a writing signed by the President of said Street Railway Company, signifying such assent, the same shall be deemed obligatory and binding upon said City of Saginaw and said Saginaw Street Railway Company.

A. F. R. BRALEY, Mayor.

ROBERT MCQUEEN, Recorder.

The Saginaw Street Railway Company by the signature of its President, hereby expressly assents to the terms and conditions contained in the foregoing ordinance, adopted on the 19th day of September, A. D. 1867, by the Common Council of said City of Saginaw, and hereby accepts of the rights and franchises granted them. Assent of the Saginaw Street Railway Company.

D. H. JEROME,

President Saginaw Street Railway Company.

Dated the 19th day of September, A. D. 1867.

*[Record Ordinance Book, page 72.]*

---

*An Ordinance granting the right to the Jackson, Lansing and Saginaw Railroad Company, to run its Railroad through the City of Saginaw.*

*It is hereby ordained by the Common Council of the City of Saginaw:*

SECTION 1. That the Jackson, Lansing and Saginaw Railroad Company be and hereby is authorized and empowered to locate, construct, operate and maintain its Railroad within and through the City of Saginaw, by the most direct and convenient route from a point where the said road crosses the Tittabawassee river to a point in Water street at or near its southerly end, and thence down and along said Water street, to a point at or near the northerly end thereof, and from thence by such direct and convenient route as said company may select and acquire the right to use upon the conditions following, and not otherwise: Route of road. Conditions.

1st. Only a single track shall be laid on said road between Williams street and Throop street, except as the Common Council of said city may hereafter allow. Single track in certain limits.

Depots, location of.

2d. The said company shall locate and forever maintain its passenger and freight depots for said city at some point on or east of Water street, between Williams street and Throop street.

Track on Water St., how laid and maintained.

3d. The track along Water street shall be laid upon the grade of the street, and shall be so maintained as to afford the least obstruction to the passage of vehicles over and along said Water street, from Saginaw street to Throop street, and the said company shall construct, maintain and keep in repair at all times the same planking or pavement over that part of the street occupied by the Railroad for a width equal to the length of the ties of the said road, which is now or may be constructed by the order of the city over that part of the street adjoining such track.

Speed of trains, &c., through the city under control of Common Council.

Common Council to make rules and regulations again't accidents.

4th. The speed at which trains shall be run through the city, the stationing of flagmen, the obstruction of the street by cars not in motion, and the planking, paving and keeping in repair of that part of the street occupied by the road, shall be at all times under the control and direction of the Common Council of said city, which shall have full power to make any order, rules and regulations which such Council may deem necessary for guarding against accidents, the protection of property, and the keeping of such streets in good and safe condition for use as such.

Principal offices and shops, location of.

5th. The principal offices of the company for the transaction of business on the Saginaw River, and the principal repair, manufacturing, machine and car shops of the company on the Saginaw River shall be located and forever maintained in the City of Saginaw, at some point south of Throop street, provided the City of Saginaw shall furnish ample and sufficient grounds within the prescribed limits, for said manufacturing, machine and car shops.

6th. The said company shall procure a relinquishment from the Saginaw Street Railway Company, of any rights which it may have to use said Water street, in the operation of its railway. **Street Railway.**

The said company shall also have the right to put down in said Water street such side track and switches as may be deemed necessary for entering and leaving their depots, the location thereof to be under the direction of the Common Council. **Side track and switches on Water street.**

Nothing herein contained shall be construed to prevent the Common Council of said city from authorizing any Street Railway Company to construct its railway across said railroad track, and the right to do so is hereby expressly reserved to said Common Council. **Rights reserved by Common Council.**

When the said Railroad Company shall have assented to the foregoing terms and conditions, and have filed with the Recorder of said city a writing signed by the proper officers of said company, signifying such assent, the same shall be deemed obligatory and binding upon both parties. **Assent of Company to foregoing conditions required.**

Adopted April 16, 1867.

A. F. R. BRALEY, Mayor.

ROBERT MCQUEEN, Recorder.

[*Record Ordinance Book, page 64.*]

## *An Ordinance relative to Street Railroad.*

Preamble. WHEREAS, differences have arisen between the Common Council of the City of Saginaw and the Saginaw Street Railroad Company, as to the control which said Council has over said company, and.

WHEREAS, The limits of such control have been settled and fixed by the mutual agreement and understanding of the parties, as hereinafter set forth, now, therefore,

*It is hereby ordained by the Common Council of the City of Saginaw:*

Rights to be subject to Control of Council. That the rights and privileges held and enjoyed by said Saginaw Street Railway Company, under an ordinance of said Council, entitled, "An Ordinance relative to the removal of the track of the Saginaw Street Railway Company," adopted September 19th, 1867, shall be continued and enjoyed by said Saginaw Street Railroad Company, subject to the control of said Common Council, as hereinafter stated and defined; and that section one of said ordinance be amended so as to read as follows:

Right to build and maintain road. Term of right. Streets, on what. SECTION 1. That in consideration of the covenants and agreements hereinafter set forth, and to be executed by and on the part of said Saginaw Street Railway Company, said company shall for the period of thirty years from and after the sixth day of October, 1863, being the date on which the aforesaid ordinance was passed, have the exclusive right to build, maintain and operate a street railway in, along and upon Mackinaw street, from the west side of Hamilton street to the Saginaw River, or the eastern line of the city limits, also down Hamilton street from Mackinaw street to Jefferson street, thence up Jefferson street to Washington street, thence along Washington street and the State Road to the west line of the village of Florence, and also through Hamilton street to the northerly limits of the City of Saginaw, and also from Hamilton street to Washington street, on either Madison or Monroe street, as the said Saginaw Street Railway Company may elect, with all necessary switches, turn-outs, side tracks and appurtenances, and in case the said Jackson, Lansing & Saginaw Railroad Company shall at any time hereafter cease to occupy said Water street for railroad purposes, at any time during the life of the present charter of said Street Railway Company, then and in such case said Saginaw Street Railway Company shall have the right to lay and extend its track, and operate the same on said Water street on the same terms and conditions as said company is now operating its railway: *Provided* said Street Railway Company shall build its road and operate the same on said Water street within one year from service of written notice, by a two-third's vote of said Common Council, that a street railway is required on said Water street: *Provided*, That said company shall not be required, in order to secure its right to said Water street, to build its railroad on said Water street, without its consent, below or north of Throop street, in said city, and in case said company are required to build on said Water street, then it shall have granted to it the right to get from Water street to Washington street. *Provided*, always, that the Mayor, Recorder and Aldermen of said city shall have at all times the right, and such right is hereby expressly reserved, to grant the privilege to any railway company, either street or steam railway, that may hereafter be chartered and constructed, to cross the track of said Saginaw Street Railway Company at any point within the limits of said City.

**Proviso.**

**Company not required to build road on Water St.**

**Power reserved to grant right of way to other companies.**

Consideration. In consideration of and upon the conditions following, this ordinance is to be in force and effect, and not otherwise, that is to say :

Street R. R. Co. to surrender its rights on Water St. That the said Saginaw Street Railway Company agree to and do hereby surrender and give up its rights and franchises in and to said Water street, and to remove its railway track on such terms as to price for work in removing the same, to be paid by said railroad company; as may be agreed upon between said companies, from said Water street so soon or at such time as the said railroad company may desire said street for laying their track therein, and for preparing such street for that purpose, ten day's notice in writing to be given by said Jackson, Lansing & Saginaw Railroad Company of the time when it desires said street railway track to be removed. But, notwithstanding such surrender, no grant shall be made by the said Common Council to any other person or corporation of the right to construct, maintain or operate any street railway in or upon said Water street, north of Mackinaw street, until the said Saginaw Street Railway Company shall have forfeited all right to re-enter upon said street, as provided by this ordinance.

When this ordinance to have effect. When the said Saginaw Street Railway Company shall have assented to the foregoing terms and conditions and have filed with the Recorder of said city a writing signed by the President of said Street Railway Company, signifying such assent, the same shall be deemed obligatory and binding upon said City of Saginaw and said Saginaw Street Railway Company. And that said ordinance be further amended by the addition of the following sections :

How track shall be laid. SEC. 2. The track of said Street Railroad shall be laid in a manner as shall not unnecessarily obstruct the free passage of vehicles and carriages. The rails shall be laid four feet eight inches apart, and not to exceed one and one-fourth inches above the surface of the street, and shall conform to the grade of the street as established from time to time by the Common Council; and whenever the said Street Railroad Company shall, for the purpose of constructing or repairing its road, take up or remove any planking or paving in any street in said city, the company shall, as soon as such repairs or construction can reasonably be effected, restore such planking or paving to the condition in which it was before such removal: *Provided, also,* That said Street Railway Company shall not remove their present track to any other part of streets now occupied by said track; and that no new track be laid by said company, except by consent of the Common Council as to vacation of track on such street.

Track to conform to grade of street.

Duty of Company respecting repairs.

Proviso as to change of track.

SEC. 3. The cars to be used on said street railroads shall be drawn by animals, and at a speed not exceeding the rate of six miles per hour, and shall be run as often as public convenience shall require and the Common Council shall prescribe: *Provided,* That the said Common Council will not require them to run oftener than once in thirty minutes during fourteen hours every day from the 15th day of April to the 15th day of October, and twelve hours per day from the 15th day of October to the 15th day of April. *Provided further,* That the provisions of this section shall not be binding upon said company when any portion of the line of road now operated by said company is rendered impassable from any cause beyond the control of the company.

Cars to be drawn by animals.

Speed, rate of.

How often to run.

Proviso.

SEC. 4. The rate of fare shall not exceed, for any distance within the limits of said city and on the line

Fare, rate of.

of road now operated within said limits, five cents for each passenger in any one car: *Provided*, The rate of fare mentioned above shall only apply between the hours of seven o'clock A. M. and nine o'clock P. M., and shall not interfere with special contracts.

Proviso as to time.

Light.

SEC. 5. The cars, after sunset, shall be provided with signal lights.

Construct'n as to rights of Council.

SEC. 6. Nothing in this ordinance shall be so construed as to prevent the Common Council authorizing the laying down of water or gas pipes and sewers, or repairing the same; and the grantees or their assigns shall have no claim for damages against said city, gas or water company: *Provided*, The work of laying said water or gas pipes and sewers shall be done in such a manner as not unreasonably to damage or injure said railways or their use.

Proviso.

Cars not to stop on crosswalks.

SEC. 7. No car shall be allowed to stop on a crosswalk, nor in front of any intersecting street, except to avoid collision or to prevent danger to persons in the street.

Exception.

Stop at what points

SEC. 8. When the conductor of any car is required to stop at the intersection of streets to receive or leave passengers, the cars shall be stopped so as to leave the rear platform slightly over the crossing.

Duty of Company in respect of employes

SEC. 9. The said company shall employ careful, sober and prudent agents, conductors and drivers to take charge of their cars while on the road, who shall use every precaution not to do any injury to any team, carriage, or person on foot.

Children and women not to enter or leave moving cars.

SEC. 10. Conductors shall not allow ladies or children to enter or leave the cars while in motion. Each conductor shall have full power, and it shall be his duty, to

preserve order on the car under his charge, and to remove therefrom any drunken or disorderly person and any person who shall use profane or obscene language on such car, and shall have the same power to arrest any drunken or disorderly person on such car as is possessed by the Marshal or any Deputy Marshal of said city within the limits thereof. **Conductor may remove and arrest persons disorderly.**

SEC. 11. The cars shall at all times be entitled to the track, and any vehicle on the track of said railroad shall turn out when any car comes up, so as to leave the track unobstructed; and the driver of any vehicle refusing to do so, shall be liable to a penalty not exceeding five dollars, on conviction before the Recorder's court of the said city of Saginaw, and costs of prosecution. **Right of cars as to track.** **Penalty for not yielding track.**

SEC. 12. The ordinance passed by the Common Council of the City of Saginaw, on the sixth day of October, A. D. 1863, granting the right to Thomas S. Sprague, Henry Barnes and George Jerome to construct and operate a street railway, and the amendments thereto, are hereby repealed. **Repealing clause.**

SEC. 13. When the said Saginaw Street Railroad Company shall have assented to the foregoing terms and conditions, and have filed with the Recorder of said city a writing signed by the President of said Street Railway Company, signifying such assent, the same shall be deemed obligatory and binding upon said City of Saginaw and said Street Railroad Company. **Assent of Company necessary to this ordinance.**

Adopted March 20, 1871.

GEORGE F. WILLIAMS, Mayor.

JOHN B. SCHICK, Recorder.

[*Record Ordinance Book, page 141.*]

NOTE.—The following acceptance of this ordinance was filed with the Recorder, and may be found attached to page 380 of Journal No. 3, 1871:

Assent of Company.

"The Saginaw Street Railway Company by the signa-"ture of its President, hereby assents to the terms and "conditions contained in the foregoing ordinance, adopted "on this 20th day of March, A. D. 1871, by the Com-"mon Council of the City of Saginaw, and hereby accepts "of the rights and franchises granted therein.

"D. H. JEROME,
"President Saginaw Street Railway Company."

---

*An Ordinance to restrain and regulate the use of Locomotive Engines and Cars, upon the Jackson, Lansing and Saginaw Railroad, within the limits of the City of Saginaw.*

*It is hereby ordained by the Common Council of the City of Saginaw:*

Restricti'ns &c., contained in succeeding sections.

SECTION 1. All locomotives, tenders and cars, used or run upon the Jackson, Lansing and Saginaw Railroad, within the limits of the City of Saginaw, shall be under the restrictions and regulations contained in the following sections of this ordinance.

Rate of speed within certain limits.

SEC. 2. The rate of speed of all locomotives, tenders and cars on said road within the limits of the City of Saginaw, except between the crossings of Elm street and Farley street in said city, shall not exceed eight miles per hour, and between Elm street and Farley street it shall not exceed five miles per hour.

Ringing locomotive bell.

SEC. 3. No locomotive on said road shall be run or put in motion between the crossings of Elm street and Farley street in said city without first ringing the locomotive bell and continuing so to ring, as a signal during the time the locomotive shall be in motion.

SEC. 4. The fire pans of all locomotives of said road shall be kept closed while locomotives are in motion between the crossings of Emerson street and Farley street in said city. Fire pans to be kept closed, when

SEC. 5. No engine, tender, freight or other car shall be placed, left or allowed to remain for any purpose, so as to obstruct, in whole or in part, free access to the Saginaw River through any street of said city leading thereto, for more than ten minutes at any one time, without permission first obtained from the Common Council; and no engine, tender or car of any kind shall be left, either for loading or storage, on any track of said railroad company, running along Water street, in front of any lots, blocks or premises in said city, without permission first obtained from the Common Council, or from the owners of said lots, blocks or premises.

[*Record Ordinance Book, page 150.*]

SEC. 6. No locomotive, tender, car, or other vehicle or conveyance on said road shall be run or driven over or across any hose or other apparatus used in connection with any fire engine, or used for the extinguishing or prevention of fires, while being used for that purpose. No locomotive, &c., to run across fire hose, &c.

SEC. 7. Any person or persons who shall violate or cause any other person or persons to violate directly or indirectly any of the provisions of this ordinance, shall, upon conviction thereof, be punished by a fine of not less than five dollars and not exceeding one hundred dollars, or by imprisonment in the county jail of Saginaw County for a term not exceeding ninety days, or by both such fine and imprisonment, in the discretion of the court making such conviction. And in case of default made in the payment of such fine, the court imposing Penalty for violation of this ordinance.

said fine shall forthwith upon such conviction and default, commit the offenders to the county jail of said county until such fine be paid: *Provided*, That no person remain imprisoned for the non-payment of such fine more than thirty days.

Power of Recorder and Justices to try offences under this ordinance.

SEC. 8. The Recorder and Justices of the Peace of said city shall have power to try and determine all offences arising under the provisions of this ordinance; and upon complaint made in writing and on oath before the Recorder or any Justice of the Peace of said city, of any violations of the provisions of this ordinance, he shall issue his warrant, directed to the Marshal, or any Constable of said city, or to the Sheriff, or to any Under or Deputy Sheriff of the county of Saginaw, which warrant shall recite the substance of the complaint and require the officer to whom it is directed forthwith to arrest the accused and bring him before such Recorder or Justice of the Peace, to be dealt with according to law, and in the same warrant require the officer to summon such witnesses as shall be named therein, to appear and give evidence at the trial. On the return of the warrant with the accused, the said Recorder or Justice shall proceed to hear, try and determine the cause within ten days after the return of said warrant.

Practice and proceedings.

SEC. 9. The practice in such prosecutions as shall arise under the provisions of this ordinance, shall be as prescribed by the laws of this State, regulating the rules and practices of Justices' Courts, except as otherwise provided for in this ordinance and the charter of the city of Saginaw.

Adopted January 19, 1869.

A. F. R. BRALEY, Mayor.

JOHN B. SCHICK, Recorder.

[*Record Ordinance Book, page 96.*]

*An Ordinance relative to the construction of sidewalks and improvement of streets.*

*Be it ordained by the Mayor, Recorder and Aldermen, of the City of Saginaw City, in Common Council convened:*

SECTION 1. All sidewalks shall be constructed upon the grade of the streets, and shall be constructed by the owners or occupants of the adjoining lots, or by assessments upon the same, and shall be constructed at least four feet in width, of sound, durable pine plank, one and a half inches in thickness, and a distance of five feet from the line of said lots, except on Washington and Court streets, which shall be four feet from the line of lots, and shall be constructed under the direction of the Street Commissioners of the different wards in which the work is constructed: *Provided*, That the Common Council may at any time order a sidewalk to be constructed any width greater than four feet that they may deem necessary, and *Provided, further*, That the Common Council may order any sidewalks to be built nearer the lines of lots.

**Manner of constructing sidewalks.**

**Proviso.**

SEC. 2. The expense of grading for, and laying all sidewalks, together with all materials for the same, shall be assessed upon the lots adjacent thereto, and the crossings or cross-walks shall be built by assessments upon the adjacent quarter block, except on the east or river side of Water street, where the crossings or cross-walks shall be assesed upon the adjacent half block.

**Expense of constructing sidewalks, how assessed.**

SEC. 3. The expense of grading all streets ordered to be graded by the Common Council, shall be defrayed, together with the Treasurer's fees for collecting and the

**Expense of grading streets, how assessed.**

expense of publishing the requisite notice of assessment, by assessment on the half block adjoining such street or streets in manner following, to wit: When the streets to be improved run the longest way of the lots the corner lots adjoining such street so improved shall be assessed each three dollars and seventy-five cents, ($3.75), and the other lots in that half of the block next the street shall each be assessed one dollar and twenty-five cents ($1.25), and parts of lots in equal proportion; and where the street to be improved runs the shortest way of the lots, each lot in that half of the block adjoining such street shall be assessed the sum of two dollars and fifty cents ($2.50): *Provided*, That if it shall not be necessary to assess the aforesaid lots the amounts aforesaid to defray the said expense, then and in that case they shall each be assessed such sums less in the same proportion as shall be sufficient to pay the expense aforesaid: *Provided further*, That where a greater sum shall be necessary than the sums herein limited to be raised by assessment as aforesaid, such sum shall be paid out of the moneys raised for general highway tax.

Proviso.

Expense of grading streets through lands unplatted.

SEC. 4. In case any street or highway shall be ordered to be opened and graded by said Common Council through any portion of said city not laid out in lots and blocks and recorded, the assessments for the expense of opening and grading of said streets or highways, and the culverts on the same, together with the expense of publishing of the requisite notice of assessment and the Treasurer's fees for collecting the same, shall be assessed upon all lands adjoining such streets or highways so ordered to be opened and graded in equable proportion (as near as may be) to the length said lands shall adjoin such

How assessed.

street or highway: *Provided,* That the Common Council may appropriate from the general highway fund such sums as they may deem right, when in their opinion the expenses of improving such street or highway shall exceed in amount what the adjoining lands should in justice be assessed for. **Proviso.** **Common Council may appropriate from general highway fund.**

SEC. 5. The ordinance approved May 13, A. D. 1857, relative to the construction of sidewalks, improvement of streets, etc., is hereby repealed and annulled, together with an amendment or addition to section four of said ordinance aforesaid, October 17th, A. D. 1857. **Ordinance of May 13th, 1857, repealed.**

SEC. 5. This ordinance shall take immediate effect.

Adopted June 19, A. D. 1858.

GARDNER D. WILLIAMS, Mayor.

NEWTON D. LEE, Recorder.

[*Journal No. 1, page 111. Record Ordinance Book, page 13.*]

---

*An Ordinance relative to billiard tables and saloons.*

*It is hereby ordained by the Common Council of the City of Saginaw:*

SECTION 1. No person shall keep a billiard table or saloon within the limits of the City of Saginaw, without first obtaining a license therefor, as hereinafter provided. **License required.**

SEC. 2. To keep a billiard table, within the meaning of this ordinance, is to own, keep or have in posssession a billiard table whereon others are permitted to play for the profit or benefit, in any manner, of the person owning, keeping or having the same in possession. **Definition of billiard keeper.**

Definition of saloon.

SEC. 3. To keep a saloon, within the meaning of this ordinance, is to keep any place whereat drink of any kind (except soda, tea and coffee) shall be sold at retail by the glass or measure, or in any other manner, to be drank in the house or upon the premises where sold.

Application for license.

SEC. 4. Any person desiring a license to keep a billiard table or saloon, within the limits of this city, may make application therefor to the Common Council, in writing, which application must be recommended by twenty resident freeholders of the city. On such application being approved by the Common Council, the Recorder, on receiving two dollars for his fees, and on payment to him of the amount required by this ordinance to be paid for such license, and on receiving the bond required by section five of this ordinance, shall, in the name of the City of Saginaw, issue to such applicant a license for one year to keep a billiard table or saloon, as the case may be.

Bond required.

SEC. 5. Before any person shall receive a license under this ordinance, he shall execute and deliver to the Recorder his bond to the city of Saginaw, in the penal sum of five hundred dollars, with two sureties, who shall each under oath, justify their pecuniary responsibility in double the amount of said bond, before the Recorder, which justification shall be in writing and endorsed on the back of such bond ; and the condition of such bond shall be, that the person receiving such license, will faithfully observe, keep and obey the charter and ordinances of the City of Saginaw, and that he will not suffer or permit any gambling, drunkenness or other disorderly or immoral conduct in the house or on the premises kept by him during the time such license shall be in force: *And Provided,* The Recorder shall not accept such bond unless the City Attorney shall endorse thereon that the same is correct in form.

SEC. 6. The amount to be paid for a license to keep a billiard table, shall be ten dollars per year for each table proposed to be kept; and the amount to be paid for a license to keep a saloon, shall be fifty dollars per year.

**Amount of billiard license.**

**Amount of saloon license.**

SEC. 7. No person licensed under this ordinance, shall at any time suffer or permit any gaming for money, or other property of any value whatever, on any table kept by him, or in the house, or on the premises occupied by him. Nor shall any person licensed under this ordinance, suffer or permit any drunkenness, gambling, quarreling, fighting, profanity, or other immoral, indecent or disorderly conduct; nor keep, permit or suffer any saloon kept or occupied by him, to be open or any business whatever to be done thereat on Sunday, or between the hours of twelve o'clock at night and the hour of five o'clock in the morning; nor shall any person licensed as aforesaid, suffer or permit any saloon to be open on any day upon which any election shall be held in this city, or sell, give away, or in any manner whatever suffer or permit any person to obtain thereat or therefrom any drink of any kind whatever.

**Duty of person having license.**

**Drunkenness, gambling, &c., prohibited.**

**Saloons to be closed on Sunday and election days.**

SEC. 8. Any person who shall keep a billiard table, or a saloon, without first obtaining a license therefor, as provided in this ordinance, shall be punished by a fine of not less than one hundred dollars, and not more than three hundred dollars, and the costs of prosecution; and the Court imposing such fine, shall make a further sentence, that in default of payment of such fine and costs

**Penalty for keeping saloon without license.**

within twenty-four hours, the person so convicted be imprisoned in the county jail of Saginaw County until the payment of such fine and costs: *Provided*, That such imprisonment shall not exceed ninety days.

License may be forfeited. SEC. 9. Any person holding a license under this ordinance, and violating any provision thereof, shall, on conviction thereof, be punished by a fine of not less than ten dollars, and not more than fifty dollars, and costs of prosecution, and shall in addition thereto forfeit his license; and the Court before whom such conviction shall be had, shall forthwith enter judgment declaring the license of the person so convicted to be forfeited, and thereupon and thereafter such license shall be at an end and of no effect; and any person holding a license under this ordinance, and convicted and fined for a violation of the same, shall not thereafter be entitled to another license, so long as the fine and costs shall remain unpaid.

License to state place of business. SEC. 10. Every license issued under this ordinance shall state particularly where the billiard table or tables, or where the saloon is to be kept; and it shall not be lawful for any holder of a license to put a billiard table or saloon at any other place in this city, than the one stated in the license, without permission of the Common Council, granted at a regular meeting.

Recorder's duty. SEC. 11. On issuing any license under this ordinance, the Recorder shall forthwith notify the Comptroller thereof, and within five days pay over the money received therefor, to the City Treasurer and take his receipt therefor.

SEC. 12. This ordinance shall take effect on the 10th day of August, 1873, and an ordinance entitled "An Ordinance relative to billiard tables, saloons, victualing houses and the licensing thereof," adopted July 8th, 1873, is hereby repealed.

Saloon license, in certain cases without payment of $50.

SEC. 13. When any person has made the application to the Common Council for a license to keep a saloon, provided for by section four of this ordinance, and his application has been approved by the Common Council, and who has filed with the Recorder the bond required by section five of this ordinance, shall present to the Recorder due proof that he has at any time within one year prior to the date of his application, paid to the person entitled to collect the same, without protest or reservation, the liquor tax imposed by an act of the State Legislature, entitled "An Act for the taxation of the business of manufacturing and selling spirituous and intoxicating, malt, brewed, or fermented liquors, &c.," passed at the last session of the State Legislature, the Recorder shall issue to such person, without payment of the fifty dollars provided for in section six, a license to keep a saloon, for one year, from and after the date thereof, upon the same terms (except as to the fifty dollars) and upon and subject to all the conditions governing other like licenses, issued under this ordinance. It shall be the duty of the Recorder to keep a record of all licenses issued by him, under this ordinance, showing when, to whom issued, and where the saloon or billiard table is to be kept, and in all prosecutions for keeping a saloon or billiard table, without having obtained the license therefor required by this ordinance, such record shall be received in evidence, and if it shall not appear on such record that the person so prosecuted has a license in force, it shall be *prima facie* proof that he has not such license. *Record Ord. Book, page 183.*

Adopted July 22, 1873.

BENTON HANCHETT, Mayor.

JOHN B. SCHICK, Recorder.

[*Record Ordinance Book, page 158.*]

---

*An Ordinance to prevent the use of velocipedes on certain sidewalks of the City of Saginaw.*

*It is hereby ordained by the Common Council of the City of Saginaw :*

Use of velocipedes prohibited on certain streets.

SECTION 1. That no person shall hereafter use, run or ride, and it shall be unlawful to use, run or ride a velocipede on any of the sidewalks of the following named streets of said city of Saginaw, within the limits of said streets herein designated, that is to say: Water and Hamilton streets from the center of Jefferson to the center of Mackinaw streets, and Court street from the centre of Washington street to the east line of Water street.

Penalty.

SEC. 2. Any person violating any of the provisions of this ordinance shall be punished by a fine not less than one dollar, and not exceeding ten dollars, besides costs of prosecution, or imprisonment in the jail of Saginaw County not exceeding five days, or by both fine and imprisonment in the discretion of the Court.

Adopted May 18, 1871.

GEORGE F. WILLIAMS, Mayor.

JOHN B. SCHICK, Recorder.

[*Record Ordinance Book, page 148.*]

*An Ordinance to protect Washington street from injury by driving on certain portions thereof.*

*It is hereby ordained by the Common Council of the City of Saginaw:*

SECTION 1. No person shall be allowed to drive any wagon, sleigh or other vehicle, or to lead, ride or drive, any horse or horses, mule or mules, or any other animal, or team, on that portion of the sides of Washington street lying and being between the sidewalk, on each side of said street, and the gutter or ditch on either side of the centre graded road-bed of said street.

Portion of street not to be driven on.

SEC. 2. Any person violating the provisions of this ordinance, shall, on conviction thereof, be punished by a fine of not less than ten dollars, and not more than twenty-five dollars, and the costs of prosecution; and the Court imposing such fine shall make a further sentence that, in default of payment of such fine and costs, the person so convicted be imprisoned in the Saginaw County jail for a period of time not less than fifteen days, and not more than thirty days.

Penalty.

SEC. 3. It shall be the duty of the City Marshal, and of each Policeman and Constable of said city, to arrest without process, any person seen by them or either of them in the act of violating this ordinance.

Duty of Marshal to arrest persons violating this ordinance.

Adopted October 17, 1873.

BENTON HANCHETT, Mayor.

JOHN B. SCHICK, Recorder.

[*Record Ordinance Book, page 167.*]

*An Ordinance prohibiting the use of smoke-stacks not provided with spark-catchers.*

*It is hereby ordained by the Common Council of the City of Saginaw:*

Use of smoke-stacks not provided with spark-catchers prohibited.

SECTION 1. From and after the 1st day of January, A. D. 1873, it shall be unlawful to use for the ordinary purpose, any high brick, stone or iron chimney, commonly known as and called a smoke-stack, within the limits of said city, unless said chimney or smoke-stack shall be provided with a spark-catcher or screen, properly and securely adjusted thereon.

Penalty.

SEC. 2. Any person violating this ordinance shall be punished by a fine not exceeding one hundred dollars and the costs of prosecution; and in the imposition of any fine the Court may make a further sentence, that the offender be imprisoned in the Saginaw County jail until the payment of such fine: *Provided, however,* That the period of such imprisonment shall not exceed thirty days.

Adopted December 12, 1872.

WILLIAM H. SWEET, Mayor.

JOHN B. SCHICK, Recorder.

[*Record Ordinance Book, page 153.*]

---

*An Ordinance to organize a Police force for the City of Saginaw, and to prescribe the duties of the Police.*

*It is hereby ordained by the Common Council of the City of Saginaw:*

Regular police, how constituted.

SECTION 1. The regular Police force of the City of Saginaw shall consist of the Marshal, who shall be Chief of Police, and such number of Deputy Marshals as the

Common Council may, by a majority vote of all the Aldermen elect, from time to time prescribe. The Deputy Marshals shall serve as, and perform the duties of policemen, and they shall be appointed by the Marshal on the written recommendation of the Mayor, subject to the approval of the Common Council. All appointments of Deputy Marshals, and recommendations therefor, when approved by the Common Council, shall be filed by the Recorder, in his office, and shall be entered at length on the journal of the Council, immediately preceding the resolution approving the same. The Marshal, and all Deputy Marshals appointed under this ordinance, shall at all times be subject to the orders of, and under the control and direction of the Mayor ; and the Mayor and Marshal may make such rules for the government of the Police force, not inconsistant with this ordinance, as they may deem proper, and alter the same at pleasure.

Deputy Marshals, how appointed.

Police force subject to orders of Mayor.

SEC. 2. The appointment of a Deputy Marshal, when duly approved by the Common Council, shall remain in force until the same shall be revoked by a majority vote of all the Aldermen elect, or until the resignation of such Deputy Marshal shall have been filed with the Recorder, and accepted by the Council, and no appointment of a Deputy Marshal shall be revoked by the Council, except as provided for in section three (3) of this ordinance.

Term of Deputy Marshal.

SEC. 3. Whenever the Common Council shall determine to reduce the number of Deputy Marshals, the Mayor and Marshal shall designate the Deputy Marshal to be dismissed, and the Council shall thereupon revoke the appointment of such Deputy Marshal. Whenever charges shall be presented to the Common Council

Council may reduce force.

Mayor and Marshal to designate who to be dismissed.

Proceedings when charges are preferred.

against any Deputy Marshal, the Council shall, at the meeting when the same are presented, appoint a time for the consideration thereof, and the time so appointed shall not be longer than until the next regular meeting of the Common Council, unless such next regular meeting will occur within one week, in which case the time shall not be longer than to the next regular meeting thereof; and the Recorder shall furnish such Deputy Marshal a copy of such charges, at least five days before the time fixed for the consideration thereof, with notice endorsed thereon of the time when the Council will consider the same, and such copy and notice may be served by depositing the same in the postoffice, duly addressed to such Deputy Marshal and prepaid. When charges are preferred against any Deputy Marshal, the Mayor and Marshal may, in their discretion, suspend such Deputy Marshal from duty until the same shall be finally disposed of; and any Deputy Marshal may be suspended by the Mayor, on his written order filed with the Recorder, briefly stating the cause of such suspension, and thereupon it shall be the duty of the Marshal forthwith to prepare specific charges against such Deputy, and to present them to the Council at the next meeting thereof. Whenever the appointment of a Deputy Marshal shall be revoked, by the Council, upon charges preferred against him, his pay shall cease from the time he was suspended from duty, and he shall not thereafter be eligible to any appointment under this ordinance.

Recorder to furnish copy of charges.

Mayor and Marshal may suspend a Deputy.

Mayor may suspend a Deputy Marshal.

When pay of Deputy Marshals to cease.

Pay of Deputy Marshals, how fixed.

SEC. 4. The pay of the Deputy Marshals shall be uniform, and shall be fixed by the Common Council, by resolution, passed by a majority vote of all the Aldermen elect, and from time to time may be changed by a like majority vote.

SEC. 5. Every Deputy Marshal appointed under this ordinance, before entering upon the discharge of his duties, shall take, subscribe and file with the Recorder the oath of office prescribed by section one, of article eighteen, of the Constitution of this State. Oath of office.

SEC. 6. Each Deputy Marshal appointed to serve upon the regular Police force of the city, shall be required to procure, and, while on duty, wear the following described uniform, viz: Dark blue cloth, single-breasted frock coat, with a narrow standing collar, and one row of "M P" brass buttons in front, seven buttons in the row, and four similar buttons on the skirt behind; pants of dark blue cloth, with light blue strips, one-half inch wide on the outer seam; cap of dark blue cloth, wide band, large round top, leather frontispiece, with leather half band and chin strap fastened with small brass buttons. Uniform of regular Police.

SEC. 7. Each Deputy Marshal of the regular Police force shall be furnished by the city with a silver star, to be worn on the left breast, proper numbers for the cap, locust club, and a pair of handcuffs, all of which shall be charged to him by the Marshal, to be returned when discharged from the Police force, or paid for at cost, in case of loss or breakage, unless such loss or breakage occurred in the discharge of duty, and without fault of such officer. Articles to be furnished by city.

SEC. 8. The Mayor and Marshal shall assign the numbers and hours for duty to the several members of the Police force of the city, and a record thereof shall be kept by the Marshal, and in case of vacancy or dismissal, or if the number of the force be increased or diminished, a new assignment shall be made. And the Policemen assigned for duty.

Record to be kept, what to contain. Marshal shall keep a complete record, to be called the "Police Record," showing the number of arrests made by the Police force, the names of the persons arrested, for what and by whom arrested, and the disposition of each case, and before what Court or Justice the same was disposed of. And at the first regular meeting of the Common Council in each month, the Marshal shall submit to the Council a written report for the month ending on the last day of the preceding month, showing fully and in detail the facts of which he is by this section required to keep a record, and he shall certify such report to be correct and full to the best of his knowledge; and in his report he may make such suggestions, relative to the business of his office, as he may consider of use to the Council.

Police prohibited doing certain things. SEC. 9. No member of the Police force of the city shall appear on duty without the uniform prescribed by this ordinance; or during the hours assigned him for duty neglect the same; or while on duty drink any intoxicating or spirituous liquors, or enter or resort to any saloon, shop, store, office, dwelling, or other building, except in the discharge of his duty; or loiter or stand upon the street corners or elsewhere, or sit upon boxes, steps, sidewalks, or elsewhere, to the neglect of his duty.

Penalty for violation by Policemen. SEC. 10. Any member of the Police force who shall violate any of the provisions of section nine (9) of this ordinance, or any law of this State, or any ordinance of this city, or any rule or regulation of the Police force established by the Mayor and Marshal, or disobey any lawful order of the Marshal or Mayor, may be suspended from duty by the Mayor, or in his absence from the city, by the Marshal, until the next meeting of the Common Council, which suspension shall be by a written order, filed with the Recorder, and entered upon the police record by the Marshal. And the Marshal, in all cases of suspension, shall, at the next meeting of the Council thereafter, present charges against the officer so suspended, for the advice and action of the Council, and the Council shall forthwith consider such charges, and unless the same shall be withdrawn or dismissed, the Council shall proceed in relation thereto as prescribed by section three of this ordinance.

Duty of Marshal and Police, and they may arrest without process.

SEC. 11. It shall be the duty of the Marshal and of each Deputy Marshal of the Police force, to abate all nuisances, to suppress all riots, disturbances and breaches of the peace, to apprehend and arrest without process, all persons who shall be found by them, or either of them, in the act of committing any offense against the laws of this State or the ordinances of this city, whenever such persons may be found within the limits of this city ; and, for the purpose of making such arrest, they may without process, enter any house or building into which any person may flee, who has in their presence, or in the presence of either of them, violated any law of this State, or any ordinance of this city. And it shall be their duty to enter any house or building from which any extraordinary noise, alarm or cry of distress may proceed ; and they may, and it shall be their duty to arrest any and all persons by them there found violating any law of this State or any ordinance of this city. And it shall be their duty, upon reasonable information, to procure process for the arrest of any person charged with a breach of the peace, or the violation of any ordinance of this city, and at all times faithfully and diligently to enforce all ordinances and regulations of the city.

Disposition of persons arrested.

SEC. 12. Whenever the Marshal, or any Deputy Marshal, shall arrest any person, under the authority given by section eleven (11) of this ordinance, he shall forthwith take the person so arrested before the Recorder or some Justice of the Peace, before whom he shall make the proper complaint against the person so arrested, and the Recorder, or such Justice of the Peace, shall thereupon proceed to hear and determine such case according to law: *Provided*, That when the arrest shall be made on Sunday, or in the night time, or the Recorder or no Justice can be found in his office, the officer making the arrest, shall convey the person arrested to the county jail, where he shall be safely kept by the keeper thereof, until he shall be taken away by the same or some other officers possessing like powers, or until such person shall have remained in jail twenty-four hours, or in case the imprisonment commenced on Sunday, then until four o'clock of Monday following. And it shall be the duty of the officer conveying any person to jail under the provisions of section eleven (11) of this ordinance, within twenty-four hours thereafter,—or in case such person was taken to jail on Sunday, or on Saturday afternoon previous to four o'clock of Monday following, to cause such person to be brought before the Recorder, or some Justice of the Peace of the city.

Special Deputy Marshals.

SEC. 13. The Marshal, when in his judgment the public interest may require it, with the consent and approval of the Mayor, may appoint not exceeding six special Deputy Marshals, whose appointments shall continue in force not more than three days at any one time, and whose pay shall not exceed three dollars per day, to be fixed in each case by the Council, after the service has been rendered, and whose powers and duties shall be the same as the Deputy Marshals appointed to serve on the regular Police force, but they shall not be required to furnish or wear the uniform prescribed by this ordinance.

SEC. 14. Any person who shall abuse, resist, oppose, or in any manner obstruct the Marshal, any Deputy Marshal, Special Deputy Marshal, or member of the Police force, while in the exercise of his duty, or who shall violate any provision of this ordinance, shall, upon conviction thereof, be punished by a fine not less than ten dollars, and not more than one hundred dollars, and the costs of prosecution ; and the Court before whom such conviction shall be had, may make a further sentence, that in default of the payment of such fine and costs, the person so convicted be imprisoned in the Saginaw County jail for a term not exceeding ninety days. **Penalty for resisting Police.**

SEC. 15. The Marshal and Mayor, with the approval of the Common Council, may appoint such number of Special Deputy Marshals to serve without pay from the city as the public interest may require, and such Special Deputy Marshals shall have the same power to serve process, and make arrest without process, as other Deputy Marshals appointed according to the provisions of this ordinance. **Special Deputy to serve without pay.**

SEC. 16. An ordinance entitled "An Ordinance relative to uniforming Policemen and Watchman, and regulating their duties in certain cases, as amended February 2d, 1869," adopted February 2d, 1869, and an ordinance entitled "An Ordinance relative to preventing the abuse, resisting and obstructing members of the Police force, while in the exercise of their duties," adopted February **Repeal.**

2d, 1869, are both hereby repealed ; and this ordinance shall take immediate effect.

Adopted May 20, 1875.

FRED H. POTTER, Mayor.

J. J. SWARTWOUT, Recorder.

[*Record Ordinance Book, page 176.*]

---

*An Ordinance relative to the letting of contracts by the Street Commissioner.*

*It is hereby ordained by the Common Council of the City of Saginaw :*

Sealed proposals for job work.

SECTION 1. All contracts for the doing of work on the streets, or for furnishing plank or other material therefor, hereafter let by the Street Commissioner, shall be let to the lowest responsible bidder, and shall be let only upon sealed proposals. When the Common Council shall order any work to be done upon the streets, the Street Commissioner shall advertise for sealed proposals, and all proposals shall be accompanied by security for the performance of the contract to be let.

Adopted May 20, 1875.

FRED H. POTTER, Mayor.

J. J. SWARTWOUT, Recorder.

[*Record Ordinance Book, page 192.*]

---

*An Ordinance to provide for the cleaning of certain streets.*

*It is hereby ordained by the Common Council of the City of Saginaw :*

Hamilton street to be cleaned.

SECTION 1. All persons owning or occupying any premises on Hamilton street, between Mackinaw street and Madison street, and on Court street, between Water street and Washington street, shall cause all dirt, and accumulation of matter of every kind, to be neatly scraped up in a pile, convenient for removal, in front of the premises owned or occupied by them, before twelve o'clock, at noon, on Friday of every week, from the time the frost is out of the ground in the spring, until the ground shall be frozen in the fall.

SEC. 2. It shall be the duty of the Street Commissioner, immediately after such dirt is placed in piles, to cause the same to be removed from the street. Duty of St. Commiss'r.

SEC. 3. Any person who shall be convicted of a violation of this ordinance, shall be punished by a fine of not less than five dollars, and not more than fifty dollars. Penalty.

SEC. 4. It shall be the duty of the City Marshal to see that this ordinance is obeyed, and to complain of any person found violating it. Duty of Marshal.

Adopted August 2, 1873.

BENTON HANCHETT, Mayor.

JOHN B. SCHICK, Recorder.

[*Record Ordinance Book, page 190.*]

---

*An Ordinance relative to the Fire Department of the City of Saginaw.*

*It is hereby ordained by the Common Council of the City of Saginaw, as follows:*

SECTION 1. That the Fire Department of the city shall consist of a Chief Engineer, a First Assistant Engineer, a Second Assistant Engineer, and as many fire engine, hose and hook and ladder companies as the Common Council shall from time to time prescribe, and the Fire Wardens of said city. Fire Department, how constituted.

Chief and Assistant Engineers, how appointed.

SEC. 2. The Chief and Assistant Engineers shall be appointed by the Common Council in the month of April in each year, and shall continue in office for one year, and until their successors are duly appointed and qualified. They shall take the oath of office prescribed by the Constitution of this State.

No. of men to a company.

SEC. 3. Each fire engine, hose, and hook and ladder company shall consist of not less than eight, nor more than fifty members, who shall be men of good moral character, over sixteen years of age, and residents of the city, and shall be appointed members of companies by the Chief Engineer, subject to the approval of the Common Council: *Provided*, That no person shall be appointed a member of any organized company, until he shall have been duly elected by such company a member thereof.

Who constitute firemen of city.

SEC. 4. The Engineers, Fire Wardens, and members of engine, hose, and hook and ladder companies, shall constitute and be the firemen of said city.

Companies may appoint Foreman.

SEC. 5. Each fire engine, hose, and hook and ladder company shall appoint from their own members a Foreman, First Assistant Foreman, and Second Assistant Foreman, and such other officers as they may by their own by-laws and rules prescribe.

Duty of Chief and Assistant Engineers on alarm of fire.

SEC. 6. The Chief and Assistant Engineers, upon an alarm of fire, shall immediately repair to the place where such fire is, and the Assistant Engineers shall report themselves to the Chief, and obey his orders. Any person wilfully violating the provisions of this section, shall be punished by a fine not to exceed fifty dollars, or by imprisonment not to exceed two months.

SEC. 7. The Chief Engineer shall have full charge of the Fire Department, and full power, command, and control over all persons whatever at fires within said city. He shall station the engines and apparatus of companies, and any person who shall disobey the lawful orders of the Chief Engineer or any other officer for the time being lawfully discharging the duties of Chief Engineer, or shall obstruct, hinder, resist or delay him or such other officer as aforesaid, in any manner whatever, in the performance of the duties prescribed for such Chief Engineer by this ordinance, shall be punished by a fine not to exceed one hundred dollars, or by imprisonment not to exceed three months.

Chief Engineer to have full charge of Fire Department.

Duties of. Penalty for resisting Chief Engineer.

SEC. 8. It shall be the duty of the Chief Engineer, at all fires, to direct all such measures as he may deem most advisable for the effectual extinguishment of said fires; and also once in each three months to examine the condition of the apparatus belonging to the Fire Department, and report the same to the Common Council, at least once in six months; and whenever any of said apparatus shall need repairs or need replacing, he shall report the same to the Common Council; and he shall also from time to time prescribe such rules and regulations for the government of the Fire Department as he may deem proper, and a copy of the rules and regulations so prescribed by him shall be filed with the Recorder, and the same shall be effectual and binding when approved by the Common Council; and any violation thereof shall be punished by a fine not exceeding twenty-five dollars. He shall also have power to suspend any fireman from duty, for cause; but such suspension and cause therefor shall be reported without delay to the Common Council. He shall divide the city into fire districts, and establish a system of fire signals.

Duties of Chief Engineer.

May prescribe rules for Department.

Copy of rules to be filed with Recorder.

May suspend firemen.

Badge of office.

SEC. 9. The Chief Engineer and Assistant Engineers, when on duty, shall wear some suitable hat, belt or badge, indicating their rank.

Who to act in absence of Chief Engineer.

SEC. 10. In case of the absence or sickness of the Chief Engineer, or in case of vacancy in said office, the First Assistant Engineer shall act as Chief Engineer, and in case of the absence, or sickness, or vacancy in office of both Chief and First Assistant Engineer, the Second Assistant Engineer shall act as Chief Engineer during such absence, sickness, or vacancy, and in case neither the Chief or any Assistant Engineer are present at a fire, the senior Foreman present at such fire shall act as Chief Engineer, and the person so acting as Chief Engineer shall be vested with all the authority of such Chief at such fire.

Duty of Fire Wardens.

SEC. 11. It shall be the duty of all Fire Wardens to be present at all fires, and under the direction of the Chief Warden to act as a fire guard, and as such fire guard to take possession and charge of all property removed from buildings at fires, and to deliver the same to the City Marshal, Deputy Marshal, or, in their absence, to a City Constable, to store or otherwise protect until the same shall be claimed by the owner or owners; and upon such claim, to deliver up the same to such owner upon payment to such Marshal of all expenses actually and necessarily incurred in and about the care and protection of such property. At every fire each Warden shall report himself to the Chief Warden, and be subject to his direction.

Duty of Fire Companies on alarm of fire.

SEC. 12. There shall be assigned to each fire engine company, and hose, and hook and ladder companies, such engines, machines, and apparatus as the Common Council may deem necessary for the extinguishment of fires; and it shall be the duty of each of said companies, as often as any fire shall break out within said city, to repair, immediately upon the alarm thereof, to their respective engines, machines and apparatus, and convey them to or near the place where such fire shall happen, and then, in conformity to the directions given them by the Chief or an Assistant Engineer, they shall work and manage their said engines and apparatus with all their skill and power; and when the fire is extinguished they shall not remove therefrom until directed by the Chief or an Assistant Engineer, when they shall return with their respective engines and apparatus to their several places of deposit, unless otherwise ordered. Companies, when the season of the year will permit, shall, by order of the Chief Engineer, bring out their hose carts, trucks, or other fire apparatus for work, exercise and inspection; and if any fireman shall neglect said duty, or shall willfully neglect to attend at any fire as aforesaid, or leave his post of duty, while at any fire, without permission, or not perform his duty on such occasion without reasonable excuse, he shall be punished by a fine not to exceed twenty-five dollars, or by imprisonment not exceeding thirty days.

**Companies to be exercised.**

SEC. 13. Whenever any person shall be appointed as a fireman, it shall be his duty to procure from the Recorder a certificate within one month from the date of his appointment, specifying the name and number of the company to which he has been appointed, and if he has neglected to procure such certificate, within one month from the date of his appointment, such appontment shall be null and void. And it shall be the duty of each company to report on the first Monday of January in

**Firemen to procure certificate.**

each year, and oftener, if required, the names of their members to the Common Council.

Resistance of officer at fire, punished, how.

SEC. 14. All persons who, at a fire, shall refuse to obey any order or direction given by a person duly authorized to order or direct, or who shall resist or impede any officer or other person in the discharge of his duty shall, in the absence of sufficient excuse, be punished by a fine not exceeding fifty dollars, or by imprisonment not exceeding two months. The Chief or an Assistant Engineer, or any Fire Warden, Foreman or Assistant Foreman of any engine, hose, or hook and ladder company may arrest any such person and deliver him into the custody of the Marshal or any Constable of said city, who shall, as soon as may be, and within twenty-four hours thereafter, convey him before the Recorder or some Justice of the Peace of said city, and such Justice or Recorder shall thereupon, after notice to the person making such arrest, and to the City Attorney, proceed to hear the complaint of the person making such arrest, and the plea of the accused, and to try and determine such cause.

Foreman and others may require assistance.

SEC. 15. It shall be lawful for the Foreman or Assistant Foreman of any engine, hose, or hook and ladder company, or of any member of the Common Council, Chief or an Assistant Engineer, or any Fire Warden, to require the aid of any citizen or individual in drawing an engine or other apparatus to a fire, or the aid of any bystander at a fire to work any engine or apparatus at the same, or perform any other duty or work which may be deemed necessary for the effectual extinguishment of said fire; and, on neglect or refusal to comply with such requisition, the offender shall be punished by a fine not exceeding twenty dollars, or by imprisonment not exceeding twenty days, unless some sufficient cause for such refusal or neglect is alleged at the time and made to appear upon the trial; and any such person may be arrested and proceeded with as is provided by the last preceding section of this ordinance.

Penalty for refusing to assist at fire Duty of Marshal, &c., on alarm of fire.

SEC. 16. The Marshal and every Constable of said city, and such Deputy Marshals or Policemen of said city, as shall be detailed by the Marshal for that purpose, shall, on an alarm of fire, repair immediately to the place where the fire may be, and preserve the public peace, and protect and take charge of property in the vicinity of the fire; and shall, when directed by the Chief Engineer, prevent the access of any person to the immediate vicinity of the fire, except firemen, members of the Common Council, and such other persons as the Chief Engineer or Chief Fire Warden may direct; and for any neglect to comply with the provisions of this section, the person so neglecting shall be punished by a fine not exceeding fifty dollars, and shall be subject to removal from office.

Duty of Marshal, on alarm of fire, &c.

SEC. 17. The hook and ladder and axe men at a fire shall, under the direction of the Chief Engineer, or person acting as such, with the Mayor, or in his absence, an Alderman of said city, cut down and remove any building, structure or material for the purpose of checking the progress of the fire.

When buildings may be removed, &c.

SEC. 18. No fire engine, hose cart, hook and ladder wagon, or truck, or other apparatus belonging to said city, or owned therein by the Fire Department, shall be conveyed or removed beyond the limits of said city without the consent of the Chief Engineer or Common Council, and any person or persons who shall remove, or

Apparatus of Fire Department, not to go out of city.

attempt to remove, the same without such permission, shall be punished by a fine not exceeding fifty dollars, or by imprisonment not exceeding sixty days.

SEC. 19. An ordinance entitled "An ordinance in relation to the Fire Department of the City of Saginaw," approved August 21, 1863, and the amendments thereto, are hereby repealed.

Adopted May 20, 1875.

FRED H. POTTER, Mayor.

J. J. SWARTWOUT, Recorder.

[*Record Ordinance Book, page 184.*]

---

*An Ordinance relative to special assessments and collection thereof.*

*It is hereby ordained by the Common Council of the City of Saginaw, as follows:*

Expense of grading, paving and planking streets and sidewalks, how assessed.

SECTION 1. Whenever the Common Council shall have caused any street, lane or alley to be made, paved, planked, graveled or lighted, or caused the grading, paving or planking of any sidewalk, or making of any drain, sewer or other local improvement, or shall have directed said work to be done, the Comptroller of said city, when so directed by said Common Council, shall make an assessment against the owners or occupants of the lots or premises which are in front of, or adjoining such work or improvement, and against any other lots or premises which in his opinion are benefited thereby.

[*Record Ordinance Book, page 124.*]

Comptroller to make out and report to the Council, assessment roll.

SEC. 2. The said Controller shall make out a written report and an assessment roll connected therewith, showing the names of the owners or occupants of the lots or premises liable to be assessed for such work or improvement, describing such lots or premises ; and when the same are unoccupied, and the names of the owner or owners are unknown to said Comptroller, the fact thereof shall be stated in said assessment roll, by being mentioned and described therein as "non-resident." Said Comptroller shall also ascertain, and in his assessment roll state, as near as may be, the sum of money that each such owner or occupant, and each of such lots or premises should, in his judgment, be assessed for such work or improvement, which report and assessment roll said Comptroller shall present to the Common Council.

Contents of such roll.

[*Record Ordinance Book, page 124.*]

SEC. 3. The said Comptroller shall then cause to be published, in a newspaper printed and published in said city, once in each week, for two successive weeks, a notice containing a description of such work or improvement, and the names of the owners or occupants of the lots or premises to be assessed, and pay for the expense thereof, so far as such names appear in said assessment roll, warning them that they are about to be assessed to defray the expense of such work or improvement, and that an assessment roll is on file in the office of the Comptroller of said city for inspection, and that at a certain time and place, to be mentioned in said notice, the Common Council will meet and review said assessment roll, on the request of any person conceiving himself aggrieved.

Notice of assessment to be published.

Contents of notice.

[*Record Ordinance Book, page 125.*]

SEC. 4. The Common Council shall, at the time and place in said notice specified, or at some session thereafter to which they may adjourn, take said assessment roll into consideration, and if no person appears to object to the same, and no good cause to the contrary

Common Council to take assessment roll into consideration.

Affidavit of publication to be presented to the Council. Council to approve of assessment.

appears and an affidavit of the publication of the requisite notice having been made and presented to said Common Council, they shall, by resolution to be entered upon ther journal, declare that they approve of said assessment roll; that the lots and premises described in said roll, as benefited by such work or improvement, are, in the opinion of said Common Council, actually benefited thereby; that they receive as correct the description of the lots or premises, and the names of the owners or occupants therein contained; and that the sum stated in said assessment roll which each such owner or occupant should be assessed and pay, be assessed and collected from such owner or occupant according to law. But if any sufficient reason appear or be shown to said Common Council, they shall review said assessment roll, and make such an assessment as shall be just and right in the premises; and they may, if necessary, adjourn from time to time for the purpose of finishing said review of said assessment roll.

Resolution of approval. Contents of.

Council may review assessment roll, and may make a new one.

[*Record Ordinance Book, page 125.*]

Mistakes, certain not to invalidate assessment roll.

SEC. 5. Whenever, by mistake or otherwise, any person may be improperly designated as the owner or occupant of any lot, block or premises in proceedings under this ordinance, or any other ordinance of said city relative to taxes or assessments, the tax or asssessment shall not for such cause be vitiated, but the same shall be a lien on such lot, block or premises, and shall be collected as in other cases.

Sidewalks to be repaired by owner of lot.

SEC. 6. Whenever any paved or planked sidewalk within said city shall require repairing, the Street Commissioner shall notify the owner of the lot, block or premises in front of which such sidewalk requires repairing, forthwith to repair the same; and if such owner or occupant neglect for the space of two days after being served with such notice to proceed with all due diligence to make the necessary repairs, it shall be the duty of the Street Commissioner to cause such repairs to be made, and the expense thereof shall stand as an assessment against such owner or occupant, and shall be collected in the manner provided for in the collection of special assessments: *Provided,* That if such owner be a non-resident, or unknown, such notice shall be published, once a week, for two successive weeks, in a newspaper published in said city.

Refusal to repair, how dealt with.

Commiss'er, when to repair; cost of repair, how collected.

Notice to non-residents to be published.

SEC. 7. All expenses of special assessments, ordered by the Common Council, together with the expense of printing notices, and all other charges relative to such assessments, and the collection thereof, together with the Treasurer's fees, shall be justly apportioned to the persons and property liable to pay such assessments, and shall be collected at the same time and in the same manner.

Expenses of assessment, how collected.

[*Record Ordinance Book, page 125.*]

SEC. 8. Whenever any special tax or assessment shall have been laid or imposed by authority of the Common Council of said city, the Comptroller shall issue a warrant under his hand and the seal of said city, directed to the Treasurer of said city, commanding such Treasurer to collect from the several persons named in the tax or assessment roll, to which said warrant shall be annexed, the several sums mentioned in the last column of said roll, opposite their respective names; and in case any person or persons named in said roll shall neglect or refuse to pay his, her, or their tax, to levy the same, together with said fees, by distress, and the sale of the goods and chattels of such person or persons, and fur-

Warrant for collection of roll, issued by Comptroller.

Comptroller's warrant, contents of; to be annexed to roll.

ther commanding said Treasurer to make returns to the Common Council within sixty days, of his doings thereon, and shall deliver said assessment roll and said warrant so annexed thereto, to said Treasurer, and shall charge said Treasurer with the amount of said tax or assessment mentioned in said assessment roll.

Comptroller to deliver warrant and roll to Treasurer, and charge him with the amount thereof.

[*Record Ordinance Book, page 126.*]

Treasurer to collect assessment on such roll.

SEC. 9. On receiving said assessment roll with the warrant thereto annexed, said Treasurer shall proceed to collect the assessments therein mentioned, and in case any person shall refuse or neglect to pay the assessment against him, to levy the same by distress and sale of the goods and chattels of said persons, wherever the same may be found within said city. Said Treasurer shall give public notice of the time and place of sale, and of the property to be sold, at least five days previous to the sale, by advertisement to be posted up in three public places in said city, and the sale shall be by public auction; and any surplus, after deducting the amount of said assessment and all costs and charges from the proceeds of such sale, shall be paid over to the person entitled thereto. Said Treasurer shall be entitled to two cents on the dollar, on the amount of the assessment collected; and in the case of a levy upon and sale of property for the satisfaction of the assessment, he shall, for his services in each such case of levy and sale, be entitled to one dollar and twenty-five cents, to be retained out of the proceeds of such sale.

May levy upon goods and chattels.

Notice of sale to be given. Contents of such notice.

Notices, how posted up.

Sale, how made.

Proceeds of property sold, how disposed of.

Treasurer's fees.

[*Record Ordinance Book, page 126.*]

Treasurer to return roll, when.

SEC. 10. The Treasurer shall make returns of his doings within the time mentioned in said warrant, to the Common Council if in session, and if not, then at their next meeting. If any person or persons against whom or upon whose lands and premises any such assessment may have been made, are non-residents of such city, or unknown, or if goods and chattels of any such person or persons can not be found, and the tax or assessment remains unpaid, the Treasurer shall state such fact verified by affidavit, and annex the same to a list of such land on which the taxes or assessments have not been paid, and the Recorder, under the direction of the Common Council, shall give to the Treasurer such credit as may be just.

Treasurer's return, contents of.

Return to be sworn to.

Delinquent list.

SEC. 11. Said warrant may be renewed from time to time, if the Common Council shall so direct, not to exceed sixty days in all.

Warrant may be renewed.

SEC. 12. If the special assessments on any real estate shall be returned as aforesaid, unpaid, any person may pay the tax on any part or undivided interest in such lands or premises, with interest calculated thereon, from the date of the return thereof to said Recorder, at the rate of fifteen per cent. per annum, and the sum of twenty-five cents on each certificate containing one description, and for each additional description in the same certificate, six cents for office charges to the Recorder aforesaid, for his use at any time before they are sold for taxes The said Recorder shall issue duplicate receipts for all taxes received by him, which shall not operate as a discharge until countersigned by the Mayor of said city, and one of said duplicates shall be left with such Mayor, but no additional charge shall be made for issuing duplicate receipts.

Delinquent assessments may be paid to the Recorder.

Interest on renewed assessments.

Recorder's fees.

Recorder to give duplicate receipts.

Receipts to be countersigned by Mayor.

One receipt to be left with Mayor.

SEC. 13. All land returned to the Recorder, as provided in this ordinance, upon which the taxes, interest and charges shall not be paid, shall be subject to sale and resumption as hereinafter provided.

Returned lands subject to sale.

Recorder to make a statement of returned lands.

SEC. 14. If any special assessment, or assessments and the interest thereon after being returned to said Recorder as herein aforesaid, shall remain due and unpaid for the period of two days next succeeding the time of said return to said Recorder, it shall be the duty of said Recorder to make out a statement of all such land as the assessment aforesaid shall remain due upon; specifying the amount due on each parcel, the interest thereon up to the day appointed for the sale of said land, at the rate of interest aforesaid and the office charges, together with the cost of advertising, expenses of sale and conveyances, calculated upon each description by dividing such charges by the whole number of descriptions. Preceding such statement the Recorder shall cause to be published in said city, for eight weeks successively after the same shall have been made out, in a newspaper printed and published in said city, and shall also post three printed copies of said statement in three public places within the limits of said city, for at least two weeks preceding the time of sale in said notice mentioned.

Recorder's statement, contents of.

Statement to be published before sale eight weeks.

Statement to be posted in three places two weeks.

Cost of printing and advertising.

SEC. 15. The cost of printing and publishing said statement shall not exceed forty cents for each description of land so advertised., and no printer shall be paid for publishing any such statement who shall not present to the Recorder, within three days after the last publication thereof, an affidavit of the publication therof, for the term as required herein.

Notice to be published with statement.

Contents of notice.

SEC. 16. The Recorder shall annex to, and cause to be published with each of said statements, a notice that so much of each tract or parcel of land described in said statement as will be necessary for that purpose, will be sold by him at the expiration of three months from the date thereof, at the office of the Recorder, in said city, at an hour therein to be designated, for the payment of special assessments, interest, and charges thereon.

SEC. 17. On the day designated in the notice of sale, the Recorder shall commence the sale of those lands on which the special assessments have not been paid as aforesaid, and shall continue the sale from day to day (Sundays excepted) until so much of each parcel thereof shall be sold as shall be sufficient to pay the taxes, interest, and charges thereon: *Provided*, That every description of land embraced in said notice, which has been bid off to the city at a previous sale, and which remains unredeemed or otherwise undisposed of, shall be bid off to the city by said Recorder.

Sales, when to commence.

Sale to be continued, how long.

SEC. 18. In case less than the whole of any parcel described in the statement aforesaid shall be sold for the assessments, interest, and charges thereon, the portion thereof sold shall be taken from the easterly end or side of such parcel, and shall be bounded on the westerly side by a line running parallel with the easterly line thereof, unless the same shall be an irregular fraction, in which case the portion thereof so sold shall be bounded on the west side by a line running due north and south.

When part of lot sold, where to be taken.

SEC. 19. The Recorder may, in his discretion, require immediate payment of any person to whom any parcel of such land shall be struck off, and in all cases when payment is not made in twenty-four hours, he may declare the bid cancelled, and at his discretion sell the land again.

Payment of bids, when to be made.

SEC. 20. At any such sale if any parcel so offered shall not be purchased by any person or persons at said sale, the same shall be bid off by said Recorder for and

Recorder may bid in lands for city, when.

in the corporate name of said city, and all land so bid off by the said city shall be offered at the sale next succeeding the sale at which the same was so struck off to said city, unless the same shall have been redeemed or purchased according to the provisions of this ordinance: *Provided*, That no land bid off for and in the name of said city, shall be offered at public sale until the expiration of one year from the date of said purchase by said city.

Proviso as to lands bid in by the city.

Certificate of sale to be given, and copy to be filed in Recorder's office.

SEC. 21. At the sale aforesaid, the Recorder shall give to the purchasers, on the payment of their bids, a certificate in writing, describing the land purchased and amount paid therefor, and such certificates shall be regularly numbered, and a duplicate copy of each filed in the office of said Recorder.

Redempti'n of lands sold, by whom, and how made.

SEC. 22. Any person claiming any lands sold as aforesaid, or any interest therein, may, at any time within one year next succeeding the sale, redeem any parcels of said lands, or any interest therein, by paying to the Recorder the amount for which such parcel was sold, or such portion thereof as the part or interest redeemed shall amount to, with interest thereon at the rate of twenty-five per cent. per annum, of which interest fifteen per cent. shall be paid by the Recorder to the purchaser, and ten per cent. shall belong to the city, and shall, by the Recorder, be paid over to the Treasurer of the city, and the Recorder shall take his receipt therefor, which he shall deliver to the Comptroller, who shall charge the Treasurer with the sum so paid to him by the Recorder.

Interest on lands redeemed, and how applied

[*Record Ordinance Book, page 197.*]

Interest, how computed.

SEC. 23. When any land shall be redeemed as provided in the preceding section, the interest shall in all cases be computed from the day of sale up to the end of the current quarter of the year directed for such redemption.

SEC. 24. On presentation to the Recorder of such certificate of sale as provided in section twenty-one (21) herein, after the expiration of one year from the date of such certificate, said Recorder shall execute to the purchaser, his heirs and assignees, a deed of the land in such certificate described, unless he shall have discovered that the taxes for which said land was sold had been paid according to law, and in such cases he shall, on demand of the person holding said certificate, cause the money paid therefor to be refunded, with seven per cent. interest thereon from the date of such certificate, which deed shall be *prima facie* evidence of the regularity of all the proceedings to the date of the deed inclusive, and of title in fee in the purchaser; and every such deed, when witnessed and acknowledged in the manner prescribed by law for witnessing and acknowledging deeds in other cases, and after it shall have been on record two years, in the office of the Register of Deeds, in the county of Saginaw, shall except:

Deed, when and how executed.

When Recorder may withhold deed.

Effect of Deed.

1st. When the land sold was not subject to taxation at the date of the assessment of the taxes for which it was sold;

Exceptions.

2d. When the taxes have been paid to the proper officers within the times limited by law for the payment of redemption thereof; or,

3d. When a certificate that no taxes were charged against the land, has been given by the proper officers within the time limited by the law for the payment

What deed evidence of. thereof—be positive evidence that the lands described were by such deed conveyed in fee simple to the grantee therein named, and his heirs and assigns; and no suit of ejectment shall be commenced to recover said land or title thereto, or be sustained thereafter by any person alarming, holding possession or title through any other source.

Lands unredeemed subject to taxation. SEC. 25. All such lands remaining unredeemed, except such descriptions as the city may have a title to, for the tax or taxes for another year or years, shall be subject to sale at any time, at the office of the Recorder; and upon the payment thereof to the Recorder of the amount for which such lands were bid off, with interest at the rate of twenty-five per cent. per annum, to be computed from the day upon which said lands were bid off to the city, to the time of such application, the Recorder shall issue to the purchaser a certificate of purchase.

[*Record Ordinance Book, page 197.*]

Purchaser of redeemed lands entitled to am't of bid and interest. SEC. 26. If such lands shall be redeemed, the purchaser shall be entitled to the amount bid by the city, with twenty-five per cent interest, as contemplated and provided for in section twenty-two of this ordinance: Proviso. *Provided*, That the sum refunded to the purchaser shall in no event be less than the sum paid by him upon Deed to purchaser. such purchase. But if such lands are not redeemed in accordance with the provisions of this ordinance, the Recorder shall, on the surrender of such certificate of purchase, execute to the purchaser a deed for the lands therein described, which deed shall have the same effect, in all respects, as is provided in section twenty-four of this ordinance.

[*Record Ordinance Book, page 127.*]

SEC. 27. Any description of land bid off to the city, at any sales under the provisions of this ordinance, which shall have remained undisposed of for five years from the date when it was so bid off, shall vest in the city an absolute title in fee simple. Five-year lands, when title to vest in city.

SEC. 28. The Recorder shall render to the Common Council, within fifteen days after any sale of lands as herein provided, or as soon thereafter as said Common Council may convene, a statement of all proceedings had by him under and by virtue of this ordinance, in detail, showing the description of the lands sold, the amount for which each parcel shall have been sold, the names of the purchasers at such sale, the amount of money received by him at such sale, or for redemptions or payments, together with a description of the property sold, which statement shall be verified by the affidavit of said Recorder. Recorder to render statement to Common Council of lands sold, &c. Contents of statement.

SEC. 29. All money received by the Recorder from sales made by virtue of the provisions of this ordinance, less his fees for office charges as herein provided for, shall, on the first Monday of each month, be paid over by the Recorder to the City Treasurer of said city, and the Recorder shall take his receipt therefor, and deliver the same forthwith to the Comptroller, who shall at once charge the Treasurer with the amounts thus paid to him. Proceeds from lands sold to be paid to Treasurer. Recorder to take receipt therefor. Comptroller's duty.

[*Record Ordinance Book, page 198.*]

SEC. 30. All lands bid off to the city, as provided in section twenty herein, shall continue liable to be taxed in the same manner as if they were not the property of the city, and such taxes shall be a charge upon such land. Lands bid off to city still liable to be taxed.

Repealing section.

SEC. 31. All ordinances or parts of ordinances heretofore passed, contravening the provisions of this ordinance, be and the same are hereby repealed.

Adopted April 26, 1865.

STEWART B. WILLIAMS, Mayor.

A. F. R. BRALEY, Recorder.

[*Record Ordinance Book, page 24.*]

---

*An Ordinance regulating water rates and the use of water from the City Water Works, and the assessment and collection af such water rates, and providing for the care and protection of the Water Works.*

*It is hereby ordained by the Common Council of the City of Saginaw:*

Rates for water.

SECTION 1. All persons using using water from the City Water Works, shall pay therefor at the following rates, viz:

Dwelling houses.

Dwelling houses with six rooms or less, and only occupied by one family, and using one faucet, five dollars ($5) per annum—each additional faucet, one dollar ($1)—and each additional room occupied by the family, one dollar ($1). All tenement houses, occupied by more than one family, to pay the same rates as above, for each family, faucet and room.

Hotels.

Hotels and boarding-houses, five dollars per annum, and one dollar in addition thereto, for each room therein.

Saloons and stores.

Saloons, grocery and provision stores, each, five dollars per annum.

Bathing.

Bathing apparatus for family use, three dollars per annum, and for the use of guests and boarders, at a hotel or boarding-house, ten dollars per annum. Public bathing tubs, ten dollars per annum.

Water closets for family use, three dollars per annum; water closets in public houses, six dollars per annum for each bowl therein. Urinals, five dollars per annum, each. Water closets.

Steam engines to be assessed. Engines.

Private stables for one horse or for one cow, and including the use of water for washing carriages, three dollars per annum, and for each additional horse or cow, one dollar. Livery stables, including water for washing carriages, one dollar and fifty cents per annum, for each stall therein—double stalls to be counted as two stalls, or they may be assessed. Hotel stables, each stall one dollar and fifty cents per annum, including the use of water for washing carriages. Stables.

Street sprinklers—For each cart, wagon or team employed thereon, fifty cents per day. Sprinklers.

Butcher's stalls, ten to fifteen dollars per annum. Butchers.

Fountains—One 1-16 inch jet, six dollars per annum, and each additional 1-16 inch jet, three dollars per annum, and larger jets to be subject to special assessment; and all fountains playing more than eight hours per day, shall be subject to special assessment in addition to the above rates. Fountains.

Blacksmith shops—One forge, five dollars per annum, and each additional forge, two dollars per annum. Blacksmith.

Mills and manufactories, to be assessed. Mills.

Stone work, three cents per perch. Stone work.

Brick laying, ten cents per thousand. Brick work.

Plastering, one hundred yards, twenty cents. Plastering.

Garden hose and street washers, five to fifteen dollars per annum. Garden hose

Barber shop

Barber shops, five dollars per annum for one chair, and for each additional chair, one dollar.

Private hydrants.

Private hydrants, for fire protection, and used for no other purpose, no charge.

Other purposes.

Water used for other purposes to be paid for as follows: 1,000 gallons or less, four cents per 100 gallons; 1,000 to 5,000 gallons, three cents per 100 gallons; 5,000 to 10,000 gallons, two cents per 100 gallons; over 10,000 gallons, one and a half cents per 100 gallons.

Consumers must consent to rules and regulations.

SEC. 2. All persons using water from the City Water Works, under a permit from the proper authority, shall consent to and be bound by the following rules and regulations:

1st. The Water Commissioners, and all officers appointed by, and all persons employed by the Board of Water Commissioners, when directed by the Board, to have free access, at all reasonable hours, to all houses and premises where water is used.

2d. Hydrants, plugs, stop boxes, hose and all other attachments and fixtures, must be kept in complete repair by the owner or occupant of the premises where located or used.

3d. In no case will hose be allowed for the purpose of sprinkling sidewalks, gardens, or lawns, or washing carriages or other vehicles, with outflows or nozzles larger than one-fourth of one inch in diameter.

4th. Persons using water are absolutely prohibited from allowing any leakage or waste thereof.

5th. The unnecessary flow of water, while washing sidewalks, or using water for any other purpose, is prohibited.

6th. No person, without a written permit from the proper officer, shall be allowed to turn any public or private stop cock.

7th. All service pipe must be laid at least four feet below the surface of the ground, and all pipe outside the public stop, must be extra strong, as designated.

8th. In all cases where more than one family or other consumer is supplied from a pipe or pipes governed by one stop, some one person must become responsible for the payment of all bills, and for the keeping in good repair of all pipes, hydrants and other fixtures or apparatus.

9th. Cisterns located on premises where there is no hydrant, must not be filled from the hydrants in any case without special permit, of the proper officer, in writing.

10th. When hydrants are so located as to be exposed to use by non-renting consumers, the parties renting such hydrants will be held responsible for such use, and will be charged additional rates.

11th. Upon the return of a bill to the office for non-payment, the water shall be immediately shut off, and it shall not be turned on again until the bill due is paid ; and where the ferrule is withdrawn, five dollars additional will be charged for resetting the ferrule.

12th. No owner or occupant of any building in which water is introduced, will be allowed to supply other persons or families, and if found doing so the supply will be stopped.

13th. When two or more persons shall be supplied from one pipe connecting with the distributing main, on the failure on the part of one of said parties to comply with the rules and regulations contained in this section, the Superintendent shall withhold the supply of water from such main without any liability whatever, and all payments made shall be forfeited.

14th. No addition or alteration whatever in or about any pipe or water cock shall be made, or caused to be made by persons taking water, without permission therefor, in writing, from the Superintendent.

15th. All persons taking water shall keep their service pipe, stop cocks, and all apparatus connected therewith, protected from frost, at their own expense. And it is expressly stipulated that no claim shall be made against the city for, or by reason of the breaking of any public or private pipe or cock, valve or hydrant.

16th. No hydrant shall be permitted on the sidewalk, nor to be kept running when not in actual use; and taps at wash-basins, wash-closests, baths, urinals and other places, must be kept closed in like manner.

17th. Persons using water, must at all times frankly and without evasion or concealment, answer all questions of the Superintendent, relative to the use and consumption of water.

18th. In case of any fraudulent representation or misstatement on the part of the applicant, in his application, or of any use of the water not embraced in his application, or of any wilful or unreasonable waste of the water, the Superintendent shall have the right to forfeit the payments made, and to cut of the supply of the water unless the party shall promptly pay such additional charges as the Superintendent may impose.

Fine for violation of rules.

SEC. 3. Any person who shall violate any, or either of the rules and regulations mentioned in section two of this ordinance, shall, on conviction thereof in addition to the forfeitures and liabilities therein contained, be punished by a fine of not less than five dollars, and not more than fifty dollars, and the costs of prosecution.

SEC. 4. All water rates are to be due and payable half yearly in advance, as follows: On the first Monday of March and September of each year. All payments of water rates must be made to the City Treasurer, and if not paid during the first month of the half year, five per cent shall be added thereto, and if not paid during the second month of the half year, ten per cent. shall be added thereto. After a water rate shall remain due and unpaid for two months, the Superintendent shall collect the same, and shall add ten per cent. thereto for his fees. And any person who shall refuse on demand to pay the water rate that may be due from him, he shall have his supply of water shut off, and it shall be the duty of the Superintendent at once to cut the same off, and he shall not thereafter be allowed to receive water until all arrearages are paid. **Water rates when due.**

[*Record Ordinance Book, page 168.*]

SEC. 5. No person shall in any manner obstruct the access to stop cock, valve or hydrant connected with any water pipe, in any street, alley or public place, within the city, by means of any wood, lumber, brick, stone or other articles, or thing whatever. **Obstruction of valves.**

SEC. 6. No person (other than the members of the Fire Department of the city, for the uses and purposes of said Department, and those especially authorized by the Board of Water Commissioners or the Chief Engineer of the Fire Department,) shall open, or attempt to open, any hydrant, or draw, or attempt in any way to draw **Who may open hydrants.**

water from the same, or in any manner interfere with any of said hydrants.

Injuring hydrant.

SEC. 7. No person shall wilfully or carelessly break or injure any public hydrant, or faucet, or waste the water at any such hydrant.

Wrenches not to be taken from hose house, when.

SEC. 8. No member of the Fire Department shall let, suffer or permit any person to take wrenches, furnished the hose companies, to be used by said companies in case of fire, away from the hose house of the company to which such wrenches are furnished, except as such wrenches accompany the hose carriages, on occasion of fire, or alarm of fire, or for other proper purposes of the Fire Department.

Violations of 5th, 6th, 7th, and 8th sections, fine for.

SEC. 9. Any person who shall violate any of the provisions of the fifth, sixth, seventh and eighth sections of this ordinance, shall, on conviction thereof, be punished by a fine of not less than five dollars, and not more than one hundred dollars, and costs of prosecution; and the Court imposing such fine, shall make a further sentence that the person so convicted be imprisoned in the Saginaw County jail until such fine and costs are paid: *Provided*, such imprisonment shall not exceed ninety days.

Public hydrants.

SEC. 10. All hydrants heretofore constructed, placed or located, or that may hereafter be constructed, placed or located by the Board of Water Commissioners, for the purpose of extinguishing fires in this city, are hereby declared to be public hydrants.

Water shut off, not to be let on when.

SEC. 11. Any person, from whose premises the water shall have been shut off for non-payment of his water rates, or for any violation of any provision of section two of this ordinance, who shall let or in any manner use the water from or through the pipes entering his house or upon his premises, without authority from the Superintendent, shall, on conviction thereof, be fined not less than five dollars, and not more than twenty-five dollars, for each and every offense, and costs of prosecution; and the Court before whom such conviction may be had, may in lieu of such fine and costs, sentence the person so convicted, to the Saginaw County jail for a period of not less than ten days and not more than ninety days.

SEC. 12. The Street Commissioner shall act as Superintendent of the Water Works, and, in his capacity of such Superintendent, he shall act under the direction of the Board of Water Commissioners. Superintendent.

[*Record Ordinance Book, page 171.*]

SEC. 13. All applications for a permit to use water from the Water Works, shall be made in writing, upon a book to be kept by the Comptroller for that purpose, and shall state fully where and for what purpose the applicant desires the water; and such application shall be signed by the applicant, and shall contain stipulation waiving any claim against the city for or on account of any damages that may result from or be caused by any defective hydrant, pipe, valve, stop cock, or any other apparatus or thing connected with the Water Works and used in the introduction of water to his premises; and the owner of the premises where it is proposed to introduce the water, shall consent in writing to the introduction of the water, and to all the conditions of such application. Applications, how made, contents of. Stipulations in applications.

[*Record Ordinance Book, page 171.*]

Duty of Superintendent on application.

SEC. 14. On receiving notice of such application, the Superintendent shall forthwith proceed to examine the premises named in the application, and, no objection appearing thereto, he shall join with the Comptroller in issuing to the applicant a permit to use the water according to the terms of the application. The Superintendent shall make, or cause to be made, the necessary connections with the public pipes ; and all the work of trenching and laying the pipe, and the connection thereof with the public pipe, shall be done under the immediate inspection and subject to the direction of the Superintendent ; and all such work shall be done at the cost of the applicant, and the city shall not in any event be liable to pay therefor.

Permit, who to issue.

Connections by whom made

Cost of connections, how paid.

[*Record Ordinance Book, page 171.*]

Applicati'ns to be preserved.

SEC. 15. All applications for water shall be carefully preserved by the Comptroller, in his office, and he shall keep a full record of all permits issued, and a record of all permits revoked, or withdrawn by order of the Board of Water Commissioners, which last record shall state fully the cause of such revocation or withdrawal ; and the Board shall have power to revoke or withdraw any permit for a violation of any provision of the rules and regulations contained in this ordinance.

Permits, records of and of withdrawal.

[*Record Ordinance Book, page 172.*]

Plumbers must be licensed.

SEC. 16. No person shall be employed or allowed to make any connection with the public pipes of the Water Works, or do any work of a plumber thereabout, unless he shall be duly licensed by the Board of Water Commissioners ; and the charges and fees of plumbers for their work shall be fixed by the said Board.

Treasurer to be notified of permits issued.

SEC. 17. When a permit is issued to any person to use water, the Comptroller shall forthwith notify the

City Treasurer thereof. If the amount due thereof shall remain unpaid for one month, the Treasurer shall immediately thereafter give the Comptroller and Superintendent notice thereof; and if the same shall not be paid on demand of the Superintendent, he shall at once cut off the supply of water from such delinquent, and the Board shall thereupon revoke and withdraw such person's permit to use water. [*Record Ordinance Book, page 172.*]

When water may be cut off for non-payment of water rates.

Adopted August 21, 1873.

BENTON HANCHETT, Mayor.

JOHN B. SCHICK, Recorder.

[*Record Ordinance Book, page 161.*]

# INDEX TO THE CHARTER.


| | Page. | Sec. |
|---|---|---|
| ACCOUNTS—Council may endorse amount due on | 37 | 28 |
| must be verified by oath | 40 | 40 |
| must set forth details thereof, | 40 | 40 |
| ALDERMEN—when and how elected, | 9 | 5 |
| to be inspectors of election, annual, city, state and county, | 10 | 6 |
| duty of to attend all meetings of the council, | 39 | 37 |
| to act on committees, &c., | 39 | 37 |
| may order arrest of persons violating the laws, | 40 | 37 |
| ALLEYS—council may lay out and vacate, | 27 | 15 |
| proceedings to vacate, | 28 | 15 |
| ANNUAL ELECTION—when and where held, | 10 | 6 |
| notice of | 10 | 6 |
| duties of ward inspectors, | 10 | 6 |
| APPEAL—from award of damages, | 29 | 15 |
| when and how made, | 29 | 15 |
| costs on appeal, when not to be recovered, | 30 | 15 |
| person convicted of offences may appeal, | 49 | 60 |
| APPOINTMENTS—of city officers, | 13 | 8 |
| to office, how made. | 31 | 17 |
| ANNUAL STATEMENT—when to be made, | 37 | 29 |
| to be signed by mayor and recorder, | 37 | 29 |
| copy to be published in newspaper, | 37 | 29 |
| ARRESTS—may be ordered by aldermen, | 40 | 37 |

| | Page. | Sec. |
|---|---|---|
| ASSESSMENTS—annual, when and how made, | 40 | 39 |
| council may provide by ordinance for collection of | 36 | 27 |
| invalid, special, may be reassessed, | 32 | 20 |
| for improvements, how made, | 31 | 20 |
| how collected, | 32 | 20 |
| interest on such assessment, | 32 | 20 |
| lien on real estate for | 32 | 20 |
| only to be ordered by majority of all aldermen elect | 31 | 17 |
| ASSESSMENT ROLL—when to be completed, | 41 | 42 |
| to be delivered to board of review, | 42 | 44 |
| ASSESSOR—of the city, | 40 | 41 |
| ATTORNEY—to be appointed by council, | 13 | 8 |
| to be member of board of review, | 41 | 43 |
| duties of——member of council. | 47 | 54 |
| may complain in writing of offences, | 49 | 61 |
| AWNING POSTS—council may regulate setting of | 22 | 10 |
| BATHING—council may regulate in public places, | 21 | 10 |
| BARNS—council may prescribe location of, | 27 | 14 |
| BOARD OF HEALTH—council may establish, | 27 | 14 |
| council may invest it with necessary powers. | 27 | 14 |
| may impose on it certain duties, | 27 | 14 |
| BOARD OF REVIEW—how composed and duties of | 41 | 43 |
| BOARD OF SEWER COMMISSIONERS— | | |
| common council may create and prescribe powers and duties of | 61 | 95 |
| BONDS—council may require officers to file new bonds, | 31 | 18 |
| of city only to be given as provided in sec. 84, | 37 | 28 |
| recorder to give bond, | 38 | 33 |
| official, where to be deposited, | 39 | 34 |
| treasurer's, when to be given, | 45 | 49 |
| of the city, how authorized, to be issued, | 58 | 84 |
| when the common council may issue, | 59 | 85 |
| proceedings on special election to vote bonds, | 58 | 84 |

| | PAGE. | SEC. |
|---|---|---|
| BOOKS—indecent, council may prohibit sale of, | 21 | 10 |
| papers, books, &c., to be delivered to successor, | 48 | 55 |
| BOUNDARIES—of the city, | 6 | 2 |
| of wards, | 6 | 3 |
| CEMETERIES—and grave yards, council may regulate, | 22 | 10 |
| may acquire without the city, | 22 | 10 |
| may purchase land beyond city boundaries for | 25 | 10 |
| may make contract with township of Saginaw to build road to, | 60 | 92 |
| council may make road beyond city limits to the cemetery, | 60 | 92 |
| CHARTER ELECTION—election, when and where held | 10 | 6 |
| how conducted, | 10 | 6 |
| when and how result determined, | 10 | 6 |
| persons elected at, to file oath, | 11 | 6 |
| CITY—boundaries, | 6 | 2 |
| division into wards, | 6 | 3 |
| hall, council may build, | 18 | 10 |
| council may buy real estate therefore, | 18 | 10 |
| assessor, | 40 | 41 |
| attorney, member of board of review, | 41 | 43 |
| funds in treasury of, interest on, | 61 | 96 |
| CITY OF "SAGINAW CITY"—acts of confirmed, | 58 | 82 |
| act to incorporate repealed, | 59 | 87 |
| COMMITTEES—aldermen to act on, | 39 | 37 |
| COMMON COUNCIL—how constituted, | 11 | 7 |
| to decide tie vote, | 11 | 6 |
| quorum, | 12 | 7 |
| may be summoned by mayor, | 12 | 7 |
| may be summoned by recorder in mayor's absence, | 12 | 7 |
| power to compel attendance, | 12 | 7 |
| may impose fine for non-attendance, | 12 | 7 |
| who to preside over, | 12 | 7 |

| | PAGE. | SEC. |
|---|---|---|
| COMMON COUNCIL—(Continued.) | | |
| in absence of mayor and recorder, may appoint president and recorder *pro. tem.*, | 12 | 7 |
| no member to vote when he has an interest in the question, | 12 | 7 |
| no business to laspe, or fail for want of a quorum, | 12 | 7 |
| may pass questions over the mayor's veto, | 13 | 7 |
| may appoint attorney, | 13 | 8 |
| may remove members of the council, | 14 | 8 |
| may remove all appointed officers, | 14 | 8 |
| may issue subpœna, | 14 | 8 |
| may appoint to fill vacancy, | 14 | 9 |
| special election ordered by, to fill vacancy, when, | 15 | 9 |
| may fill vacancies in office held by appointment, | 15 | 9 |
| to have control of finances of city, | 15 | 10 |
| to preserve purity of water in Saginaw river, | 15 | 10 |
| to erect wharves at foot of streets, &c., | 16 | 10 |
| to license ferries, | 16 | 10 |
| to regulate dock line, | 16 | 10 |
| to regulate private wharves, | 16 | 10 |
| may lease wharves at foot of streets, | 16 | 10 |
| to provide for draining swamps in, or within three miles of city, | 16 | 10 |
| to pay damages when caused by drains, | 16 | 10 |
| proceedings to drain, | 16 | 10 |
| to prohibit construction of wooden buildings, | 17 | 10 |
| to establish fire limits, | 17 | 10 |
| to appoint inspectors of articles to be measured, | 17 | 10 |
| to provide for paupers, | 17 | 10 |
| may prohibit the bringing of paupers to the city, | 17 | 10 |
| may build city hall, | 18 | 10 |
| may purchase real estate for, | 18 | 10 |
| may prevent vice, preserve the peace, | 18 | 10 |

| | Page. | Sec. |
|---|---|---|
| COMMON COUNCIL—(Continued.) | | |
| may maintain a police, | 18 | 10 |
| may restrain houses of ill fame, | 18 | 10 |
| may prevent gaming, | 18 | 10 |
| may restrain and prevent sale of liquor, | 18 | 10 |
| may punish drunkards, vagrants, &c., | 18 | 10 |
| may prohibit and license public exhibitions, | 18 | 10 |
| may prohibit and abate nuisances, | 19 | 10 |
| may regulate slaughter houses, | 19 | 10 |
| may prevent obstructions of streets, &c., | 19 | 10 |
| may prevent fast driving, | 19 | 10 |
| may prohibit dogs running at large, | 20 | 10 |
| may regulate use of locomotives, | 20 | 10 |
| may require railroad companies to light track, | 20 | 10 |
| may prevent indecent exposure of the person, | 21 | 10 |
| may regulate bathing in public places, | 21 | 10 |
| may prohibit sale of indecent books, &c., | 21 | 10 |
| may punish disorderly language, | 21 | 10 |
| may establish pounds, | 22 | 10 |
| may prevent gaming, | 22 | 10 |
| may prevent violation of the sabbath, | 22 | 10 |
| cemeteries and grave yards, may regulate, | 22 | 10 |
| dead carcass, may prohibit bringing or leaving within city, | 22 | 10 |
| market place, may lay out and establish, | 22 | 10 |
| fire-wood, may regulate the sale of | 22 | 10 |
| hay, may regulate the sale of | 22 | 10 |
| farm produce, may regulate sale of | 22 | 10 |
| meetings of electors, council may call, | 22 | 10 |
| pay of city officers, may regulate, | 22 | 10 |
| pay of city officers, how changed by council, | 23 | 10 |
| boundaries of city, streets, parks, &c., fixed by council, | 23 | 10 |
| license, may grant, for what purpose, | 23 | 10 |

| | Page. | Sec. |
|---|---|---|
| COMMON COUNCIL—(Continued.) | | |
| sealers of weights and measures, may appoint. | 24 | 10 |
| may punish violation of ordinances, | 24 | 10 |
| may put persons imprisoned at work on streets, | 25 | 10 |
| power of, to make ordinances relative to fire, | 25 | 11 |
| power of, to organize fire companies, | 25 | 11 |
| power of, to regulate working on the streets, | 27 | 15 |
| how to acquire land for streets, | 27 | 15 |
| may purchase land for streets, | 28 | 15 |
| council may appeal from award of damages, | 29 | 15 |
| judge of election and qualification of members of, | 30 | 16 |
| may compel attendance of members, | 30 | 16 |
| may require any officer to file new bond, | 31 | 18 |
| meetings of, to be public, | 31 | 19 |
| majority of aldermen elect necessary to pass any ordinance, | 31 | 19 |
| may assess poll tax, | 34 | 21 |
| to perform duties of township boards, | 34 | 22 |
| may raise by tax money to pay expenses of city, | 34 | 24 |
| highway tax to be raised by—limit of | 35 | 24 |
| not to issue bonds except as provided in sec. 84, | 37 | 28 |
| two-thirds vote necessary to grant special rights, | 31 | 19 |
| COMPLAINTS—who may make, how made, | 49 | 61 |
| proceedings on, | 50 | 62 |
| made by city attorney, in writing, | 49 | 61 |
| duty of recorder, when made, | 50 | 61 |
| COMPTROLLER—how appointed, | 14 | 8 |
| to be assessor of the city, | 14 | 8 |
| to make annual assessment of taxable property, how and when, | 40 | 39 |
| to perform such duties as may be prescribed by ordinance, | 40 | 41 |
| to be member of board of supervisors, | 40 | 41 |
| to be member of common council, but not to vote, | 41 | 41 |

| | PAGE. | SEC. |
|---|---|---|
| COMPTROLLER—(Continued.) | | |
| when to complete assessment roll, | 41 | 42 |
| member of board of review, | 41 | 43 |
| to deliver assessment roll to board of review, | 42 | 44 |
| to apportion taxes, &c., | 43 | 46 |
| CONSTABLES—when and how elected, | 9 | 5 |
| to receive same fees as township constables, | 56 | 75 |
| CONTRACT—for deposits of city money, by the council, | 61 | 96 |
| COPIES—certified, made evidence, | 57 | 79 |
| CORPORATE—name, | 5 | 1 |
| boundaries, | 6 | 2 |
| officers, | 8 | 4 |
| taxes, council may assess, | 24 | 10 |
| act, a public act, &c., | 60 | 89 |
| COSTS—officers sued, may recover double costs, when. | 56 | 78 |
| DAMAGES—for land taken for streets, | 29 | 15 |
| party claiming may appeal, | 29 | 15 |
| council may appeal from an award of | 29 | 15 |
| DEPUTY MARSHALS—appointment of | 46 | 51 |
| powers and duties of | 46 | 51 |
| DEPUTY TREASURER—how appointed, | 45 | 49 |
| may perform duties of treasurer, | 45 | 49 |
| DETROIT HOUSE OF CORRECTION—commitment to, when, | 51 | 63 |
| DIRECTOR OF THE POOR—how appointed, | 13 | 8 |
| duties and powers of | 47 | 52 |
| DISORDERLY HOUSES, and houses of ill fame, council may prevent, | 18 | 10 |
| DISORDERLY LANGUAGE—council may punish, | 21 | 10 |
| DOCK—council may fix line of | 16 | 10 |
| DOGS—council may prohibit running at large, | 20 | 10 |
| DRAINS—council may make drains, &c., | 31 | 20 |
| cost of, how assessed, | 31 | 20 |

| | PAGE. | SEC. |
|---|---|---|
| DRUNKARDS—council may punish, | 18 | 10 |
| ELECTION—annual, when and where held, | 10 | 6 |
| all elections conducted as in townships, | 10 | 6 |
| special, when to be ordered, | 15 | 9 |
| ENGINEER FIRE DEP'T—how appointed, | 14 | 8 |
| EXECUTION—may issue for non-payment of fine, | 50 | 62 |
| may command imprisonment, | 50 | 62 |
| FARM PRODUCE—council may regulate sale of, | 22 | 10 |
| FEES—on special assessments, | 32 | 20 |
| of treasurer, for collecting general taxes, | 44 | 48 |
| FERRIES—may be licensed by council, | 16 | 10 |
| FINANCES—subject to control of couucil, | 15 | 10 |
| FINES—may be sued for by attorney, | 49 | 58 |
| common council may remit, | 51 | 62 |
| how collected, | 50 | 62 |
| imprisonment for non-payment of | 24 | 10 |
| must be paid into the city treasury, | 52 | 67 |
| limit of, | 24 | 10 |
| council may make ordinances relative to | 25 | 11 |
| FIRE COMPANIES—duties of | 26 | 12 |
| council may organize, | 25 | 11 |
| powers of, as to rules, election of officers, | 26 | 11 |
| members of, to obtain from recorder certificate, | 26 | 11 |
| FIRE LIMITS—council may establish, | 17 | 10 |
| FIREMEN—exempt from juries, &c., | 26 | 11 |
| FIREWOOD—council may regulate sale of | 22 | 10 |
| council may appoint inspector of | 17 | 10 |
| GAMING—council may prevent, | 18 | 10 |
| GRADING—streets by council, | 31 | 20 |
| cost of, how paid, | 31 | 20 |
| GRAVELING—council may gravel streets, | 31 | 20 |
| cost of, how paid, | 31 | 20 |

| | PAGE. | SEC. |
|---|---|---|
| HAY, AND FARM PRODUCE--council may regulate sale of | 22 | 10 |
| HEALTH—council may pass ordinance to preserve the public health, | 27 | 14 |
| board of, council may establish, | 27 | 14 |
| HOUSE OF CORRECTION—persons may be committed to | 51 | 63 |
| IMPRISONMENT—for non-payment of fine, | 24 | 10 |
| limit of | 24 | 10 |
| person imprisoned may be employed on streets, | 25 | 10 |
| persons may be imprisoned, or for non-payment of fine, | 50 | 62 |
| IMPROVEMENTS—assessments for, require majority of all the aldermen elect, | 31 | 17 |
| INDECENT EXPOSURE—council may prohibit and punish, | 21 | 10 |
| INSPECTORS—of articles to be measured, weighed, &c. council may appoint, | 17 | 10 |
| INSPECTORS OF ELECTION—who are, | 10 | 6 |
| INTEREST—on special assessment, | 32 | 20 |
| on city funds in the treasury, | 61 | 96 |
| contract with banks to pay interest on deposit of city money, | 61 | 96 |
| INTOXICATION—council may punish, | 18 | 10 |
| INVALID—special assessments may be vacated and re-assessed, | 33 | 20 |
| JAIL—city to have use of county jail, | 51 | 64 |
| JURY—to open streets and fix damage, | 28 | 15 |
| inhabitants may serve on, | 49 | 59 |
| persons charged with violation of city ordinances, entitled to, | 49 | 60 |
| proceedings to draw jury, | 49 | 60 |

| | PAGE. | SEC. |
|---|---|---|
| JUSTICES OF THE PEACE—when, and how elected, | 9 | 4 |
| number of, | 9 | 4 |
| term of office, | 9 | 4 |
| powers and duties of, | 9 | 4 |
| recorder to be justice of the peace, | 38 | 32 |
| may issue warrant to sheriff of any county in the state in cases of escape, | 52 | 65 |
| must report on oath, monthly, the amount of fines collected, | 53 | 67 |
| may be removed in certain cases, | 53 | 68 |
| security to be given by, | 53 | 69 |
| to give bond to the city, | 54 | 69 |
| docket of, subject to inspection by council, | 54 | 70 |
| must produce docket when required by common council, | 54 | 70 |
| circuit judge may make an order for production of justice's docket, | 54 | 70 |
| must account on oath for stolen property unclaimed in their possession, | 54 | 71 |
| must give notice to persons claiming stolen property, | 55 | 71 |
| may sell perishable property, when and how, | 55 | 71 |
| shall, on sufficient proof, deliver stolen property to the owner, | 55 | 72 |
| expense of keeping stolen property to be paid by owner, | 55 | 72 |
| when unclaimed stolen property shall be sold, | 55 | 73 |
| to receive same fees of township justices, | 56 | 75 |
| not incompetent, because a freeholder of the city, | 57 | 81 |
| LICENSE—council may grant, for what, | 23 | 10 |
| LIGHTING OF STREETS—council may light, | 31 | 20 |
| cost of, how assessed, | 31 | 20 |
| LIQUORS—council may prevent sale of, | 18 | 10 |
| LOCAL IMPROVEMENTS—council may make, | 31 | 20 |
| cost of, how assessed, | 32 | 20 |

| | Page. | Sec. |
|---|---|---|
| MARKET PLACE—council may lay out and establish, | 22 | 10 |
| MARSHAL—how appointed, | 13 | 8 |
| must promptly attend all fires, | 26 | 13 |
| duty of, at fire, | 26 | 13 |
| may require aid of all bystanders at a fire, | 27 | 13 |
| subject to order of mayor and aldermen at fire, | 27 | 13 |
| security to be given by, | 46 | 51 |
| chief of police, | 46 | 51 |
| duty of, in respect to process, | 46 | 51 |
| to obey orders of mayor, | 46 | 51 |
| may command aid of all persons, | 46 | 51 |
| may appoint deputies, | 46 | 51 |
| fees of, | 56 | 75 |
| MAYOR—when and how elected, | 9 | 4 |
| to preside over common council, | 12 | 7 |
| may vote upon all questions, | 12 | 7 |
| may suspend certain proceedings, | 12 | 7 |
| may veto certain measures, | 12 | 7 |
| veto may be nullified by council, | 13 | 7 |
| may issue *venire facias*, | 28 | 15 |
| to preside at meeting of inhabitants, to raise tax | 35 | 24 |
| to sign annual statement, | 37 | 29 |
| to be chief executive officer of the city, | 37 | 30 |
| shall supervise other officers of the city, | 37 | 30 |
| shall see that by-laws are observed, | 37 | 30 |
| may recommend to council measures, | 38 | 30 |
| may take acknowledgment of deeds, | 38 | 31 |
| may administer oaths, &c., | 38 | 31 |
| MEETINGS—of common council to be public, | 31 | 19 |
| of inhabitants, to vote taxes, when and how called and power of voters at meetings of inhabitants | 35 | 24 |
| taxes voted at meeting of taxpayers, how raised, | 36 | 26 |
| MONEY—how drawn from treasury, | 45 | 50 |

| | PAGE. | SEC. |
|---|---|---|
| NOTE—of city not to be given, | 37 | 28 |
| NUISANCE—council may prohibit, | 19 | 10 |
| OATH—false, punished, how, | 56 | 77 |
| OFFICERS—elected, | 8 | 4 |
| when and how elected, | 8 | 4 |
| elected, can only be removed on charges, | 14 | 8 |
| pay fixed by annual salary, how and when altered | 23 | 10 |
| council may regulate fees of, | 23 | 10 |
| may be required to file new bond, | 31 | 18 |
| resignation of, | 48 | 55 |
| additional powerr and duties of, | 48 | 56 |
| common council to prescribe term of, | 48 | 57 |
| salary and compensation fixed by council, | 48 | 57 |
| suits against city officers, where must be commenced, | 56 | 78 |
| may receive double costs in certain cases, | 56 | 78 |
| OFFICE—when vacant by neglect to qualify, | 11 | 6 |
| term of, fixed by council, | 48 | 57 |
| no defaulter to be elected to, | 58 | 83 |
| ORDINANCE—not to have immediate effect, when, | 12 | 7 |
| not to go into effect until after one day, | 13 | 7 |
| creating an offence, must prescribe the punishment, | 24 | 10 |
| majority vote necessary to pass any, | 31 | 19 |
| certain, require two-thirds vote, | 31 | 19 |
| style of, | 34 | 23 |
| recorder to keep record of, | 39 | 33 |
| must be published one week, | 39 | 33 |
| mayor may veto, | 13 | 7 |
| record of, when evidence, | 57 | 79 |
| proof of publication, how made, | 57 | 80 |
| printed by authority of council, evidence, | 57 | 80 |
| of the "City of Saginaw City," to remain in force, | 59 | 86 |

| | Page. | Sec. |
|---|---|---|
| PAUPERS—council may provide for, | 17 | 10 |
| council may prohibit the bringing of, to the city, | 17 | 10 |
| PAVING STREETS—how paid, | 31 | 20 |
| council may pave, | 31 | 20 |
| PENALTY—limit of, | 24 | 10 |
| PLANKING STREETS—how paid, | 31 | 20 |
| council may plank streets, | 31 | 20 |
| PLATS—must be approved by common council, | 61 | 94 |
| certificate of, approval must be endorsed thereon, | 61 | 94 |
| POLICE—council may maintain, | 18 | 10 |
| POLL TAX—how assessed, | 33 | 21 |
| how expended, | 33 | 21 |
| POSTS—council may regulate setting of, | 22 | 10 |
| POUND—council may establish, | 22 | 10 |
| PRIVIES—council may prescribe location of, | 27 | 14 |
| PROCESS—how directed, | 52 | 66 |
| by whom executed, | 52 | 66 |
| PROSECUTIONS—to be in name of city, | 34 | 23 |
| PROSTITUTES—council may punish, | 18 | 20 |
| PUNISHMENT—must be fixed in the ordinance creating the offence, | 24 | 10 |
| QUORUM—how constituted, | 12 | 7 |
| less than a, may adjourn, | 12 | 7 |
| no business to laspe or fail for want of a quorum, | 12 | 7 |
| RAILROAD—council may require to light track, | 20 | 10 |
| REAL ESTATE—sale of, for special assessment, | 32 | 20 |
| effect of deed of, on sale for special tax, | 32 | 20 |
| how returned and sold for special assessment, | 32 | 20 |
| RECORDER—when and how elected, | 9 | 4 |
| term of office, | 9 | 4 |
| to give notice of annual election, | 10 | 6 |
| charter elections, to give notice of, | 10 | 6 |
| to make and file with county clerk certificate of election of justices, | 11 | 6 |

| | PAGE. | SEC. |
|---|---|---|
| RECORDER—(Continued.) | | |
| may summon the council to a meeting in the mayor's absence, | 12 | 7 |
| to keep a record of council proceedings, | 12 | 7 |
| to vote only in absence of mayor, | 12 | 7 |
| must lay before council any order of mayor suspending an ordinance, resolution, or vote, | 13 | 7 |
| duty of, in street opening cases, | 28 | 15 |
| duty of, in appeals from an award of damages, | 30 | 15 |
| —and mayor to sign roll for taxes voted at property holders meeting, | 36 | 26 |
| to sign annual statement, | 37 | 29 |
| to be ex-officio justice of the peace, | 38 | 32 |
| title of recorder's court, | 38 | 32 |
| records to be kept by, and delivered to successor, | 38 | 32 |
| to be clerk of common council, | 38 | 33 |
| shall give bond, | 38 | 33 |
| shall perform duties of township clerk, | 39 | 33 |
| compensation of, as clerk, | 39 | 33 |
| official bonds to be deposited with, | 39 | 34 |
| to perform duties of mayor in his absence, | 39 | 35 |
| subject to impeachment, | 39 | 36 |
| duty of, in respect to assessment roll, | 41 | 42 |
| to certify amount of taxes, | 43 | 45 |
| duty of, on complaint for violation of city ordinances, | 51 | 63 |
| power and authority of, in cases of prosecution, | 51 | 63 |
| may issue warrant to sheriff of any county in the state in certain cases, | 52 | 65 |
| must make monthly report of fines collected, | 53 | 67 |
| may be removed for failure to report fines, | 53 | 67 |
| may be removed for failure to pay over money, | 53 | 68 |
| may be removed for unfaithful conduct, &c., | 53 | 68 |
| shall report to council names of officers neglecting to give bonds, | 55 | 74 |

| | Page. | Sec. |
|---|---|---|
| REMOVALS—from office, how made, | 31 | 17 |
| duty of officer on being removed, | 48 | 55 |
| recorder may be removed in certain cases, | 53 | 68 |
| justice of the peace may be removed, | 53 | 68 |
| RESIDENCE—of elector, | 56 | 76 |
| RESIGNATIONS—how made, | 14 | 9 |
| duty of officers on resigning, &c., | 48 | 55 |
| RESOLUTIONS—certain, not to have affect until after one day, | 13 | 7 |
| mayor may veto, | 12 | 7 |
| REVIEW—board of, how constituted, duties of, | 41 | 43 |
| comptroller to deliver assessment roll to, | 42 | 44 |
| RIGHT OF WAY—council may grant to railroad co. | 31 | 20 |
| for streets, how acquired by city, | 28 | 15 |
| SABBATH—council may prevent violation of, | 22 | 10 |
| SAGINAW—corporate name, | 5 | 1 |
| may sue and be sued, | 5 | 1 |
| may have a common seal, | 5 | 1 |
| may purchase, hold, lease and convey real estate and personal property, | 5 | 1 |
| SALARY—of officers not to be changed during time to be prescribed by council, | 48 | 57 |
| SCHOOL LAW, | 63 | |
| SEALER, of weights and measures, council may appoint | 24 | 10 |
| SEWERS—council may construct, &c., | 31 | 20 |
| cost of, how paid, &c., | 31 | 20 |
| SEWER COMMISSIONERS—council may appoint, | 61 | 95 |
| council may prescribe powers and duties of, | 61 | 95 |
| SHADE TREES—council may regulate planting of | 22 | 10 |
| SHOWS—council may license, | 18 | 10 |
| SLAUGHTER HOUSES—council may regulate, | 19 | 10 |

| | Page. | Sec. |
|---|---|---|
| SPECIAL ASSESSMENTS—for local improvements, | 31 | 20 |
| how made, on what property, | 32 | 20 |
| how collected, | 32 | 20 |
| invalid, may be vacated and re-assessed, | 33 | 20 |
| council may provide for collection of, by ordinance, | 36 | 27 |
| SPECIAL ELECTION—when to be ordered, | 15 | 9 |
| how conducted, | 15 | 9 |
| STATEMENT—annual, when to be made, | 37 | 29 |
| STOLEN PROPERTY—duty of justice in respect of, | 54 | 71 |
| owner of, to pay cost of keeping, &c., | 55 | 72 |
| to be delivered to owner, when, | 55 | 72 |
| may be sold by justice, when, | 55 | 73 |
| proceeds of, how disposed of, | 53 | 73 |
| STREETS—cost of lighting, how assessed, | 31 | 20 |
| council may light streets, | 31 | 20 |
| council may prevent obstruction of, | 19 | 10 |
| council may lay out and establish, | 28 | 15 |
| council may vacate, | 27 | 15 |
| manner of vacating streets and alleys, | 28 | 15 |
| land for, how acquired, | 28 | 15 |
| compensation for land taken for, | 29 | 15 |
| council may appeal from award of damages for, | 29 | 15 |
| council may pave, plank, &c., | 31 | 20 |
| cost of planking, paving, grading, how paid, | 31 | 20 |
| STREET COMMISSIONER—how appointed, | 13 | 8 |
| duties and powers of, | 47 | 53 |
| must take oath of office, | 47 | 53 |
| SUITS *vs.* city, inhabitants competent witnesses, jurors, &c. | 49 | 59 |
| SUPERVISOR—when and how elected, | 9 | 5 |
| powers and duties of, | 10 | 5 |
| to perform duties of township supervisors in certain cases, | 34 | 22 |
| shall be member of board of supervisors of Saginaw county, | 40 | 38 |

| | PAGE. | SEC. |
|---|---|---|
| SWAMPS—council may drain within three miles of city limits, | 16 | 10 |
| proceedings to drain, | 16 | 10 |
| TAXES—council may assess and collect, for what, | 24 | 10 |
| for paying expenses of city, how raised, and amount of, | 34 | 24 |
| highway, how raised, amount of, | 35 | 24 |
| tax-payers meeting may vote, when, | 35 | 24 |
| state, county, city, and school taxes, how raised and collected, | 35 | 25 |
| proceedings for return and sale of land for, | 36 | 25 |
| authorized by property holders, how raised, | 36 | 26 |
| mayor and recorder to sign roll for taxes voted at tax-payers' meeting, | 36 | 26 |
| council may provide for collection of taxes not mentioned in section 25, | 36 | 27 |
| amount necessary to be raised, when and how determined, | 43 | 45 |
| to be a lien on property, | 44 | 47 |
| sale of property for, | 44 | 47 |
| fees for the collection of, | 44 | 48 |
| duty of treasurer, in collection of, | 44 | 48 |
| TIE VOTE—result, how determined, | 11 | 6 |
| TAX ROLL—when tobo delivered to treasurer, | 43 | 46 |
| duty of common council, when treasurer fails to give the proper security, | 43 | 46 |
| TREASURER—when and how elected, | 9 | 4 |
| term of office, | 9 | 4 |
| to be collector of taxes, | 9 | 4 |
| to collect taxes voted at meeting of tax-payers, | 36 | 26 |
| to be member of board of review, | 41 | 43 |
| failing to give proper security, council shall appoint a collector, | 43 | 46 |
| fees for collecting taxes, | 44 | 48 |
| duty of, in collecting taxes, | 44 | 48 |

| | Page. | Sec. |
|---|---|---|
| TREASURER—(Continued.) | | |
| collection of all taxes, | 45 | 49 |
| when to give bond to city and to county treasurer, | 45 | 49 |
| powers of, same as township treasurer, | 45 | 49 |
| may appoint deputy, | 45 | 49 |
| to keep account of money drawn from treasury, | 46 | 50 |
| to exhibit to council statement of receipts, &c., | 46 | 50 |
| may be required to deposit money with bank, | 61 | 96 |
| and his sureties not liable for moneys deposited by order of the council, | 62 | 96 |
| TOWNSHIP CLERKS—recorder to perform for city, duties of, | 38 | 33 |
| TAX SALES—comptroller may attend, when, | 60 | 93 |
| city may bid in lands sold at, annually, | 60 | 93 |
| may quit title to such lands, | 61 | 93 |
| VACANCY—by neglect to qualify, | 11 | 6 |
| VAGRANTS—council may punish, | 18 | 10 |
| VICE—council may prevent, | 18 | 10 |
| VETO—mayor may veto certain ordinances and resolutions, | 13 | 7 |
| VOTE—mayor may vote, | 12 | 7 |
| certain votes not to take effect until after one day, | 13 | 7 |
| majority, necessary to pass any ordinance, | 31 | 19 |
| two-thirds vote to pass certain ordinances, | 31 | 19 |
| two-thirds vote necessary to grant right of way, | 31 | 20 |
| who may vote at tax-payers' meeting, | 35 | 24 |
| elector to vote in the ward where he resides, | 56 | 76 |
| elector to vote in the ward where he takes his meals, | 56 | 76 |
| WARRANT—for money to be drawn from treasury, contents of, | 45 | 50 |
| may issue, to sheriff of any county in the state, in certain cases, | 52 | 65 |
| WITNESS—jurors, &c., inhabitants may be, | 49 | 59 |
| not incompetent, because a freeholder, | 57 | 81 |
| WHARVES—council may construct, | 16 | 10 |
| council may fix line of, | 16 | 10 |
| council may lease at foot of streets, | 16 | 10 |
| WOODEN BUILDINGS—council may prohibit the erection of, | 17 | 10 |

# INDEX TO THE ORDINANCES.

PAGE.

**AFFIDAVIT**—publication of, assessment, 208

**ANIMALS**—dead, not be left in city, 78

prohibited from running at large, 88

who may drive to pound, 88

impounded to be fed and when to be sold, 89

impounded when, and how redeemed, 89

money received from sale of, how disposed of, 90

penalty of pound master for refusing to receive, 90

penalty for illegally impounding, 90

penalty for hindering the impounding of, 90

fees for taking to pound, 91

fine for permitting, to run at large, 91

**ARREST**—may be made without process, when, 74

city attorney to be notified of, 74

**ASHES**—how and where to be kept, 105

penalty for not keeping as required, 105

**ASSAULT AND BATTERY**—how punished, 75

**ASSESSMENTS**—special, ordinance relative to, 206

expense of grading, &c., streets, 206

comptroller to make and report —roll, 206

notice of, to be published, contents of, 207

council to consider roll, 207

affidavit of publication to be presented to council, 208

mistake in, not to invalidate roll, 208

PAGE.

ASSESSMENTS—(Continued.)

sidewalks to be repaired by owner, ........ 208
refusal to repair, how dealt with, ........ 209
street commissioner to cause sidewalk to be repaired,... 209
expense of, how collected,........ 209
warrant for collection of, ........ 209
contents of warrant,........ 209
treasurer to collect and return roll. ........ 210
treasurer's return must be sworn to, ........ 211
warrant for collection of, may be removed. ........ 211
delinquent, ........ 211
interest on delinquent, ........ 211
recorder's fees on,........ 211
recorder to make statement of lands returned,........ 212
cost of advertising delinquent, ........ 212
statement of delinquent, to be published and posted,.... 212
notice to be annexed to statement of delinquent, ........ 212
sales of land, when and how made,........ 213
payment of bids when to be made, ........ 213
recorder may bid off lands to city, ........ 213
certificate of sale, ........ 214
redemption of lands sold,........ 214
interest on lands redeemed,........ 214
interest, how computed,........ 214
deed for lands sold on,........ 215
recorder may withhold deed, when, ........ 215
effect of deed,........ 215
deed, evidence of what,........ 216
lands, redeemed subject to tax,........ 216
purchasers of redeemed lands, entitled to bid and interest 216
five year lands,........ 217
recorder to render statement to council of lands sold,... 217
proceeds of lands sold, to be paid to treasurer, ........ 217
recorder to take treasurer's receipt, ........ 217
lands bid off to city liable to taxation,........ 217

PAGE.

ATTORNEY—city, to be notified of arrests, ---------------- 74

may make complaint for violating ordinance relative to burying ground, ---------------------------------- 98

AUCTIONEERS—must have license,------------------------ 95

officers of the law, do not require license as, ------------ 95

fine for doing business of, without license, ------------- 97

BILLIARD TABLES--see page,-------------------------- 183

BOARD OF HEALTH—may incur indebtedness, ----------- 155

infected persons excluded from city,--------------------- 155

to make monthly reports, -------------------------- 155

pest houses and hospitals under control of,------------ 155

penalty for violating ordinance of,---------------------- 156

when and how may abate nuisance,------------------- 156

may enter houses, &c., to abate nuisances,-------------- 84

members to, to enforce ordinance relative to health,---- 87

members of, how appointed, ------------------------- 150

ordinance relative to,-------------------------------- 150

city physician, to be member of,----------------------- 150

president of, ---------------------------------------- 150

recorder to be clerk of,-------------------------------- 150

powers of, ------------------------------------------- 150

duties of keepers of public houses, -------------------- 153

may examine houses, &c., ------------ ----------- 154

BOND—of poundmaster, --------------------------------- 87

of saloon-keepers and billiard table keepers,------------ 184

BUILDING—materials, obstructing street with,------------- 79

BUTCHERS—to keep slaughter houses clean,---------- 86

BURYAL—of the dead, prohibited in the city,-------------- 99

BURYING GROUNDS—ordinance relative to,------------- 98

no one but sexton to dig grave in, -------------------- 98

penalty for violating ordinance relative to,------------- 98

CARAVAN—license for,-------------------------------- 111

PAGE

CEMETERY—ordinance relative to, ........................ 99
Oakwood cemetery, where located,........................ 99
government of,........................................ 99
commissioners, how appointed. ........................ 99
powers and duties of commissioners of,................. 100
lots in, how purchased, ............................... 101
roads and walks in, not to be obstructed, ............. 101
trespass in, or upon fences, &c., of..................... 101
penalty for any violation of ordinance relating to,....... 102
poor persons, how burried in,.......................... 101
CHIMNEY—how to be constructed,....................... 105
CITY OFFICERS—same duties as township officers,......... 130
receiving fines or license money to pay same over to treasurer, .......................................... 123
penalty for not paying over money, .................... 124
CITY PHYSICIAN—to be member of board of health,....... 150
duties of, as member of board of health,................ 154
CIRCUS—license for, .................................... 111
COMBUSTIBLE matter, where not to be kept, .............. 106
fine for placing, in certain places, .................... 106
COMMON COUNCIL—may permit building material in streets 79
may revoke draymen's license,........................... 94
COMPTROLLER—To open account with street commissioner on poll tax, ......................................... 126
ordinance relative to duties of,........................ 131
chief financial officer of the city, ..................... 131
demands *vs.* city must be referred to,................... 131
to make all purchase of personal property,.............. 131
to report his action to the council, .................... 131
shall examine reports of street commissioner, treasurer, recorder and justice of the peace, ..................... 132
shall keep a complete set of books, ..................... 132
to keep list of all property belonging to city, ........... 132
shall keep account with treasurer, ..................... 133

PAGE.

COMPTROLLER—(Continued.)
- to make and extend all special assessment rolls, ........ 133
- to be secretary of water board, ........ 146
- to audit accounts of water works, ........ 146
- shall keep an account with water consumers, ........ 147
- to make and report assessment roll, ........ 206
- to publish notice of special assessment, ........ 207
- to issue warrant for collection of assessments, ........ 209

CONCERT—license for, ........ 111

CONSTABLES—may arrest without process, when, ........ 74

CONTRACTS—ordinance relative to, for street work, ........ 198

CROSSWALKS—ordinance relative to, ........ 149

CURIOSITIES—license for exhibition of, ........ 111

DEAD—burial of, prohibited within city, ........ 99

DEPUTY MARSHALS—to arrest certain persons without process, ........ 74 and 195
- how appointed for police force, ........ 191

DISORDERLY persons and drunkards, ........ 73
- disorderly persons, how punished, ........ 73
- marshal and deputies to arrest without process persons found intoxicated, &c., ........ 74
- disorderly conduct and language, ........ 75
- may be arrested by conductors of street cars, ........ 177

DRAYMEN—to be licensed, ........ 93
- amount of license, ........ 93
- price to be paid to, for single load, ........ 94
- mayor, recorder or common council may revoke license of 94

DRIVING—fast, prohibited and penalty for, ........ 81

DRUNKARDS and disorderly persons, how punished, ........ 73
- drunkards, how punished, ........ 73
- liquor not to be sold or given away to, ........ 75
- drunkeness in saloons prohibited, ........ 185

DWELLING HOUSES—certain, to have scuttle, ........ 105

PAGE.

FEES—of poundmaster, ... 89
for taking animals to pound, ... 91
of inspector of fire wood, ... 139
of sealer of weights of measures, ... 161
recorder's, for saloon license, ... 184
recorder's, on delinquent assessments, ... 211

FENCE VIEWER—street commissioner to be, ... 91

FINES—for selling liquors on sunday, ... 77
for selling liquors to an intoxicated person, ... 75
for assault and battery, ... 75
for indecent, immoral and disorderly conduct, ... 75
for being intoxicated, ... 73
for creating, or permitting a nuisance, ... 79
for obstructing streets, ... 79
for leaving horse in streets untied (penalty) ... 79
for permitting animals to run at large, ... 91
for digging, &c., in streets, ... 92
for draying without license, ... 95
for peddling, &c., without license, ... 97
for violating ordinance relative to burying ground, ... 98
for using a stove pipe not conducted into a brick or stone chimney, ... 104
for violation of fire limits ordinance, ... 111
ordinance relative to deposition of, ... 123
for violating ordinance relative to public decency, ... 134
for firing gun on Sunday, or within certain limits, ... 134
for violating ordinance relative to shade trees, ... 135
for hitching horses to shade trees, ... 135
for injuring shade trees, ... 135
for violating ordinance relative to fire wood, ... 140
for violating ordinance relative to market place, ... 158
for violating ordinance relative to board of health, ... 156

PAGE.

FINES—(Continued.)
for violating ordinance relative to sealers of weights and measures, 161
for violating ordinance relative to lamp posts, 163
for violating ordinance relative to planking street railway 164
for violating ordinance relative to use of locomotives of J. L. & S. R. R., 179
for keeping saloon without license, 185
for violating velocipede ordinance, 188
for illegal driving on Washington street, 189
for violating smoke stack ordinance, 190
for violating police ordinance, 197
for resisting policeman, 197
for violating ordinance relative to street cleaning, 199
for neglect of duty by chief, and assistant engineers of fire department, 200
for resisting chief engineer of fire department, 201
for resisting officer at fire, 201 and 204
for refusing to assist at fire, 204
for violating rules and regulations of water rate ordinance 222
for violating certain sections of water rate ordinance, 225

FIRE—prevention of, 102
stove-pipe must lead into brick chimney, 104

FIRE DEPARTMENT—chief engineer to have charge of water works, when, 148
ordinance relative to, 199
how constituted, 199
chief and assistant engineers, 200
number of men to a company, 200
firemen, who constitute, 200
foreman, companies may appoint, 200
duty of engineers on alarm of fire, 200
penalty for neglect of duty, 200
chief engineer to have full charge of, 201

PAGE.

FIRE DEPARTMENT--(Continued.)

penalty for resisting chief engineer, ........ 201
duties of chief engineer of, ........ 201
rules of chief engineer, ........ 201
copy of rules to be filed with recorder, ........ 201
chief engineer may suspend firemen, ........ 201
badge of office, ........ 202
absence of chief, who to act as chief, ........ 202
fire wardens, ........ 202
duty of companies on fire alarm, ........ 203
companies to be exercised, ........ 203
firemen to procure certificate, ........ 203
resistance of officers at fire, punished, ........ 204
foreman may require assistance, ........ 204
penalty for refusing to assist at fire, ........ 204
marshal, duty of on alarm of fire, ........ 205
buildings may be removed, when, ........ 205
apparatus of, not to go out of city, ........ 205

FIRE LIMITS—each week building remains, a distinct offence 110
boundaries of, ........ 109
wooden buildings prohibited in, ........ 109
wooden buildings, eight feet square may be built, ........ 109
wooden building not to be repaired in, ........ 109
wooden building not to be removed from one lot to another lot in, ........ 109
when wooden buildings in, may be repaired, ........ 109
proceedings to acquire right to repair wooden buildings, partially destroyed by fire, ........ 110
when and how blocks may be included in, ........ 110
resolution to include other blocks in, must be published, 110
penalty for violation of fire limits ordinance, ........ 111
(See section 9 and 10.)

FIRE WARDENS—board of, duties of, ........ 102

PAGE.

FIRE WOOD—see ordinance on page ---- 139

GAMBLING—in saloons prohibited, ---- 185

GAS—ordinance relative to lighting streets with, ---- 115

preamble to gas ordinance, ---- 115

proposition of gas company, ---- 115

acceptance of gas company's proposition, ---- 116

council may designate location of gas posts, ---- 116

gas company to have charge of posts and pipes, ---- 117

gas company liable for loss of, and damage to property, when, ---- 117

bills to be verified, by whom. ---- 117

payment of gas bills, when and how paid, ---- 117

measurement of, how made, ---- 117

when and how lamps to be lighted, ---- 118

council may direct when lamps are to be lighted, ---- 118

ordinance to provide for establishment of gas works, ---- 118

exclusive right to establish gas works, ---- 119

time when gas company had to organize. ---- 119

time when to erect gas works, ---- 120

rates for gas to citizens, ---- 120

rates for gas to city, ---- 120

office of gas company, where to be kept. ---- 120

directors, where to reside, ---- 120

company to give notice of laying pipe, ---- 121

company not to obstruct streets, ---- 121

to save city harmless of damage, ---- 121

company may forfeit conditions, when, ---- 121

company, right of to removal of ordinance, ---- 122

right of company to continue thirty years, ---- 122

city may purchase gas works, when, ---- 122

how city may purchase, ---- 122

price of gas to be fixed, when and how, ---- 123

acceptance of gas company of gas ordinance, ---- 122

PAGE.

GUNPOWDER—when, may be seized, ........ 106
where and how to be kept, ........ 107
forfeited, how disposed of, ........ 107
penalty for unlawful keeping, ........ 107
GUNS—not to be fired on Sunday, ........ 134
not to be fired within certain limits, ........ 134
HAWKERS—must have license, ........ 95
license as, cost of, how obtained, ........ 96
fine for doing business without license, ........ 97
HOGS—not to be confined within fifty feet of street, ........ 78
HORSES—not to be left in streets untied, ........ 79
not to be lead or driven on sidewalks. ........ 83
may be impounded, when, ........ 88
not to be hitched to shade trees, ........ 135
penalty for hitching horse to shade tree, ........ 135
not to be hitched to lamp posts, ........ 163
HOUSE OF ILL FAME—(see ill fame.)
ILL FAME—houses of, not to be kept, ........ 136
no person shall reside in house of, ........ 136
general reputation *prima facia* proof of, ........ 136
penalty for residing in house of. ........ 137
marshal, and police force may arrest without process persons residing in house of. ........ 137
marshal to see ordinance relative to, inforced. ........ 137
INSPECTOR OF FIRE WOOD—how appointed. ........ 139
to give bond, ........ 139
oath of office, ........ 139
to keep an office, ........ 139
fees of for inspecting, ........ 139
wood must be inspected before sale, ........ 139
to give certificate ........ 140
how to make measurement, ........ 140
to keep a record book, ........ 140
penalty for taking illegal fees, or for fraud, ........ 140
penalty for refusing to pay legal fees of, ........ 141
punishment for violating ordinance relative to, ........ 140

PAGE.

JUSTICE OF THE PEACE—duty of, in cases of intoxication, 74

J. L. & S. RAILROAD—ordinance granting right of way to .. 169

route of road and conditions, ........................ 169

single track, ........................................ 169

location of depots, .................................. 170

track on water street, how laid, ..................... 170

speed of trains, ..................................... 170

common council may make certain rules, ............... 170

principal offices and location of shops, ............. 170

street railway, ...................................... 171

side tracks and switches, ............................ 171

rights reserved to common council, ................... 171

ordinance relative to use of locomotives of, ......... 178

rate of speed, ....................................... 178

fire pans, how to be kept, ........................... 179

cars not to obstruct streets, ........................ 179

cars, &c., not to be run across fire hose, ........... 179

penalty for violating ordinance relative to, ......... 179

recorder and justice to have certain jurisdiction, ... 180

LAMP POSTS—who to control, ........................... 162

not to be injured, ................................... 163

who to light lamps, .................................. 163

horses not to be hitched to, ......................... 163

to be located by the council, ........................ 163

penalty for violating ordinance relative to, ......... 163

LANGUAGE—disorderly, how punished, .................... 75

LICENSE—draymen to take, ............................. 93

fee for draymen, ..................................... 94

of draymen may be revoked, ........................... 94

for public exhibitions, .............................. 111

for public exhibitions, how obtained, ................ 111

penalty for not having, for circus, theatres, &c., ... 113

saloon and billiard tables, .......................... 183

for saloon may be forfeited, ......................... 186

PAGE.

LIQUOR—not to be sold on Sunday, ... 76

stores, shops, &c., not to be kept open for sale of, on Sunday, ... 76

LIVERY STABLES—lighted candles must not be used in, ... 108

MARKET PLACE—ordinance relative to, ... 158

where established, ... 153

vehicles, how placed on, ... 158

vehicles not to stand in streets, ... 158

marshal's duty, in respect of, ... 158

penalty for violating ordinance relative to. ... 158

MARSHAL—to arrest without process, certain persons, ... 74

duty of, in respect of persons so arrested, ... 74

to arrest without process, when, ... 75, 114, 137 and 195

to abate and remove nuisance, when, ... 78

to enforce ordinance relative to nuisance, ... 87

may enter any house or place, to abate nuisance, ... 84

to dispose of forfeited gunpowder, ... 107

may arrest persons found violating ordinance relative to public exhibitions, ... 114

duty of, relative to house of ill fame, ... 137

to serve notices for board of health, ... 157

duty of, in respect to market place, ... 158

to enforce Washington street ordinance, ... 189

to keep a police record, contents of, ... 194

may arrest without process, when, ... 195

duties of, under police ordinance, ... 195

mayor and marshal may appoint special deputy marshals, 196

to arrest without process, unlicensed showmen, ... 114

duty of, in respect of cleaning Hamilton and Court streets, 199

duty of, on an alarm of fire, ... 205

MAYOR—may permit building material in streets, ... 80

and marshal may appoint special deputy marshal, ... 196

to recommend deputy marshals, ... 191

PAGE.

MISTAKE—in assessment roll, not to invalidate, ............ 208

NUISANCE—ordinance relative to, ........................ 78

nuisances prohibited, .................................. 78

offensive and unwholesome trades not to be carried on, .. 78

dead animals not to be deposited in any part of city, .... 78

may be removed at expense of author, ................ 78

duty of marshal in respect of, ........................ 78

fine for creating or permitting, ....................... 79

owners and occupants to keep premises clean, .......... 80

rubbish, &c., not to be put in drains, gutters or sewers, .. 81

dead animals, &c., not to be placed or left in streets, .... 81

2d ordinance relative to, ............................. 84

dead animals, &c., not to be deposited in streets, ........ 84

dead animals, &c., not to be placed in Saginaw river, .... 84

board of health may enter houses to abate, ............ 84

impure water and substances not to be cast in streets, ... 85

——nor upon adjoining property, ..................... 85

brewers and others not to permit impure water to run in to street, or on adjoining lands, ..................... 85

butchers to keep slaughter houses clean, ................ 86

marshal, street commissioner and board of health, to enforce ordinance relative to, ........................ 87

marshal, street commissioner and board of health, may enter any house or place to abate or remove, ....... 84

when and how board of health may abate, ...... 156 and 157

when and how board of health may abate, ............. 157

ORDINANCE—*Drunkards* and disorderly persons, .......... 73

*Selling Liquor*, and closing stores on Sunday, .......... 76

*Nuisances*, ........................................... 78

*Obstruction of Streets* and nuisances, .................. 79

*Nuisance*, (2d ordinance, relative to, ) ................. 84

*Pounds*, animals impounded, ......................... 87

*Streets and Public Grounds*, excavation in, ............ 92

PAGE.

ORDINANCE—(Continued.)

*Licensing Draymen* and others........................ 93
*Peddlers and Hawkers*, and auctioneers,................ 95
*Burying Grounds*,....................................... 98
*Cemeteries*, ........................................... 99
*Fire*, relative to prevention of,...................... 102
*Fire Limits*, relative to, ............................ 109
*Public Exhibitions*, relative to,...................... 111
*Gas*, and lighting streets with, relative to,.......... 115
*Gas Works*, to provide for establishing. .............. 118
*Poll Tax*, relative to................................. 125
*Supervisors*, relative to duties of, .................. 130
*Comptroller*, relative to duties of, .................. 131
*Public Decency*, relative to,.......................... 133
*Shade Trees*, relative to, ............................ 135
*Ill Fame*, relative to houses of,...................... 136
*Vagrants*, relative to,................................ 137
*Fire Wood*, relative to inspectors of,................. 139
*Water Works*, relative to. ............................ 141
*Crosswalks*, relative to, ............................. 149
*Public Health*, relative to............................ 150
*Market Place*, relative to,............................ 158
*Sealer of Weights and Measures*, relative to, ......... 159
*Lamp Posts* and protection of same, relative to,....... 162
*Planking Street Railway*, relative to,................. 163
*Street Railway*, relative to removal of track of, ..... 165
*J. L. & S. R. R.*, granting right of way to, .......... 169
*Street Railway*, (second ordinance) relative to,....... 172
*Locomotives, &c.*, regulating use of, ................. 178
*Side Walks*, relative to construction of,.............. 181

PAGE.

PENALTY—for leaving vehicles in streets, 79
for leaving horse in street untied, 79
for leaving building materials in street, 80
for placing building materials in street, 79
for not keeping drains and gutters clear, 80
for throwing, &c., rubbish in drains, gutter and sewers, 81
for placing or leaving rubbish in streets and alleys, 81
for leaving wagon, timber, &c., in streets and alleys, 81
for fast driving, 81
for leaving team, &c., or wagon, or other vehicle on crosswalk, 82
for permitting property to remain in streets and alleys, 82
for placing obstructions, boxes, &c., on streets, 82
for taking dirt away from street, 82
for leading or driving horse on sidewalks, 83
for nuisances committed in steets, or in Saginaw river, 84
for not removing nuisance when lawfully ordered, 82 and 83
of poundmaster, refusing to receive animals, 90
for illegally impounding animals, 90
for hindering the impounding of animals, 90
for breaking pound, 91
for violating ordinance relative to cemeteries, 102
for not keeping ashes as required, 105
for not placing scuttle in roofs of certain houses, 106
for unlawful burning of shavings, 106
for placing combustible matter in certain places, 106
for the unlawful keeping of gunpowder, 107
for steamboats not having proper spark catchers, 107
for using exposed lights in livery and other stables, 108
for not paying over money collected from fines and licenses, 124
for idleness while working poll tax, 127
for street commissioner not returning poll tax, 129
for being a vagrant, 138

PAGE.

POLICE FORCE—ordinance relative to, .................... 190

regular, how constituted, .................... 190

deputy marshals, how appointed, .................... 191

subject to orders of mayor, .................... 191

deputy marshal, term of, .................... 191

council may reduce force, .................... 191

mayor and marshal to designate what deputy marshal to be dismissed, .................... 191

charges against members of, .................... 192

recorder to furnish copy of charges, .................... 192

mayor and marshal may suspend deputy marshal, ..... 192

pay of deputy marshal, when to cease, .................... 192

pay of deputy marshal, how fixed, .................... 192

oath of office, .................... 193

uniform of, .................... 193

articles to be furnished members of, .................... 193

members of, how and by whom assigned to duty, ....... 193

Police Record to be kept by marshal, .................... 194

members prohibited certain things, .................... 194

may arrest without process, .................... 195

duty of, section 11, .................... 195

care of persons arrested by, .................... 196

special deputy marshals, pay of, .................... 196

certain special deputy marshals to serve without pay, ... 197

resisting, penalty for, sec. 14, .................... 197

penalty for violation of ordinan ce, sec. 10, ............. 194

penalty for violation of ordinance, sec. 14, ............. 197

POLICE RECORD—marshal to keep, .................... 194

contents of, .................... 194

PLANKING--streets, expense of, how assessed, ............. 206

PAGE.

POLL TAX—ordinance relative to, 125
street commissioner to make list of persons liable to, 125
who liable to pay, 125
recorder to make duplicate rolls for collection of, 125
one roll to be filed in recorder's office, 126
warrant to be annexed to roll, 126
comptroller to open account with street commissioner, 126
names omitted from roll to be inserted by street com'r, 126
notice to persons liable to pay poll tax, 127
persons assessed for, may work, 127
penalty for idleness while working tax, 127
tax not worked, street commissioner may levy same, 128
notice of sale of property for, 128
proceeds of sale, how disposed of, 128
when city may sue for, 128
street commissioner shall pay over money collected to treasurer, 128
street commissioner to return roll in writing, 129
return of, to show what, 129
penalty of street commissioner for refusing to account for moneys, 129

POUNDS—animals impounded, 87
poundmaster, how appointed, 87
who may drive animals to, 88
animals impounded, when and how redeemed, 89
penalty for breaking, 91
fees for taking animals to, 91

PEDDLERS and hawkers, must have license, 95
license fee for, 96
fine for peddling without license, 97

POUNDMASTER—how appointed, 87
bond and oath of office, 87
duty of, in respect to animals impounded, 88

PAGE.

POUNDMASTER—(Continued.)
- to register animals impounded, ........ 89
- to feed animals impounded, ........ 89
- when and how to sell animals impounded, ........ 89
- fees of, ........ 89 and 90
- money from sale of animals by, how disposed of, ........ 90
- penalty of, for refusing to receive animals, ........ 90

POOR PERSONS—when and how to be burried in cemetery, 101

PUBLIC DECENCY—ordinance relative to, ........ 133
- penalty for violation of ordinance relative to, ........ 133

PUBLIC EXHIBITIONS—license for, ........ 111

RECORDER—may revoke drayman's license, ........ 94
- to issue license to draymen, ........ 93
- to issue license to peddlers, hawkers and auctioneers, ........ 96
- to make duplicate roll for poll tax, ........ 125
- to be clerk of board of health, ........ 150
- to have certain jurisdiction by ordinance relative to J. L. & S. R. R., ........ 180
- duty of, in respect to saloon license, ........ 184 and 187
- fees of, on saloon license, ........ 184
- to furnish copy of charges *vs.* member of police force, ........ 192
- fees of, on delinquent assessment, ........ 211
- to give duplicate receipts for delinquent assessments, ........ 211
- lands returned to, subject to sale, ........ 211

(Should read whole ordinance relative to special assessments.)

RESISTING OFFICER at fire, fine for, ........ 204
- police force, fine for, ........ 197

RIOT—how punished, ........ 75

SAGINAW RIVER—filth not to be put in, penalty for, ........ 84

SALOONS—license to keep, required, ........ 183
- saloon defined, section 3, ........ 184
- application for license, section 4, ........ 184
- bond required, section 5, ........ 184

PAGE.

SALOONS—(Continued.)
amount of license for, sec. 6, ---- 185
drunkeness and gambling in prohibited, sec. 7, ---- 185
to be closed on Sunday and on election days, sec. 7, ---- 185
penalty for keeping, without license, sec. 8, ---- 185
license for, may be forfeited, sec. 9, ---- 186
license for, must state place of business, sec. 10. ---- 186
recorder's duty in respect of, sec. 11, ---- 186
recorder's fees on issuing license for, sec. 4, ---- 184
license, without payment of $50, when, sec. 13, ---- 187

SEALER OF WEIGHTS AND MEASURES— ---- 159
term of office, ---- 159
powers and duties of, ---- 159
to be provided with book, ---- 159
to make yearly inspection, ---- 160
fees of, ---- 161
penalty for violating ordinance relative to, ---- 161

SHADE TREES—ordinance relative to, ---- 135
how to be set, ---- 135
horses not to be hitched or tied to, ---- 135
fine for hitching horses to, ---- 135
penalty for injuring or taking away, ---- 135

SHOWS—license for, ---- 111

SIDEWALKS—penalty for obstructing with boxes, &c., ---- 82
horses and carts, &c., not to be led or driven on, ---- 83
relative to construction of, ---- 181
expense of constructing, how paid, ---- 181
expense of grading all streets, how to be paid, ---- 181
to be repaired by owner, ---- 208

SLAUGHTER HOUSES—to be kept clean, penalty for not, -- 86
not to be built or used in city without permission from common council, ---- 86
penalty for building unauthorized, ---- 86

PAGE.

SMALL POX—persons having, may be confined, ............. 154
persons having, not to go about city, ................... 154
infected persons excluded from city, .................... 155
SMOKE STACKS—ordinance relative to, ..................... 190
must have spark catchers on, ............................ 190
penalty for violating ordinance, ........................ 190
SPARK CATCHERS—see smoke stacks, ........................ 190
SPECIAL ASSESSMENTS—see assessments also, ............... 206
STABLES—exposed lights not to be used in, ............... 108
penalty for using exposed lights in, .................... 108
penalty for keeping hay and straw in, near fire place. ... 108
STEAMBOATS—to have spark catchers, when, ................ 107
penalty for not having spark catcher, ................... 107
STORES—to be closed on Sunday, .......................... 76
STREETS—ordinance relative to obstruction of, ........... 79
vehicles not to be left in, ............................. 79
horses not to be left in, untied, ....................... 79
obstructing, with building materials, ................... 79
dead animals, &c., not to be placed or left in streets. .... 81
penalty for above, ...................................... 81
dirt not to be removed from, penalty for, ............... 82
property not to be left in street, ...................... 82
excavations in, prohibited, ............................. 92
fine for digging in. .................................... 92
expense of grading, how paid, sec. 3, ................... 181
expense of grading street through lands not platted, how assessed and paid, ........ 182
contract for work on, how to be let, .................... 198
ordinance to provide for cleaning certain, .............. 198
STREET CLEANING—certain streets to be cleaned, .......... 198
duty of street commissioner, ............................ 199
duty of marshal, ........................................ 199
penalty for violating ordinance, ........................ 199

PAGE.

STREET COMMISSIONER—to enforce ordinance relative to nuisance, 82
to enforce 2d ordinance relative to nuisance, 87
may enter any house or place to abate nuisance, 84
to be a fence viewer, 91
to make list of persons liable to poll tax, 125
to return poll tax, 129
penaly for not accounting for poll tax and not returning roll, 129
duty of, in respect to street cleaning, 199
to cause sidewalks to be repaired, 209
to act as superintendent of water works, 225

STREET RAILWAY—ordinance relative to planking, 163
track of, to be on grade of street, 164
to be planked on certain streets, 164
how to be planked, 164
penalty for violating ordinance relative to, 164
ordinance relative to removal of track of, 165
rights of company in certain streets, 166
rights reserved to common council, 167
to surrender rights on Water street, 168
acceptance of ordinance by company, 169
2d ordinance relative to, 172
rights to be subject to control of council, 172
right to build and maintain road, 172
term of right, on what streets, 172
company to surrender right on water street, 174
when ordinance to take effect, 174
track, how to be laid, 174
track to conform to grade of street, 175
duty of company as to repairs on streets, 175
how cars to be drawn, 175
speed, rate of, 175

PAGE.

STREET RAILWAY—(Continued.)
how often to be run, ---------- 175
fare on, ---------- 175
cars to be lighted, when, ---------- 176
cars not to stop on crosswalks, ---------- 176
cars of, where to stop, ---------- 176
duty of company, as to its employes, ---------- 176
children and women not to leave running cars, ---------- 176
conductors may arrest disorderly persons, ---------- 177
right of cars to track, ---------- 177
penalty for not yielding track to cars, ---------- 177
acceptance of company of ordinance, ---------- 178
common council may lay gas pipe under, ---------- 176
common council may build sewers under, ---------- 176
city not liable for damage for laying pipes, &c., under, ---------- 176

TREASURER of city, receiving fine or license money, to give receipt, ---------- 124
to keep a water works account, ---------- 143
to collect special assessments, ---------- 210
to collect water rates, ---------- 227

VAGRANTS—ordinance relative to, ---------- 137
who to be deemed vagrants, ---------- 137
fine for being a vagrant, ---------- 138
punishment of, ---------- 138
duty of marshal and other officers to arrest vagrants without process, ---------- 138

VELOCIPEDES—ordinance relative to, ---------- 188
prohibited on certain streets, ---------- 188
penalty for unlawful use of, ---------- 188

WARRANT—for collection of special assessments, ---------- 211
to be issued by comptroller, for collection of special assessment, ---------- 209

PAGE.

WASHINGTON STREET—ordinance relative to, ............ 189

part of the street not to bé driven on, ................ 189

penalty for illegal driving on, ........................ 189

marshal to enforce ordinance relative to, .............. 189

WATER RATES—ordinance relative to, ..................... 218

rates for water, .................................218 to 220

consumers must consent to and sign regulations, ........ 220

fine for violation of rules, ........................... 222

when due, .............................................. 223

obstruction of valves of water works, .................. 223

who may open hydrants of water works. .................. 223

injuring hydrants, ..................................... 224

wrenches of hydrants, where to be kept, ................ 224

penalty for violating certain sections of ordinance relative to, ................................. 224

public hydrants, ....................................... 224

water shut off, not to be let on, ...................... 224

superintendent of water works, ......................... 225

applications for water, how made, ...................... 225

duty of superintendent on application, ................. 226

permit, when and how to issue, ......................... 226

costs of connections, how paid, ........................ 226

record of permits, ..................................... 226

plumbing and plumbers, ................................. 226

treasurer to be notified of permit, .................... 226

treasurer to collect water rates, ...................... 227

WATER WORKS—ordinance relative to, ..................... 141

first commissioners of, ................................ 141

term of office of, original commissoiners of, .......... 142

president of board, .................................... 142

commissioners of, may make by-laws, .................... 142

city treasurer, to keep accounts of, ................... 143

quorum, how constituted, ............................... 143

PAGE.

WATER WORKS—(Continued.)

duty of board of commissioners, ---------- 143

plan for, to be devised by commissioners, ---------- 143

plan must be confirmed by council, ---------- 144

alterations of plan, ---------- 144

board may recommend to council to construct works, ---------- 144

board of, to purchase real estate and machinery, ---------- 144

work on to be let by public notice, ---------- 145

commissioners not to be interested in work or materials for, ---------- 145

commissioners to have control of, ---------- 145

board of, may enter upon land, &c., ---------- 145

board to certify amount due on contract, ---------- 146

comptroller to audit accounts of, ---------- 146

board of, how constituted after April 15, 1875, ---------- 146

appointment of commissioners after April 15, 1875, ---------- 146

vacancies in board, how filled, ---------- 146

secretary of board, comptroller to be, ---------- 146

comptroller to keep record of proceedings of board, ---------- 147

comptroller to purchase supplies for, ---------- 147

comptroller to keep account with consumers of water, ---------- 147

board may appoint employes and fix pay, ---------- 147

chief engineer of fire dep't may have charge of, when, ---------- 148

WEIGHTS AND MEASURES—sealer of, ---------- 159

www.ingramcontent.com/pod-product-compliance
Lightning Source LLC
LaVergne TN
LVHW010237110826
845151LV00004B/1318
* 9 7 8 1 4 2 5 5 2 4 3 0 2 *